BRIDGESPOTTING

PART 2

A GUIDE TO EVEN MORE BRIDGES THAT
CONNECT PEOPLE, PLACES, AND TIMES

Bob Dover

Bridgespotting Part 2:
A Guide to Even More Bridges that Connect People, Places, and Times
© 2022, Bob Dover. All rights reserved.
Published by Sewell Pond Press, Columbia, MD

ISBN 978-1-7379003-2-0 (paperback)
ISBN 978-1-7379003-3-7 (eBook)
Library of Congress Control Number: 2022919634

www.robertdover.com

Without limiting the rights under copyright reserved above, no part of this publication may be reproduced, stored in or introduced into a retrieval system, or transmitted in any form or by any means (electronic, mechanical, photocopying, recording or otherwise whether now or hereafter known), without the prior written permission of both the copyright owner and the above publisher of this book, except by a reviewer who wishes to quote brief passages in connection with a review written for insertion in a magazine, newspaper, broadcast, website, blog or other outlet in conformity with United States and International Fair Use or comparable guidelines to such copyright exceptions.

This book is intended to provide accurate information with regard to its subject matter and reflects the opinion and perspective of the author. However, in times of rapid change, ensuring all information provided is entirely accurate and up-to-date at all times is not always possible. Therefore, the author and publisher accept no responsibility for inaccuracies or omissions and specifically disclaim any liability, loss or risk, personal, professional or otherwise, which may be incurred as a consequence, directly or indirectly, of the use and/or application of any of the contents of this book.

Publication managed by AuthorImprints.com

ALSO BY BOB DOVER

BRIDGESPOTTING:
A GUIDE TO BRIDGES THAT CONNECT PEOPLE, PLACES, AND TIMES (2022)

TABLE OF CONTENTS

Introduction 1
Chapter 1: Landmark Bridges 6
   Ponte di Rialto, Venice 6
   Forth Railroad Bridge, Edinburgh 8
Chapter 2: Historic Bridges 10
   Roman Bridge, Córdoba, Spain 10
   Romerbrücke, Trier, Germany 13
   Stone Bridge, Regensburg, Germany 14
   Sint-Michielsbrug and Hoofdbrug, Ghent, Belgium 16
   Pont Adolphe, Luxembourg City 18
   Hyde Hall Covered Bridge, Cooperstown, New York, and
      Hassenplug Covered Bridge, Mifflinburg, Pennsylvania 21
   West Cornwall Covered Bridge, West Cornwall, Connecticut 28
   Eads Bridge, St. Louis 29
   Roebling Suspension Bridge, Cincinnati 33
   South Portland Street Footbridge, Glasgow 36
   Builder Plaque Mysteries, Wrought Iron Bridge Company Bridges,
      Various Locations, Eastern and Mid-Atlantic United States 38
   Milford Swing Bridge, Milford, New Hampshire, and Keeseville
      Suspension Bridge, Keeseville, New York 45
   Columbia-Wrightsville Bridge, Pennsylvania 48
   Benjamin Franklin Bridge, Philadelphia 54

Burnside Bridge, Antietam, Maryland..58
Ludendorff Bridge, Remagen, Germany..60
Chapter 3: Community Bridges..64
Mittlerebrücke, Basel, Switzerland..64
Charles River Bridges, Boston, and Kenneth F. Burns Bridge,
  Worcester, Massachusetts 65
Ashtabula County Covered Bridge Festival, Ohio 67
Krämerbrücke, Erfurt, Germany...73
Queensboro Bridge, New York City 76
Bridge Between Continents, near Keflavik, Iceland 77
Dundas Aqueduct, Limpley Stoke, England 78
Barrage Vauban and Ponts Couverts, Strasbourg, France............81
Frederick Douglass Bridge, Washington, DC 85
Chapter 4: Decorated Bridges 88
Hammersmith Bridge, London 88
Lower Trenton Bridge, Trenton, New Jersey 89
Calvin Coolidge Memorial Bridge, Northampton, Massachusetts......90
Market Street Bridge, Wilkes-Barre, Pennsylvania 91
Panther Hollow Bridge, Pittsburgh 93
Dumbarton (Q Street) Bridge, Washington, DC 96
Chapter 5: Decorative Bridges..99
Liberty Bridge, Greenville, South Carolina.....................................99
Gateshead Millennium Bridge, Newcastle-upon-Tyne, England 102
Iowa Women of Achievement Bridge, Des Moines, Iowa.................103
Gray's Lake Park Bridge, Des Moines, Iowa 104
High Trestle Trail Bridge, Madrid, Iowa...105
Public Garden Footbridge, Boston..109
Valley Drive Suspension Bridge, Youngstown, Ohio 110
River Ness Bridges, Inverness, Scotland 113
Chapter 6: Cultural Bridges 116
Alcántara Bridge, Toledo, Spain..116
Longfellow Bridge, Boston..118
Bridge of Sighs, Venice 118
Rip Van Winkle Bridge, Catskill, New York..................................120
Chapter 7: Recreational Bridges..123
Woodrow Wilson Bridge, Washington, DC....................................123
O'Callaghan-Tillman Bridge, Boulder City, Nevada 125

Sydney Harbour Bridge, Sydney, New South Wales, Australia 128
Padlocked Bridges, Paris 132
Rhine Falls Bridge, Schaffhausen, Switzerland 136
Marienbrücke at Neuschwanstein, Germany 140
Bear Mountain Bridge, Peekskill, New York 142

Chapter 8: Repurposed Bridges 148
Walnut Street Bridge, Chattanooga, Tennessee 148
Purple People Bridge, Cincinnati 152
Red, Green, and Riverside Park Drive Bridges, Des Moines, Iowa 154
Calhoun County Historic Bridge Park, Battle Creek, Michigan 155
Navajo Bridge, Arizona 158

Chapter 9: Multiple Bridge Tours 161
Vltava Bridge Tour, Prague 161
River Liffey Bridge Tour, Dublin 163
River Avon Bridge Tour, Bath, England 170
River Dee Bridge Tour, Chester, England 173
Three Rivers Bridge Tour, Pittsburgh 179
Central Park Bridge Tour, New York City 185
Wienfluss Bridge Tour, Vienna 193
Delaware River Bridge Tour, Bucks County, Pennsylvania 198

Chapter 10: Bridges Not For Tourists 223
Billboard Bridges, Various Locations 223
Manhattan and Williamsburg Bridges, New York City 227
Hanover Street Bridge, Baltimore, Maryland 230
Theodore Roosevelt Bridge, Washington, DC 232
Chesapeake Bay Bridge, Annapolis, Maryland (Update) 236

Epilogue 240
Bridge Index 245
About the Author 251

INTRODUCTION

READERS OF THE ORIGINAL BRIDGESPOTTING: *A Guide to Bridges that Connect People, Places, and Times*, published in early 2022, may recall that the epilogue discussed how the objective changed as the resulting book progressed. In the introduction to that book, which I will refer to here as "*Bridgespotting: Part 1,*" I stated that the objective was to provide a travel guide for frequent travelers and casual bridgespotters to identify and learn about bridges in tourist centers, or in their local communities, that they could visit on foot.

True to this objective, the early drafts of *Bridgespotting: Part 1* were just that—a series of narrative descriptions of dozens of tourist bridges, with a focus on logistical details to support tourist visits, accompanied by maps and photos. However, there was no consolidated discussion of the reasons that people visit bridges. There was no analysis of the various roles that bridges have historically served, and continue to serve, in our communities. There was not even any attempt to defend the thesis that tourist bridges exist as stand-alone attractions, or that you can find them in hundreds of locations. I presented the narrative descriptions in no particular order, and they were not organized or discussed within the framework of any common feature such as location, construction type, construction material, age, or attraction type.

Ultimately, this unstructured approach changed as I performed additional bridge visits, conducted supporting research, and developed the book. Instead of consisting of a series of seemingly unrelated bridge profiles, *Bridgespotting: Part 1* focused on the identification and analysis of the reasons people visit bridges and concluded by encouraging readers to use this information to improve construction and rehabilitation efforts on local bridges in their communities.

Although the initial focus and objective of providing a travel guide had changed, *Bridgespotting: Part 1* presented an enormous amount of bridge-specific information that, I hoped, was still useful as a guide to bridge tourists. The index to the book listed more than 350 bridges that were discussed as having some type of attraction for tourists or for persons pursuing recreation or hobbies. Detailed profiles were provided for more than 70 of them, including most of the best known and heavily visited tourist bridges in the United States, Canada, and western Europe. Instead of being provided as ad hoc bridge descriptions outside of any organizational framework, I offered the profiles within the context of the various reasons that people visit bridges. I considered each of these reasons a "theme," and each theme formed the basis of its own subchapter—50 of them, by the time I was done. This approach acknowledges that many tourists or hobbyists enjoy focusing their activities on just one or two areas of interest. It also allows the reader to compare and contrast bridges with similar attractions, even if the examples are in widely scattered locations.

This change in objective and framework had two effects. First, by grouping the discussions of individual bridges together within the context of a single theme, the descriptions of both the themes and the bridges that are examples of those themes were vastly improved. *Bridgespotting: Part 1* was a more informative book for having analyzed the themes in detail and by combining the major examples of each theme into a single sub-chapter within the book.

The second effect was that my original objective of having the book serve as a travel guide suffered, due to space limitations. To make the book a useful travel guide, it must, physically, be of a manageable size. It must be able to fit into a traveler's day bag or backpack, and not be so large that it discourages potential users who are already concerned about lugging heavy bags from hotel to hotel. It also must have font large enough that it

INTRODUCTION 3

can be easily read when consulted, in real time, on field visits. It also must be affordable. While a coffee-table book displaying beautiful photographs of tourist bridges would have its uses, it would be both too expensive and too unwieldy to be used as a travel guide.

As the project and book developed, I started to become concerned about these issues. The process of turning the focus away from the individual bridge profiles and into an analysis of the themes improved the book, but also began to crowd out the profiles, the logistical material, the photos and maps, and a summary of how I came to pursue the project in the first place. Meanwhile, the bridge visits continued. For every bridge I visited, I discovered there were two more that also fit the theme, resulting in even more field visits. What started out as a guide to 30 or 40 important tourist bridges grew to more than 600. While I tried my best to ensure the book still presented all of the most important and prominent examples, that goal eventually became impossible.

Thus, I made the decision to split the material into two volumes and now offer *Bridgespotting Part 2: A Guide to Even More Bridges that Connect People, Places, and Times*. For casual tourists and entry-level bridgespotters, *Bridgespotting: Part 1* may be all they will need. Regarding my initial objective of providing a useful travel guide, *Bridgespotting: Part 1* still covers most of the important tourist bridges in North America and western Europe. The 350 bridges described there are likely to be far more than most casual tourists and entry-level bridgespotters will ever be able to visit.

However, the original book still leaves out dozens of important bridges. Now that the concept of tourist bridges has been thoroughly explored, and supported by hundreds of examples in *Bridgespotting: Part 1*, *Bridgespotting: Part 2* returns to my initial objective, which is to encourage tourists, business travelers, and those pursuing recreation and hobbies to go out to see some more great bridges.

An important note is that I made the decision to split the material into two volumes before the original book was too far along in the publication process. As a result, *Part 2* is not composed solely of leftover, second-tier bridges that only an advanced bridgespotter could love. Instead, I attempted to balance the profiles between the two volumes. Therefore, *Part 2* includes some internationally famous bridges that would have been important parts of the original book had there been space, as well as additional bridges that are prominent local tourist attractions.

Finally, there is one more important reason that I decided there was a large amount of important material to support a *Part 2* after the original book had been published. This was because, although the original book about tourist bridges had been completed, the learning about bridges continues to be a work in progress. As with any project, the more I learned about my subject, the more I learned how much more I need to learn. The COVID-related travel restrictions in 2020-21 forced me to quit adding new bridge visits for a while, giving me the time to concentrate on completion of *Bridgespotting: Part 1*. However, even after walking across more than 600 bridges to complete the original book, I knew that I was far from done. My "wish list" continued to grow, finally breaking out into a rash of new bridge adventures and experiences in mid-2021.

Please note that, while *Part 2* presents information on dozens of additional bridges, it does not necessarily serve as a stand-alone guide separate from *Bridgespotting: Part 1*, as the two parts are intended to be used together. In addition to its detailed bridge descriptions, the introductory paragraphs in each subchapter in *Bridgespotting: Part 1* provide a large amount of background information on bridge types, history, and attractions for tourists. This information is not repeated, but it is just as relevant to the bridge descriptions in *Part 2* as those in *Bridgespotting: Part 1*. As an example, the introduction to the subchapter on Covered Bridges in Chapter 2 of *Part 1* describes the historical development of wooden truss types in the early United States. This information is not necessarily required to enjoy visits to the Hyde Hall and Hassenplug covered bridges profiled here in *Part 2*, but does provide a historical context for understanding how the large wooden arches within each of these bridges indicates their early construction dates, and their role within the further development of wooden truss types for later covered bridges.

If you enjoyed using *Part 1* to create your own bridge adventures and experiences, then you will likely find others that are just as enjoyable in *Part 2*. You might slam on the brakes, angering the drivers behind you, when you unexpectedly see large, obelisk-shaped monuments rising from the deck of the Nurse Fairchild Memorial Bridge in Watsontown,

INTRODUCTION

Pennsylvania. Or when you pass a historical marker reading "Stone Arch Bridge" on Route 9 in New Hampshire. Or when you figure out that the dull gray barn you just passed on Route 121 near Bellows Falls, Vermont, is actually an important covered bridge.

Monuments on Pont Fragnée, Liège, Belgium

    The Ashtabula County Covered Bridge Queen may smile and wave at you, and I will bet that you wave back. Your entire Belgian vacation plans may be thrown into disarray when passing through Liège on the train, where the most prominent sight you will see from the window is the enormous, 50-foot-high monuments of the Pont Fragnée, topped by gilded angels blowing trumpets. If you have explored enough of the bridges constructed by the Wrought Iron Bridge Company of Canton, Ohio, you could visit the Noble's Mill Road Bridge in Maryland, admire the lovely ornate date plaque, but then slowly get the sinking feeling that something is not quite right about it.

    Or you might walk alone across a tiny bridge directly over the source of the 444-mile-long Susquehanna River, and then six days later walk across the mouth of the Susquehanna River on the five-mile-long Chesapeake Bay Bridge with 10,000 other people. One thing I have learned is that there are more terrific bridge experiences out there than there is time to experience them.

CHAPTER 1

LANDMARK BRIDGES

PONTE DI RIALTO, VENICE

In a city that can boast of dozens of historic bridges, it is difficult to suggest that one of them is more iconic than any of the others. However, the unusual profile of the Rialto Bridge is instantaneously recognizable as the most enduring symbol of the city of Venice.

Any view of a map of Venice quickly shows two prominent features: lots of canals everywhere, but one canal, the Grand Canal, is much wider than any of the others, meandering back and forth and splitting the city in two. By virtue of being the main waterway amidst a network of small, subsidiary waterways, the Grand Canal has always been the center of boat traffic in Venice, and this means that it is crossed by only a small number of bridges. Two of these are the 1934 Ponte degli Scalzi and the 2008 Ponte della Costituzione, both located at the far northwestern end of the Grand Canal, and serving as access for pedestrians between the railway station and central Venice. A third, the Ponte dell'Accademia, is situated at the far southeastern end of the Grand Canal, where it enters the sea. In between these two extremes, there is only one bridge providing access between the two sides of the Grand Canal, and this is the Rialto Bridge.

Venice is not like Prague, or London, or Florence, or other cities where tourists cross on the famous bridge due to its fame, but the locals use one of the other nearby bridges to avoid the crowds. Visitors and locals can cross the Grand Canal on the many water buses, but anyone walking from the railway station or the San Polo district to the central tourist area at the Piazza San Marco must cross on the Rialto Bridge.

The current Rialto Bridge is just the latest in a series of bridges constructed at this location. Because of the importance of the Grand Canal for boat traffic, bridges crossing the canal must either be high or movable. The first bridge at this site was a pontoon bridge constructed in 1181. This bridge was replaced in 1255 with a movable wooden bridge. The wooden bridge famously collapsed in 1444 due to the weight of too many people positioned to watch a boat procession during the wedding of the Marquis. The replacement bridge then collapsed again in 1524. The decision was then made to construct a more permanent replacement in stone, and many famous architects of the Renaissance, including Michelangelo, submitted designs. However, each of the designs involved multiple spans, which would have been too disruptive to boat traffic. It was not until the 1580s that the current design was selected, and the bridge was opened in 1591.

The bridge is constructed of white stone and spans the canal on a single arch. The arch is deliberately elevated so that it is high enough, 24 feet high, to allow passage of boats. This means that the deck is steeply sloped, with stairs lined with shops leading up to a central portico, resulting in the famous profile. The shops, which today sell glass, jewelry, and souvenirs, are perfectly situated for maximum exposure to shopping tourists.

Having been the only bridge crossing the Grand Canal for hundreds of years, the Rialto Bridge perfectly illustrates how the traffic-focusing property of bridges results in them becoming the communal center of early settlements. The bridge is named after the famous Rialto Market on the eastern end of the bridge, and shops were constructed directly on the bridge to take advantage of the concentrated foot traffic as early as 1255. In Act 1, Scene 3 of *The Merchant of Venice*, Shylock responds to the entrance of Antonio with the question "What news on the Rialto?" Later, in Act 3, Solanio asks the same question of Salarino. These exchanges demonstrate how early bridges served as important community trading and gathering places, even places for the exchange of news amongst townspeople. When both Shylock and Solanio ask this question, they are effectively confirming that the Rialto played a central role in the distribution of information in the city. However, an even more stunning observation is that the location was so iconic, even in the 1590s, that an English playwright who lived more than 700 miles away felt that it would be recognizable enough to his audiences to incorporate it into the plot of one of his plays.

FORTH RAILROAD BRIDGE, EDINBURGH

The hundreds of tourist bridges visited and researched for the *Bridgespotting* books have one important feature in common. With only one exception, you can walk across all of them. This makes sense, when you think about it. It would be extremely difficult for a bridge to be an attraction for tourists if they can only drive across it or view it from a distance. If you cannot walk up to it, or over it, or at least get close to it, how can it possibly be an attraction?

There is one exception. In almost any publication that claims to show the world's most important, unusual, or beautiful bridges, you will see a photograph of the gorgeous Forth Railroad Bridge near Edinburgh, Scotland. It may not be quite as much of an iconic image and household name in the United States as the Golden Gate, but it is probably the most recognizable bridge in the United Kingdom after Tower Bridge. You may not know the name of the bridge, or its location, but you know you have seen it somewhere before.

The bridge consists of three enormous, rust-orange, diamond-shaped cantilevers, each composed of gigantic steel tubes up to 12 feet in diameter. The symmetry, size, and color evoke the twenty-first century sculptural bridges, so some people are shocked when they hear that it was constructed in 1890. Instead of being a modern sculptural bridge, it is actually an early industrial-age bridge whose stunning appearance is still inspiring bridge designers 130 years later. The bridge is still used for rail travel but, unfortunately, rail passengers do not get to see the iconic shape in full profile. Also, the bridge is located about nine miles from central Edinburgh, so it is not visible to tourists in the historic town center. If you climb to the top of Arthur's Seat mountain in eastern Edinburgh, you can just see the very tippy-top of the northernmost truss of the bridge in the distance.

Despite these challenges, there is enough demand to see it that accommodations have been made for visitors. Approximately a half-mile to the west of the railroad bridge is the Forth Road Bridge, a 1960s-era suspension bridge that carries traffic. This traffic bridge has an accessible sidewalk, on its eastern side, from which the iconic railroad bridge can be admired and photographed. The road bridge makes a perfect platform, at the perfect angle and distance, from which to view and photograph the railroad bridge. The view is so perfect that the relatively uninteresting road bridge actually has a visitor center, viewing platform, exhibition plaques, and snack bar on its southern end, accessible by a short bus ride from central Edinburgh. It is an unusual case in which one bridge has been outfitted with accommodations so tourists can view a different bridge. For good measure, the Forth Road Bridge can also be used to view the new, cable-stayed Queensferry Crossing Bridge on its west side.

The iconic status of the railroad bridge is reflected by a proposal by Network Rail to build a walkway to the top of the southern truss, accompanied by a visitor center. The plan to lead guided tours of 12 to 15 people at a time was approved by the Edinburgh City Council in June 2022. Given that the bridge remains one of Scotland's most iconic landmarks, it is likely that that there will be enormous tourist demand when the project is actually constructed.

CHAPTER 2

HISTORIC BRIDGES

ROMAN BRIDGE, CÓRDOBA, SPAIN

Tourists interested in historic architecture are often attracted to cities that underwent a golden age of prosperity, accompanied by a massive building spree that still dominates the street patterns and architectural styles centuries later. Many of the cities in southern Spain, including Córdoba, are unusual in having undergone multiple golden ages—and multiple building sprees—over a period of more than 2,000 years. The resulting architecture reflects a mixture of the different periods, often in proximity to each other, or even superimposed onto each other within a single structure.

In southern Spain, population growth and associated large-scale construction projects flourished under Roman rule. Almost every tourist center in southern Spain proudly displays the remnants of Roman temples, baths, amphitheaters, paved roadways, and bridges. These include Córdoba, where the Roman Bridge was constructed in the first century BC. A prominent component of the Roman construction, which is still a major tourist attraction today, is the Gate of the Bridge, situated at the northern landing of the bridge. The gate served as part of the city walls for controlling entry into the city, as well as a tollhouse for collection of taxes from merchants entering the city.

From the early 700s to the early 1200s, after Roman control had waned, Spain was ruled by Muslims, who called the area al-Andalus, and Islamic architecture and art dominated. During this Islamic period, Córdoba was the capital of al-Andalus, and became one of the largest cities in Europe. It is for its Islamic architecture that Córdoba is best known, and that makes it one of the most important tourist destinations in Spain today.

The Mezquita, or Mosque, of Córdoba was designated as a UNESCO World Heritage site in 1984, one of the earliest sites to be designated. Constructed beginning in the eighth century, the Mezquita is the third largest mosque ever constructed and the interior, consisting of an apparently never-ending forest of red and white-striped arches, is iconic. In addition to the Mezquita, the Islamic period also included reconstruction of the old Roman Bridge, as well as the castle-like Calahorra Tower, which dominates the southern end of the bridge today. The original World Heritage designation for the Mezquita was expanded in 1994 to include all of central Córdoba, including the Roman Bridge, Gate of the Bridge, and Calahorra Tower.

Starting in the early 1200s, the reconquest of the Iberian Peninsula by the Christian monarchs of Castille and Aragon of northern Spain had succeeded in replacing the Muslim rulers in most of Spain except for the Emirate of Granada, a small sliver of Spain along the southern coast. Córdoba fell to Ferdinand III in 1236, and Granada was eventually conquered in 1492. As the reconquest proceeded from north to south and al-Andalus was brought under Christian rule, the former Islamic influences on art and architecture were replaced by Christian influences of the rest of Europe. The most striking example of this was the construction, starting in 1523, of a cathedral almost hidden in the center of the Mezquita. The Mezquita is so enormous that you can wander through its labyrinth of columns and arches for hours without being aware that part of it was demolished and turned into a standard, full-sized cathedral. During this same period, the bridge again underwent phases of renovation and decoration, including the seventeenth century installation of a statue of San Rafael, the patron saint of the city, on a pedestal along the parapet.

Although the Guadalquivir River has since silted in and is no longer navigable at Córdoba, it was navigable all the way from Cádiz on Spain's Atlantic coast to Córdoba, a distance of about 150 miles, when the Romans constructed the bridge. Córdoba represented the head of navigation, and therefore was the only convenient location for construction of a bridge that would not interfere with river-borne transportation. Being the location of the only bridge, overland trade and military routes converged on this crossing.

The route that crossed the bridge at Córdoba was the famous Via Augusta. The Via Augusta was the most important Roman roadway on the Iberian Peninsula, allowing the Imperial capital in Rome to communicate, control, and trade with its provinces in southern Spain. The Via Augusta was an east-west oriented route than 900 miles long, paved, and extending from Cádiz eastward to the Pyrenees, where it connected to other major roads leading south to Rome. From Cádiz to Córdoba, the Via Augusta traversed south of the Guadalquivir River. At Córdoba, the Via Augusta crossed the Guadalquivir River at its head of navigation, resulting in the growth of a city at this important intersection. The Via Augusta then continued eastward on the north side of the river.

Later, during the Muslim period in Spain, an important north-south oriented route, known as the Camino Mozarabe de Compostela, existed. This route served primarily to carry Christians from the Muslim-ruled area of Andalusia to Santiago de Compostela, as part of the famous Way of Saint James pilgrimage, or Camino de Santiago. There were multiple spurs of this route south of the Guadalquivir, including one from the important Muslim center of Granada. These southern routes converged on Córdoba, the only location of a bridge across the river. From Córdoba, the Camino Mozarabe continued north to Mérida, where it joined a similar pilgrimage route for Mozarabes from Seville north to Santiago de Compostela. Although information on this north-south route is focused on its prominent role several hundred years after the Roman period, it likely followed an earlier Roman route. In any case, by the Muslim period, the Roman Bridge represented the intersection not only of the Via Augusta with the river, but also the intersection of the Via Augusta with the Camino Mozarabe.

Today, the bridge is about 800 feet long, crossing the Guadalquivir River on 16 stone arches. The structure consists of white stone blocks set horizontally, with a radial pattern around the arch ring. At the statue of San Rafael on the parapet, worshippers burn liturgical candles on a stand.

HISTORIC BRIDGES

The entire complex of the Mezquita, Gate of the Bridge, the bridge itself, the Calahorra Tower, and the old city center is situated within a tight, easily walkable area.

The bridge's current appearance is reported to primarily reflect its reconstruction during the Islamic period. However, the bridge also underwent reconstructions in the medieval period. The bridge continued to carry traffic up until 2004, at which time it was reserved for pedestrian use only. It was renovated in 2008, resulting in the installation of pink granite pavement on the deck. This was controversial at the time because it is not a material the Romans used, but it does continue the practice of imposing the architectural style of a new era onto previous eras. The 2008 renovation also included a cleaning of the centuries-old stones of the bridge, meaning that the structure now gleams white and is famous for capturing the pink and orange shades of sunsets.

Tourists attracted to the Roman Bridge are not limited to those interested in the historic architecture. Images of the bridge were used to represent the Long Bridge of Volantis in season five of *Game of Thrones*. Aerial shots of the bridge were filmed using drone flyovers. CGI technology was then used to line both sides of the bridge deck with shops and houses, and to draw in the more distant parts of the background. Undoubtedly, some tourists visit the bridge not because of its antiquity, architecture, or proximity to world-class cultural sites, but because of its association with the popular television show.

As with several bridges discussed in this book, the Roman Bridge is not the most prominent tourist attraction in its city. In fact, it would be hard for any other structure or event to rise to the level of the Mezquita, one of the most important historical and architectural marvels in the entire world. However, although the bridge is not as iconic a tourist destination as the Mezquita, it would, on its own, be a major bridge attraction in any other city.

ROMERBRÜCKE, TRIER, GERMANY

The Romerbrücke, or Roman Bridge, crosses the Mosel River in Trier in western Germany, near the Luxembourg border. It is the oldest bridge in Germany and one of the oldest in Europe. The bridge is not large, high, or visually spectacular. It is not even completely original. A wooden bridge was erected by the Romans across the Mosel in AD 17, to serve the road connecting Lyon to Cologne. It was replaced by a stone bridge a few years later, the remains of which are still to be found in the river a few hundred feet downstream of the current Romerbrücke. That stone bridge was in turn replaced by the Romerbrücke in about AD 144. All that remains of this original Romerbrücke is the stone piers, made of black basalt from the Eifel Mountains.

The piers of the Romerbrücke are composed of the original black basalt blocks, and the arches are made of red sandstone blocks. The road deck itself has been constructed and reconstructed numerous times, most recently in the eighteenth century. The juxtaposition of the two different building materials is appealing, but also gives the appearance of construction having been started one way and then completed another, which is exactly what happened. However, even knowing that only a few parts are original, it is still impressive to consider the transport and assembly of the large blocks of basalt that make up the bridge's piers, and awe-inspiring to consider the bridge's age and the role it played in historical events for almost 2,000 years.

STONE BRIDGE, REGENSBURG, GERMANY

Regensburg is located on the Danube, a river that tourists tend to associate with the larger cities of Vienna and Budapest much further to the east. However, for several hundred miles upstream from Vienna, the Danube was a major barrier to early travelers throughout Germany. Cutting west to east from the Black Forest to the Black Sea, anyone traveling south from northern Germany into Italy, the Mediterranean, or the Holy Land needed to cross the Danube.

The river does not flow directly west to east. Instead, it flows northeast out of the Black Forest into eastern Germany, and then makes an abrupt turn to the southeast toward Austria, forming a rough, inverted V-shape. Because the river formed the northern boundary of the Roman Empire, the apex of the "V," where the river made its sharp turn, became the northernmost point of the Roman Empire in Germany. This northernmost point, in turn, became important for defense against, and trade with, the remainder of northern Germany. An overland trade route between the Roman Empire and points north developed, and the location served as the intersection of the river with this trade route, thus spurring the settlement and growth of Regensburg. Once the Romans were gone, defense and commerce continued, the river-based and overland trade routes remained, and the settlement at their intersection continued to grow.

Early wooden bridges built here were routinely washed away by floods, eventually leading to one of the best remaining examples of an early stone bridge that was linked into medieval city walls. There are a handful of medieval bridges left in Germany, but the oldest of them is the Regensburg Stone Bridge. The bridge was built in the 1130s and completed by 1147, just in time to provide passage across the Danube for the armies of King Louis VII of France on their way to the Second Crusade. The city walls are now mostly gone, but the medieval street pattern, Old Town, and the bridge leading into them have been preserved. Regensburg was largely spared from bombing damage in World War II, leaving its medieval center intact, and it is protected today by its UNESCO World Heritage status.

The fact that stone bridges served as guarded entryways into medieval city walls can be seen in historic drawings and etchings of these cities, and in studying the remnants in the form of bridge piers, wall fragments, and guard towers. The remarkable feature at Regensburg is that, although the walls are gone, the bridge, guard towers, medieval street pattern, and even many of the medieval buildings still remain. Another pleasant surprise, when you consider that the bridge is almost 900 years old, is its size. Most remaining stone bridges are visited because of an interest in their antiquity, but they are often physically underwhelming to visitors. The Regensburg Stone Bridge is an exception. You assume it will be small when you decide to visit it for its impressive antiquity, but then its enormous size is unexpected. The Danube, even this far upstream, is not a small river. The bridge is almost a quarter-mile long, crosses the river on 16 stone arches, and rises more than 30 feet above river level.

Regensburg may not be familiar to American tourists, but it is famous within Germany due to its well-preserved Old Town, of which the bridge is an integral part. Guided tours of the Old Town include the short walk to the bridge, which crosses into the Old Town through brightly colored towers attached to a seventeenth century salt warehouse.

SINT-MICHIELSBRUG AND HOOFDBRUG, GHENT, BELGIUM

Ghent may not be the most obvious destination for your next trip to Europe, unless you happen to be a major art history enthusiast seeking out one of the most iconic works of western art—the Ghent Altarpiece by Jan Van Eyck. Be careful, though, because it is easy to take the one-hour train ride from Brussels to seek out the Van Eyck and then rush back to catch whatever is happening in the Grand Place that evening. This would be a mistake, because you would miss a beautifully preserved medieval city that is home to two important tourist bridges.

Instead of turning back toward the train station after leaving St. Bavo's Cathedral, continue out to the other side of the Sint-Baafsplein to the Belfort, the fifteenth century clock tower. Then continue past the Belfort through Goudenleeuwplein to the thirteenth century St. Niklaaskerk. Then step from that church out onto the Sint-Michielsbrug, and look to your right. You will be glad you did, because the view from this beautiful medieval bridge rivals anything you will see at the Grand Place, or in nearby and more famous Bruges, or anywhere else.

To correctly capture the Sint-Michielsbrug, it is necessary to describe not the bridge but its setting. If you enjoy visiting the medieval market squares with their ornate guild houses throughout northern Europe, then you are in for a treat. The square in Ghent is enormous in size and lined with elaborately decorated guild houses straight out of a Bruegel painting. As a necessary modern touch for the tourist, the fronts of the houses are lined with outdoor cafes so you can enjoy a beer and waffle, and take it all in.

Usually, the towns with these market squares also have a cathedral nearby, sometimes even directly on the square. In Ghent, all within a few steps of the Sint-Michielsbrug, there are three enormous cathedral-sized churches, all bunched together at one end of the square. Mixed in among these is a massive medieval clock tower soaring in between two of the churches and a small, picturesque castle, the Gravensteen, at the far end of the square, with its crenulated tower visible just above the guild houses.

HISTORIC BRIDGES

This amazing scene is bisected by a small river running directly through the middle of the square. Not a large river, only about 25 feet wide, but wide enough to support an active trade in tour boat rides. Of course, the presence of the river means that you need a bridge to be able to cross it. You could do this with a boring, modern street level bridge, but a better idea is to cross on the medieval stone arch bridge elevated above the square, literally extending from the base of one enormous church to another, providing an amazing view.

This is the almost impossible setting for the Sint-Michielsbrug, crossing the Leie River in the center of Ghent. The square does not appear to have a specific name and is more L-shaped than square. The Sint-Michielsbrug sits at the corner of the "L." Extending east from the bridge are the series of squares on which you will find the churches of St. Niklaaskerk, Belfort, and St. Bavo's, in that order. On the western end of the bridge is the massive fifteenth century St. Michael's Church. Extending north from the bridge, along the river, are the guild houses of the Korenlei on your left and the Graslei quay on your right. At the far end of this scene is the Grasbrug, one of what seems like dozens of small, street level movable bridges connecting the two sides of the Old Town of Ghent. Behind the Grasbrug is the Gravensteen, a remarkably intact twelfth century castle that was home to the Counts of Flanders.

The fourteenth century Hoofdbrug, or Execution Bridge, situated on the western side of the Gravensteen, is where the Counts of Flanders had criminals and rebels decapitated, and is today a major tourist bridge attraction. To the north and east of the Grasbrug, the medieval wonders seem to have no end. Guild houses, small bridges, and warehouses continue through the Korenmarkt, the Groentenmarkt, the Pensmarkt, and the fifteenth century Vleeshuis. Each church, tower, castle, and guild house is open to visitors, and each would be an impressive tourist attraction on its own. Put together, this area should be given a full day or two to even begin to get an idea of what needs to be seen.

Sint-Michielsbrug's structure and history are interesting enough to merit a visit, but in the end, they are dwarfed by its exquisite setting. The bridge is not large, maybe a total of 200 feet long and 50 feet wide, and is supported by three arches constructed of grayish white limestone blocks.

The elevated central arch crosses the river and is flanked by two smaller arches that cross the river-level stone pavement of the Korenlei and Graslei. The slope of the bridge continues on with increasingly smaller arches to the east until it melds in with the pavement of the St. Niklaaskerk. The area is pedestrian-only, so you can linger on the bridge, check out sights on both sides, take some pictures here, sit for a beer there, pop into a major cathedral, and climb the Belfort for a view, all at your leisure.

PONT ADOLPHE, LUXEMBOURG CITY

The Pétrusse River, which forms the southern boundary of the Haute Ville area of Luxembourg, is all of about two feet wide. You can easily step over it without getting your feet wet, but to cross this little river, Luxembourg has one of the highest, most impressive, gravity-defying bridges you will ever see.

The geologic setting of the city of Luxembourg is unique, and is the reason a settlement was developed here. Although the size of the Pétrusse River and, on the eastern and northern boundary of the Haute Ville area, the Alzette River, is not substantial, both rivers flow within deep, steep-sided, narrow valleys that define a promontory, which made the area a natural location for an easily defensible fortress. The promontory was honeycombed with miles of underground tunnels to accommodate entire armies, with their horses and equipment. After the fortress was demilitarized under guarantee of neutrality by the great powers in 1867, large portions of the underground workings were demolished, but the area continued to grow as a city. However, this development was limited by the small size of the promontory and the steep, bedrock cliffs lining the edges of the Pétrusse and Alzette valleys. Therefore, further expansion, including a station to support railroad access to the city, had to occur on the sides of the valleys opposite the Haute Ville, and these developments had to be connected to the Haute Ville by bridges, the most prominent being the Pont Adolphe crossing the Pétrusse valley.

Built between 1900 and 1903, Pont Adolphe connects the heart of the Haute Ville with the railway station and suburbs on the south side of the Pétrusse. Due to the depth of the valley, the bridge does this in spectacular fashion. Instead of crossing the valley on piers, which would have been

HISTORIC BRIDGES

the obvious and easy choice, the bridge consists of a single arch, about 250 feet long, spanning the entire width of the valley. Constructed mostly of white sandstone, with some use of reinforced concrete, the bridge was the largest stone arch in existence at the time it was constructed.

The Pont Adolphe is different from most other bridges in that it cannot be investigated by walking across the deck. Because it is a substructure arch with no superstructure, nothing of the bridge structure itself can be seen when crossing on foot. The view from the bridge, which includes the Cathedral Notre Dame and Haute Ville area, is made possible not because one is elevated above the other, but because the bridge deck is situated far above the trees in the Pétrusse valley below, leaving a clear view in all directions. On its northern end, the bridge leads to several sites of national importance, including the beautiful cathedral, resulting in its status as a symbol of the nation.

The only way to appreciate the bridge is to descend into the underworld of the Pétrusse valley and walk directly beneath it. Although shown on a map to be in the middle of the city, the valley is almost its own little world. The walls of the valley are so steep that there are only a few places from which it can be accessed—and only on foot by steps or winding paths. The valley slopes are mostly wooded, although there are some houses and urban gardens lining the northern slope in some places. The floor of the valley has just enough space for the small river, flowing within a concrete-lined channel, and an adjacent walking path with some benches. Even though it is centrally-located, the trees and the elevation difference almost completely shut off the noise of the city as you descend, and all you hear is the gurgling of the tiny river. The trees also make it impossible to see the city buildings on the edges of the valley, providing a sense of isolation. The walking path is very popular, with plenty of joggers and bikers present at any time.

When walking on the valley floor, the bridge crosses more than 130 feet above your head. The central arch is flanked on each side by a large stone tower, and then a smaller arch connects the central arch to the city streets on either side. The stonework of the central arch, towers, and side arches has been carefully chosen to use subtly different stone colors and textures to create a decorative effect. The towers and base of the central arch are constructed of large, rough-faced sandstone blocks of a sturdy appearance. The arch itself is constructed of smaller, smooth-faced sandstone blocks that give it a lighter appearance. The open spandrel between the top of the central arch and the deck is then made up of a series of four graduated mini-arches, also constructed of the smaller, smooth-faced sandstone blocks. The pillars supporting the graduated mini-arches are the same white sandstone, but then yellow sandstone, almost resembling yellow brick, is used for the arches themselves.

The bridge underwent an unusual reconfiguration in 2018. Due to continued growth, the city needed to improve transport access between the Haute Ville and the southern suburbs, including the train station. This improvement included a new tram line, but a new bridge for the tram was thought to be an unacceptable intrusion to the visual attractions of the area. Instead of a new bridge, the width of the Pont Adolphe was expanded to allow construction of the tram line over what had previously been traffic lanes. However, this eliminated the bike and pedestrian sidewalks on the deck. To continue to provide bike and pedestrian access, a new bike and pedestrian trail was provide not across the deck, but beneath the deck. The large, main arch of the bridge is really two side-by-side arches, separated by a space about 20 feet wide. Within this space, a paved pathway was suspended about 15 feet beneath the deck, and now serves as the main pedestrian access from the train station into the Haute Ville.

With two rivers and deep gorges bordering the Haute Ville, there are several other bridges in Luxembourg that deserve a visit, time permitting. About a half-mile to the east of Pont Adolphe is the lovely Passerelle, constructed in about 1860 to connect the new train station to the Haute Ville on the promontory. Although it is a little bit higher and longer than the Pont Adolphe, it is not so prominent because is not as ornate. Unlike Pont Adolphe, which is supported from the valley sides, the Passerelle sits securely on high piers supporting 24 narrow, stone arches. Each of the piers is subtly tapered, being much wider at the base than at the top. Two other bridges, both railroad bridges that cross the Alzette Valley to the east of the city, were built at the same time, and using the same design. It appears that the entire complex—the railroad, the railroad station, and the road leading from the station into town—was built in a single, coordinated effort. This gives a unity to the entire design, all of which is visible in a single sweeping view from the battlements surrounding the Haute Ville.

Within the Alzette valley east of the Haute Ville is a small, medieval neighborhood called Grund. Although the Pétrusse valley is so narrow that it can only accommodate a park, the Alzette valley is wide enough that this small suburb was built at the base of the battlements shortly after the city was founded. Similar to the Pétrusse valley, Grund is a semi-isolated, quiet, and pleasant place to walk among medieval walls and gardens along the small river and to view the battlements and casemates towering above from the vantage point of an outdoor café.

At the northern end of Grund, the fourteenth century city wall connects to the cliffs and crosses the Alzette River, thus enclosing Grund within the city's fortifications. The wall crossing of the Alzette forms an interesting small bridge called the Wenceslas Wall, which is actually the oldest of the Luxembourg bridges.

Another small stone bridge crossing over the Alzette in the center of Grund is made of three low stone arches and carries car traffic on Rue Münster. This little bridge provides a lovely view of the old buildings of Grund lining the Alzette, as well as the battlements and the Haute Ville looming directly above Grund. Finally, the Pont du Stierchen at the northern end of Grund is a medieval stone arch bridge famous as the home of the Stierches geescht, the ghost of a heavy drinker who is known to attack inebriated persons, throw them to the ground, and beat them.

With all of these bridges, valleys, battlements, walls, and streams having been walked, the most welcome site near the end of this little bridge in Grund is a sign, on the battlement wall, that indicates the availability of an elevator at the entrance to a tunnel. Sure enough, this tunnel leads about 50 feet into the cliff wall, ending at a public elevator. A few minutes later, you are back at street level in the Haute Ville, ready to see more.

HYDE HALL COVERED BRIDGE, COOPERSTOWN, NEW YORK, AND HASSENPLUG COVERED BRIDGE, MIFFLINBURG, PENNSYLVANIA

Of the more than 14,000 wooden covered bridges constructed in the United States, approximately 900 of them remain and can be visited today. However, because towns relied on standard, patented designs, the number of different wooden truss types on these 900 bridges is limited. The US Department of Transportation Federal Highway Administration's *Covered Bridge Manual* documents that almost 800 of these bridges fit neatly into one of five truss type categories: variations of kingpost or queenpost, Burr arch-truss, Town Lattice, Long Truss, or Howe Truss.

The earliest of these types are the kingpost, multiple kingpost, and queenpost, which were adaptations of construction techniques used for homes and commercial buildings. These truss types could only be used for small bridges shorter than about 50 feet long. Although kingpost and queenpost bridges were constructed before the 1820s, no examples of those earliest bridges remain.

The first design to advance the technology so it could bridge wider streams was the Palmer truss, but this required that the roadway itself be arched. As early as 1804, Theodore Burr designed a wooden arch-truss that allowed the roadway to remain flat, leading him to become one of the most prominent bridge designers at the time. Burr patented this design in 1817.

Burr arch-truss bridges rely on bent wooden beams, each end secured by an abutment, to form an arch on each side of the truss. While effective at allowing longer spans than kingpost and queenpost bridges, Burr arch-trusses were labor intensive to construct. Although thick wood beams curved to make an arch are much stronger than flat beams and planks, wood is a difficult material to bend into a curved shape. It must be soaked in water until it is pliable, then compressed into a curved shape using machinery, and then allowed to dry in its curved form before it can be incorporated into the wooden truss. On some bridges, the arches are a single timber, more than 50 feet long, and more than a foot wide on each side. On other bridges, the arches are a composite made of multiple planks or beams. They may be laminated, made of ten or more planks bundled together. This makes it easier to bend the arch by needing only to bend narrower planks, and also allows slippage along the surfaces between the individual planks. Other bridges have an arch that consists of two or more thick beams spliced together, end-to-end. Again, this is easier than finding and bending a single, large-scale beam.

Burr died in 1822, and none of the original bridges constructed under his direction remain. However, Burr arch-truss bridges continued to be constructed after his death, and the *Covered Bridge Manual* reports that the Burr arch-truss is still the most common truss type remaining, with 224 examples. Although the Burr arch-truss stopped being used as the most frequent design, the wooden arch today is a strong indicator of an early date for a covered bridge. The earliest of the remaining wooden covered bridges in the United States are mostly Burr arch-truss bridges, easily recognizable because the large wooden arch is visually distinct from the straight boards and planks used to construct the later truss types. The *Covered Bridge Manual* identifies three bridges, including Hyde Hall in New York, that are documented to have been constructed prior to 1830, and all three are either entirely Burr arch-truss bridges, or include a Burr arch-truss span. A fourth Burr arch-truss bridge, the Hassenplug Covered Bridge in Pennsylvania, is not mentioned in the *Covered Bridge Manual* but was also constructed prior to 1830.

The Hyde Hall Covered Bridge is widely considered the oldest covered bridge in the United States. It crosses Shadow Brook on the northern end of Otsego Lake near Cooperstown, New York. The bridge is so named because it was constructed on the property of Hyde Hall, a 340-acre country estate established by George Clarke between 1815 and 1830. The property, including the bridge and the mansion, were eventually acquired by the state and developed into Glimmerglass State Park. In addition to the bridge, the original mansion at Hyde Hall still stands and is one of many popular historical tourist attractions in the area.

The Hyde Hall Covered Bridge is not a large bridge. It is a single span, about 50 feet long and 15 feet wide. Its sides are covered with horizontal planks, with no windows. The bridge is gray and weathered, so it is not particularly picturesque. It stands alone in a cleared, grass-covered area, with no other nearby structures, just off the main entrance road into the state park. There is a parking lot large enough for about 15 cars.

Because it was constructed on a private estate, it has never carried a public roadway, nor does it carry traffic today. The park's hiking trail system incorporates the bridge, which connects the Blue Bird Trail to the Covered Bridge Trail. In addition to the parking lot and hiking trails, several other park amenities are provided, including a historical plaque at the entrance to the parking lot, a kiosk with a map of the state park, an informative exhibition plaque at the entrance to the bridge, a picnic table, and benches.

The large wooden arch-truss is the dominant structural component visible within the Hyde Hall Covered Bridge. There are actually four separate wooden arches, two on each side. The arches are each made of composite beams, rather than a single 50-foot long beam. Each segment of the beam is connected to its neighbor using a half-lap splice joint. The arches are then used as partial support for a series of multiple kingpost panels.

The historical plaque at the parking lot states that the bridge was restored in 1967, but does not provide any details regarding the extent of the restoration, such as which components are original versus which are modern replacements. However, the plaque adjacent to the bridge entrance states that the bridge still sits in its original location.

In general, the covered bridges that are most attractive to tourists are those within regional clusters of covered bridges, where the bridges are often just an excuse to go for a scenic drive for several hours. This area of New York is not one of those regional clusters. As a result, the Hyde Hall Covered Bridge is not nearly as well-known or as heavily visited by tourists as many less interesting and less important covered bridges.

The bridge does get its share of tourists as overflow from the many other important attractions in Cooperstown, which is a popular tourist town only eight miles away. Cooperstown is certainly best known as home to the Baseball Hall of Fame, which attracts tourists year-round, but in overwhelming numbers during induction week. Cooperstown is not easy to get to and after making the effort to get there, it is likely that a large number of visitors decide to stay a day or two and see other sights, such as the Hyde Hall mansion and covered bridge. There are also many historic sites associated with the American writer James Fenimore Cooper, whose father settled and gave his name to the town. Cooper's *Leatherstocking Tales* were set on Otsego Lake, and it was in the final novel of the series, *The Deerslayer*, published in 1841, in which Cooper coined the word "Glimmerglass" to describe the lake. This name has now been adopted for the state park as well as the famous local opera company.

Another potential contender for the oldest covered bridge in the nation is the Hassenplug Covered Bridge in Mifflinburg, Pennsylvania. The construction date for Hassenplug is listed as circa 1825 on a bronze plaque at the bridge, on Bridgehunter.com, and on several tourist websites, which also refer to the bridge as the second oldest wooden covered bridge in the United States.

The bridge carries North Fourth Street across Buffalo Creek just north of downtown Mifflinburg, Pennsylvania. The bridge is one lane wide, and about 50 feet long. There is a small, muddy parking lot big enough for a couple cars on the southern end of the bridge, at a trailhead for the Koons Trail. Unlike Hyde Hall, which has no outward decoration and is completely weathered gray, the Hassenplug Covered Bridge has vertical planking on the sides that are pleasantly painted red, and then white horizontal planking on the ends. The bridge has no windows.

The bridge shares a feature with many other covered bridges, which is that it displays a warning sign over the roadway that no longer applies to people crossing in the twenty-first century but is a quaint reminder of the bridge's history. The sign reads "Any person riding or driving at any other gait than a walk, or driving more than 15 head of cattle, or carrying fire in any way over this bridge are subjected to a fine of Thirty Dollars."

Like most covered bridges that still carry traffic, the bridge is narrow, there is no sidewalk, and there always seems to be a car coming, but the interior should still be investigated. The most prominent feature is the curved wooden beams indicating that this is a Burr arch-truss bridge. The arch appears to be constructed of a single beam that is not laminated and is continuous from one end of the arch to the other.

The bronze plaque inside the southern end of the bridge provides a short history lesson, complete with diagrams, in the development of early wooden covered bridge design. The Burr arch-truss used all wood members and secured the joints with wooden pins and iron bolts. By 1840, a designer named Squire Whipple began to use iron members, developed a truss to connect the arched top chord to a straight bottom chord, and invented the bowstring truss. At about the same time, William Howe developed a wood and iron truss with straight top and bottom chords, eliminating the wooden arch which was characteristic of the Burr arch-truss.

The bronze plaque, placed in 1959, lists the date for the Hassenplug Bridge as circa 1825, and states that the Hassenplug name came from the family living in the nearby brick house.

An unusual feature of this bridge is the floor, which is a steel grate like those found on modern bridges. It is likely that all other covered bridges you might have visited have wooden floors. You may not notice the steel grate when you first walk in, but it becomes obvious when a car crosses and makes that distinct, rumbling car tire-on-steel-grate sound, which is amplified by the enclosed space. The plaque documents that the bridge was modernized in 1959 by having its wooden floor and structural supports removed and replaced with a modern steel bridge built within the outer wooden frame. This was done to preserve the original wooden walls, arch, and roof of the structure.

Similar to the discussion of the Frankford Avenue, Choate, and Glen Mill bridges in *Bridgespotting: Part 1*, there does not seem to be consensus regarding the identification of the oldest wooden covered bridges in the United States. Most sources seem to agree that Hyde Hall is the oldest, with a construction date listed as 1825 in all but two major sources. The date is listed as 1825 on two historical plaques at the site and in the *Covered Bridge Manual*, but listed as 1823 on Bridgehunter.com and circa 1830 in Richard Sanders Allen's *Covered Bridges of the Northeast*. Interestingly, there is no mention of the bridge in Miller and Knapp's *America's Covered Bridges*, published in 2013, which otherwise appears to be an encyclopedic discussion of the history of covered bridge design and survey of hundreds of covered bridges.

Despite the slightly different dates on Bridgehunter and in Allen, the 1825 date appears to be well-substantiated, as one of the historical plaques at the site even provides the names of the three men who constructed the bridge—Andrew Alden, Lorenzo Bates, and Cyrenus Clark. In addition, the historical plaques at the parking lot go a little further than just saying that this is the oldest covered bridge in the nation—it says that the bridge was "recognized" in 2006 as the oldest extant covered bridge in the United States, which appears to lend authenticity to the claim. However, it does not mention what individual or organization did the recognizing, nor the kind of documentation or criteria involved.

The situation at the Hassenplug Covered Bridge is an interesting case. The 1825 date and the claim that it is the second oldest covered bridge are widespread among internet sources, including Bridgehunter. This date, or at least "circa 1825," is also listed on the bronze plaque inside the bridge. If the construction date for Hassenplug is truly 1825, then it would be remarkable if documentation reliable enough to "recognize" Hyde Hall, also dated 1825, as the older of the two bridges existed, because the difference between the two bridges would only be a matter of a few months.

The fact that the Hassenplug Covered Bridge is not mentioned by Miller and Knapp does not signify anything, because Hyde Hall is also not listed in their book. It does seem unusual that Allen's *Covered Bridges of the Middle Atlantic* mentions the bridge and identifies it as a Burr arch-truss, but does not attempt to provide a construction date. Allen's book was published in 1959, the same year the bridge was modernized and, presumably, the same year the bronze plaque with the circa 1825 date was placed on the bridge. However, Allen was writing an extensive survey of more than 1,000 covered bridges and can be forgiven for not knowing of a specific plaque placed on a specific bridge at the same time that he was writing.

More curious, though, is that the bridge is distinctly not mentioned at all in the *Covered Bridge Manual*. Page 20 of the *Manual* even has a subsection titled "Oldest Covered Bridge in the United States," which lists the only three covered bridges in the United States that have "authenticated" dates before 1830 and, for some reason, the Hassenplug Covered Bridge is not one of them. This is an unlikely oversight, and probably not due to some recent discovery of documentation changing the understanding of the Hassenplug construction date. One possibility is that the authors of the *Covered Bridge Manual* used Allen as a source for this section and left the bridge off their list because there was no date listed in Allen. Alternatively, it may mean that the date for the Hassenplug Covered Bridge is not "authenticated," although no standard for authentication is discussed.

Most likely, the sources used by the *Covered Bridge Manual* discounted the Hassenplug Covered Bridge as an extant, wooden covered bridge because the 1959 reconstruction removed the deck and placed the walls and roof on top of a new steel bridge, eliminating the structural integrity of the wooden truss. This demonstrates the complexity in studying historic bridges, because the ongoing, and necessary, reconstructions blur the lines between what is original and what is not. Although the Hassenplug Covered Bridge was reconstructed in 1959, Hyde Hall also is reported to have been "restored" in 1967, so it is not as if Hyde Hall was completely original, either. Finally, even if the Hassenplug Covered Bridge is no longer "officially" an original wooden covered bridge, it appears that the Burr arch-truss and the roof components are just as original, and about the same construction date, as those on Hyde Hall. Although the reconstruction may have eliminated the Hassenplug Covered Bridge from listings in the official record books, it should still be high on the target list for anyone interested in studying the oldest covered bridges in the United States.

WEST CORNWALL COVERED BRIDGE, WEST CORNWALL, CONNECTICUT

At first glance, the West Cornwall Covered Bridge looks like just another pretty covered bridge, no different from hundreds of others in New England. However, it has some unusual features that attract more tourists than most covered bridges.

One common feature of covered bridges is that they are almost always found in the middle of nowhere. This does not mean that they are not easily accessible. There are often signs pointing out the direction to the bridge from the main highway. The bridges also usually have a small parking area on one or both ends but, in general, there is nothing else to see within walking distance of the bridge. Usually, they are found either in the woods or in rural agricultural areas. There may be a house or an isolated building nearby, but that is all.

The West Cornwall Covered Bridge is an exception, as it is literally a few footsteps off the quaint historic green in West Cornwall. West Cornwall is not a large town, and there is not much to its town square except for a furniture maker, pottery, and a couple other small businesses. However, the town is situated directly on Route 7, a popular scenic drive through the Litchfield Hills of northwestern Connecticut. Once you have stopped and taken a closer look, you will realize that this covered bridge is better than most.

Constructed in 1841, the bridge is much earlier and longer than other covered bridges you have seen. The river it crosses, the Housatonic, passes over rapids right at the bridge, so the setting is more scenic than other covered bridge locations. The town has recognized this special location by installing numerous benches in a park overlooking the bridge and the rapids.

Because it is so close to, and visible from, a main highway, the bridge is almost a traffic hazard. Sitting on the benches and looking across the river toward Route 7, it will not take long before you can actually see the thought patterns of the drivers playing out. Maybe the drivers know they are approaching yet another quaint New England town, or maybe they do not know. Maybe they care about covered bridges and know one is here, or maybe they do not know. However, within a few minutes you will watch as a speeding driver slams on the brakes, hesitates, decides to turn off the highway, drives across the bridge, parks on the green, and gets out to take pictures.

EADS BRIDGE, ST. LOUIS

Any plan to visit historic and prominent bridges in the United States would have to include, as a matter of course, the oldest bridge crossing the Mississippi River, especially if that bridge was historically important, architecturally interesting, and offered fantastic views of famous landmarks. All of these are found in the Eads Bridge in downtown St. Louis.

Eads was not the first bridge over the Mississippi River. A road bridge was constructed in Minneapolis in 1855, followed by a railroad bridge constructed at Rock Island in 1856. Those bridges no longer exist and Eads, constructed in 1874, appears to be the oldest bridge still standing. The bridge was conceived and constructed by James Buchanan Eads, a prominent military engineer and inventor. Eads was famous before the Civil War for having invented a diving bell that allowed him to explore steamboat wrecks on the bed of the Mississippi River, from which he became rich salvaging their materials. During the war, he was noted for constructing an entire fleet of gunboats in a short period of time, allowing the Union Army to control the river. Near the end of his career, he used his knowledge of river dynamics to constrain the banks of the mouth of the

Mississippi, which in turn increased the flow rate and kept the channel clear of silt for improvement of shipping. In the middle of this amazing career, Eads designed the first bridge to cross the Mississippi at the bustling river town of St. Louis.

As an early crossing of the largest river in the United States, you can imagine that construction of this bridge set all sorts of records for highest, longest, first use of certain materials and techniques, and other engineering achievements, and it did. As part of a common theme among bridges, or anything else new for that matter, Eads' plan was opposed by steamboat and ferry operators who feared that a bridge would obstruct the river as well as cut into their business. To avoid blocking steamboat traffic on the river during construction, cantilever supports, as opposed to scaffolding, were used for the first time to hold the arches up before they could be completed. Construction of the pneumatic caissons, which needed to be sunk more than 100 feet deep to reach bedrock so that they would not be damaged by scour during floods, resulted in one of the first recognized cases of the bends, killing 15 workers.

One of its most important distinctions is that Eads Bridge represented the first use of steel in a major bridge. Much of the complex deck structure was made of wrought-iron, but the important load bearing components of the arches were made of steel. The bridge was, at the time of construction, the longest arch bridge in the world, at more than 6,400 feet long.

The bridge is actually a complex structure with different construction techniques and materials along its length. On the riverbanks, the bridge is anchored by multi-level stone arch approaches. The lower level consists of five narrow, tall arches. These arches have red granite bases, which are then topped by yellow sandstone. From close up, you can see the cross-bedding in the sandstone, making the arches a geologic field trip all on their own. The lower arches are then topped by another row of yellow sandstone arches, much smaller, that support the upper road deck. Each of these granite and sandstone ends is then flanked by a massive black stone tower, which provides an interesting color contrast with the yellow and red of the arch sections. The black towers are then used as the abutments for the most interesting part of the bridge—the ribbed steel arches.

HISTORIC BRIDGES

The main part of the bridge consists of three of these arches, each sitting on the two end towers and on two more piers in the middle of the river.

The appearance of the steelwork comprising the arches is complex and confusing. Many steel arch bridges have a common general appearance, with a curved arch on the bottom, vertical supports making up the spandrel in the middle, and then the horizontal deck on top. On Eads Bridge, the open spandrel reveals an internal horizontal component in the center of the bridge, cutting directly across the curved arch and vertical steel supports. At first, it looks as if they were randomly running steel beams for additional support, willy-nilly. That is until you hear the sound of a train running through the bridge and realize that it has two decks instead of one. Tucked within the network of curved steel arches and vertical steel supports is another network of horizontal supports holding a lower deck that is used for running light rail trains across the river to East St. Louis in Illinois. The interweaving of these supports effectively creates two bridges within one structure.

The upper deck carries Washington Avenue out of downtown St. Louis and into Illinois. The upper deck also includes a pedestrian sidewalk on the south side of the bridge, facing downtown, and separated from traffic by a low cement wall.

The development of the downtown buildings and landmarks in St. Louis mostly occurred after 1874, so they were integrated with the bridge as part of the urban landscape. Eads Bridge and the next bridge to the south, Poplar Street Bridge, are about a mile apart, and they frame the downtown area between them like a stage set flanked by curtains. The downtown riverfront between the two bridges consists of nothing but a riverfront promenade, with no docks, warehouses, or buildings interrupting the view. On the landward side of the riverwalk, an enormously wide staircase, flanked by grassy slopes, rises to the top of the bluff. The staircase leads to a large plaza surrounding the gleaming steel of the Gateway Arch, the most prominent landmark in St. Louis. Just behind the arch, centered in the middle of it, is the sparkling white stone and green copper dome of the 170-year-old Old Courthouse, where the Dred Scott case was tried in 1857. This entire complex, stretching from bridge to bridge, is the Jefferson National Expansion Memorial, operated by the National Park

Service. To the sides and behind the Old Courthouse are the office towers and hotels of the modern city. This entire prospect lies directly at your feet, from your vantage point on the bridge.

An interesting feature of the bridge's history to contemplate is the role of St. Louis in serving as the Gateway to the West in the nineteenth century. The image we have in our heads of the great westward migration is of oxen drawing covered wagons across the prairie, radiating out from St. Louis on a series of trails to the Wild West. That was true up to the middle of the century. However, the first rail bridge over the Mississippi was built in 1855, and the Transcontinental Railroad was completed in 1869, both making rail transport a prominent method of migration. Still, covered wagon transport continued to be used late into the century, well after Eads Bridge was built in 1874. The logical conclusion, then, is that this ultra-modern looking, industrial-age steel bridge must have served as the river crossing for oxen-drawn covered wagons for at least some portion of its history.

The Eads Bridge was almost lost in the early 1990s. Even though it has a prime downtown location on the St. Louis end, the bridge no longer connected to prominent areas or roads on the eastern end. Most regional traffic was long-since diverted over larger, newer interstate highway bridges that bypassed downtown. Only a few local commuters used the bridge.

Given the enormous cost to renovate and maintain the aging structure for this small volume of traffic, the bridge was closed in 1991 and remained unused for several years. Loss of the bridge would have been a shame, visually, because it would have upset the symmetrical balance that has been designed into the Jefferson National Expansion Memorial. The park, the staircase leading up to the top of the bluff, the Arch, the Old Courthouse, and the rest of downtown were all deliberately centered on this area between the Eads and Poplar Street bridges, which act as bookends for the entire area. Removal of the Eads Bridge would have opened the view from this area to include the much less attractive, and much less historically interesting, Martin Luther King Bridge. Fortunately for bridge tourists, the Eads Bridge was renovated, with the upper deck being reopened to road and pedestrian traffic in 2003. The reconstruction included development of wider parts of the narrow sidewalk to allow pedestrians to stop and admire the view. In the case of Eads Bridge, its visual and historical contribution to the urban landscape far outweighs its role in transportation.

ROEBLING SUSPENSION BRIDGE, CINCINNATI

The Roebling Suspension Bridge crosses the Ohio River in downtown Cincinnati, connecting the city to Covington, Kentucky, on the south side of the river. Constructed in 1867, the bridge is one of the most historically important bridges in the United States. Of the bridges designed by prominent early bridge engineer John Roebling in the middle of the nineteenth century, only three remain. One of those, the Delaware Aqueduct, was not designed as a traffic bridge, and only carries traffic today after numerous modifications and reconstructions over the past 170 years. The other two remaining Roebling bridges are the world-famous Brooklyn Bridge and this bridge in Cincinnati.

From a distance, the bridge is similar in appearance to the Brooklyn Bridge. It is large-scale at more than 1,000 feet long, about 30 feet high over the river, and carries two lanes of traffic with sidewalks on both sides. It has two dark-colored stone suspension towers rising from the river, and an indecipherable mess of blue-painted steel girders and cables going every which way in between.

As is often seen in the early use of a new technology, in this case the use of wire rope in large-scale suspension bridges, the design of the support system for the Roebling Bridge is either an ingenious combination of multiple technologies designed to create a delicate balance of support systems, or it is completely over engineered. In present day bridges, we are accustomed to seeing the deck held up by a single support system. In suspension bridges, a single main cable drops through an arc between suspension towers, and vertical cables extend down to hold the deck. In cable-stayed bridges, a single set of diagonal cables connect the deck to the towers. In steel truss bridges, a single truss structure extends from shore-to-pier, pier-to-pier as many times as needed, and then pier-to-shore again.

The Roebling Bridge is all three of these, and more. The deck is part of a truss of steel girders, a steel box about 15 feet high by 20 feet wide spanning the entire length of the bridge. There are three sections to this truss—a small arched truss on either end and a larger arched truss in between the suspension towers. This truss is then held tightly in place by multiple, separate support systems. The first support for the truss is the use of piers. In a normal truss bridge, the truss rests on foundations on the shore and on piers in the middle of the river. This is true of the Roebling Bridge. The steel girders of the truss are actually built into the stone structure of the suspension towers, so the suspension towers act as piers, holding up the ends of the truss.

The second support is what we think of as a "normal" suspension bridge system. A single main cable is anchored by a stone anchor tower on the south bank of the river, draped over the two stone suspension towers, and then anchored in another stone tower on the north bank. For its full length, this main cable has vertical cables extending down to hold the truss that, in turn, holds the deck.

The bridge also has a second main suspension cable system, parallel to the first. The three different spans of the bridge are of different lengths, and, therefore, of different weights. The two spans connecting to the shores are short, weigh less, and thus do not need the redundant support system. For this part of the bridge between the anchor towers on the shore and the suspension towers, this second main cable is not weight-bearing. Because it does not have vertical cables supporting a deck across this section, it is pulled taut by the weight of the central section, and does not have the catenary arc shape we are accustomed to seeing. However, the main span between the two suspension towers is much longer and heavier, and therefore the second main cable is used to support this span along with the first main cable. In between the suspension towers, the second main cable is weight-bearing and does drop through an arc, in parallel with the first main cable. In this area, the truss is held in place by two separate vertical suspension systems.

Apparently, these three different support systems were not thought to be enough. Like the Brooklyn Bridge, the Roebling Bridge also has a separate diagonal, cable-stayed support system. In addition to holding the main suspension cables, the suspension towers hold diagonal cables, in a fan-shape, to provide additional support to the truss. In this manner, the deck is supported by a truss on piers, two separate vertical cable systems, and another diagonal cable system.

The complex cable system and stone towers are pleasant to look at, both from a distance and up close during your walk. The cables and girders of the truss are all painted marine blue. The towers are constructed of fine-grained, light-colored sandstone that has darkened with age. Each tower is a single, round-topped stone archway flanked by massive stone sides. The archway is about 25 feet high, and the total tower height is about 40 feet above the deck.

The towers are nicely decorated using textured stonework and architectural elements. The sides of each tower are slightly tapered from bottom to top. The stonework on the sides of the towers is smooth, while that of the archway and above the archway is textured to make the individual blocks stand out. The top of each tower is flat, surrounded by a stone parapet, and then topped with two octagonal stone cupolas. The cupolas, in turn, are topped by a gilded orb and cross.

The city of Cincinnati has recognized the beauty and importance of the bridge by making it the center of their downtown development. The bridge does carry traffic and can be driven over, but the traffic pattern is specifically designed to be limited to a minor amount of local traffic. The road being carried by the bridge does not directly empty into downtown Cincinnati or Covington but instead ends in a traffic circle at each end. At the northern end, the traffic circle has been developed so that the bridge frames the entrance to the National Underground Railroad Freedom Center. The riverfront in this area has been developed with the city's football stadium to the left, baseball stadium to the right, and indoor arena just past the baseball stadium, as you are looking at downtown from the bridge. The baseball stadium is open toward the river, and you can stand on the bridge and watch the score of the game on the Jumbotron.

The riverfront between the stadiums and the shore has been beautifully developed into an extensive riverfront park and riverwalk. You can rent bicycles or Segways to explore the area, and there are swinging benches to sit and watch the river. The riverwalk has a great view of both the Roebling Bridge to your right, and the Taylor-Southgate Bridge to your left.

Cincinnati has also honored the Roebling Bridge by deliberately not placing any tall buildings directly near its end. The Freedom Center is a low lying building, and both the football and baseball stadiums are set to the side from the end of the bridge. The taller office buildings of downtown are a few blocks further in from the river. Although subtle how this is beneficial to the bridge, it is contrasted with the way that Covington has crowded several tall buildings directly surrounding the southern end of the bridge. The bridge towers, which are close to the shore, are beautiful, but they are not tall. By surrounding the southern towers with much taller, modern buildings, the view of the bridge from across the river is diminished. On the Cincinnati end, there are no tall buildings within several blocks of the bridge tower, making it more visible and easier to appreciate.

SOUTH PORTLAND STREET FOOTBRIDGE, GLASGOW

Although Scotland is a major tourist destination, its most popular attractions involve either the mountains, lakes, and distilleries of the Highlands, or the history of the castles in Edinburgh and Stirling. The largest city in Scotland, Glasgow, generally does not register as highly on the tourist radar. It is not often discussed as a prominent attraction, other than as the gateway airport for the rest of the country. Ask anyone what there is to do in Glasgow as a tourist, and there is no obvious answer. While Edinburgh and the Highlands have kept busy cultivating their historical, scenic, and thirst-quenching attractions, Glasgow has been doing the business of manufacturing and shipping. These generally do not result in the creation of tourist attractions, but they do result in the construction of bridges.

Wooden bridges have crossed the Clyde for centuries, but none of them remain. The current bridges are mostly stone arch bridges constructed in the late 1800s and early 1900s. These bridges are not large, nor do they have impressive decorations. There is a new generation of sculptural bridges constructed since 1990, but only one of these, the Clyde Arc, has a prominently visible superstructure that attracts substantial tourist interest. Hidden in among these mostly innocuous bridges is an unexpected little gem, the South Portland Street Suspension Bridge.

The historic center of Glasgow was on the north bank of the Clyde but, by the early 1800s, the growing city had expanded to include suburbs on the south bank. Among the prominent developments, directly on the river opposite the Metropolitan Cathedral Church of St. Andrew, were two enormous stone apartment buildings known as Carlton Place. The bridge, centered on South Portland Street, which passed between the two buildings, was constructed in 1853 to connect the buildings to downtown Glasgow.

The pedestrian-only bridge is a cute, small-scale suspension bridge about 400 feet long and 15 feet wide. In addition to its small size for a suspension bridge, the bridge is well-known because of the ornate decoration of the stone towers. The towers are both constructed of blocks of sandstone in varying hues of beige to deep red. Each tower is about 30 feet high and ten feet wide, and forms an ornamental archway. The entries to the arches are adorned with fluted stone columns. Above the archway are two cornices, with the eyebar suspension chains passing between them. The eyebar suspension chains are painted red to complement the red sandstone of the towers, as are the deck girders and the posts and top rail of the railing. Between the posts, the railing panels are filled in with an attractive lattice of white iron bars. The railing is topped with ornate Victorian lampposts.

The historic center of Glasgow, including the train and bus stations, museums, and attractive old architecture, is on the north bank of the River Clyde. There are few attractions on the south side of the river, so it would be easy for the tourists who do visit Glasgow to do so without ever walking a few blocks to the river or investigating the bridges. However, it would be a shame to visit Glasgow, or any city, without going to the river, strolling along the riverfront promenade, and investigating the historic buildings and bridges that allowed the city to develop in the first place. It is understandable that, having come this far to Scotland, most tourists would want to immediately jump on a train to the Highlands or Edinburgh. Glasgow, though, is definitely worth an extra day stopover to see the cityscape along the river and a few nice bridges.

BUILDER PLAQUE MYSTERIES, WROUGHT IRON BRIDGE COMPANY BRIDGES, VARIOUS LOCATIONS, EASTERN AND MID-ATLANTIC UNITED STATES

In about 1893, an artist or designer at the Wrought Iron Bridge Company in Canton, Ohio, was probably excited to get an important new assignment. For years, their employer had placed cast-iron builder plaques on the top chord above the portal on their bridges, but those plaques were relatively plain in appearance. Before the 1880s, the plaques were rectangular and presented no information other than the name of the builder. Through the 1880s and into the 1890s, the plaques were slightly more complex. The rectangle was given a peaked roof on top, and the sides were curved instead of straight, but there was still limited information provided. The plaques read "WROUGHT IRON BRIDGE CO. BUILDERS CANTON OH."

In 1893, however, the designer was allowed to create a plaque that was not only informative but also decorative. The shape became more complex, with three finials along the top—one in the center and one on each end. The font was also changed to be more elaborate. Instead of upper case letters all the same size, the first letter of each word was made larger than the other letters. Also, a new space was added to the top center of the plaque, to make space for a date. Most of the numbers in the date were given the same font treatment as the wording. They were relatively square, blocky, easy-to-read numbers.

Except for the "9." The "9" was given a long, curly tail that curved upward to meet the upper part of the number. On the new, clean builder plaques, the design was gorgeous, but after the paint had peeled for a while and the plaque had rusted, the "9s" became difficult to distinguish from the "8s." This was made worse by the fact that the plaques were placed high above the roadway, so they were difficult to read in normal circumstances. If the end chords framing the portal were slanted, then the plaques were also often angled upward, away from the viewer, making it even more difficult to read. Also, the plaques on many bridges fell off or were stolen by overzealous bridgespotters, leaving only old, grainy photos to show how they once looked. One of the more pristine plaques remaining is on the 1898 Masemore Road Bridge in Maryland, where the plaque is not rusted but is freshly painted and oriented vertically, making it easily legible from the roadway. Even on this bridge, it is difficult to distinguish between the "9" and the "8s."

As it would happen, of course, the heyday of the Wrought Iron Bridge Company was the 1880s and 1890s, so a difficulty in distinguishing the "9" from the "8" means an error of ten years. All of this would just be a minor nuisance, except the date plaque is one of the most important pieces of evidence used by historical researchers and state historical agencies in establishing the construction date of a bridge. As a result, the curly tail on the "9" has caused ripples in the historical documentation on at least two Wrought Iron Bridge Company bridges.

One of these ripples is relatively minor in scale but demonstrates the issue. The construction date for the York Haven Bridge in York County, Pennsylvania, is routinely reported to be 1888. This date is reported on historicbridges.org, on bridgehunter.com, and on the Pennsylvania Department of Transportation website. The bridge has an older-style Wrought Iron Bridge Company plaque that does not list the date. However, it does have the date displayed on a button covering a joint between two iron support bars. The font used for that button is the same as that used for the post-1893 builder plaques, and appears to show that the actual date is 1889, not 1888.

A more complex situation exists at the Noble's Mill Road Bridge crossing Deer Creek in Harford County, Maryland. The bridge has a lovely Wrought Iron Bridge Company date plaque, in excellent condition, over the portal on both ends. The plaque has three finials and the date, so it is clearly of the post-1893 plaque type. However, the date listed on the plaque is 1883. Some other items about the plaque are unsettling. The font of the lettering is different from that on any of the post-1893 plaques. All of the letters on the plaque are the exact same size, which does not match the post-1893 design of having the first letter in each word larger than the other letters. The 1883 date is prominently displayed and easily legible on the old-looking plaque but seems to be incorrect.

To make matters worse, as has happened at other bridges, the 1883 date has been adopted by later sources, lending it an air of authenticity. The date of 1883 is stamped into the concrete of the new abutments that were added during a 1998 rehabilitation. Bridgehunter.com provides the

1883 date with no qualifications. The 2002 book *Historic Bridges of Maryland* by Legler and Highsmith of the Maryland Department of Transportation State Highway Administration, is an important catalog of Maryland's historic bridges, with dozens of gorgeous photographs. The book was published by the Maryland Historical Trust Press and is therefore the closest thing to an "official" history of bridges in Maryland. Legler and Highsmith also adopt the 1883 date with no qualification.

Date Plaque on Noble's Mill Bridge, Harford County, Maryland

In general, it seems that an incorrect date attribution on a bridge is an innocuous matter. In this case, the Noble's Mill Road Bridge is a contributing resource to the Lower Deer Creek Valley Historic District, along with the enormous Noble's Mill building itself, which sits at the northern end of the bridge. The mill building dates to 1854. An incorrect date on the bridge could result in further errors for researchers studying the historic district.

The historicbridges.org website noticed the discrepancy on the date plaque and, noting the plaque was a recent replacement, surmised that reviewers of historical photos of the original date plaque had misread the "9" as an "8." Based on specific details of the truss type, historicbridges.org suggested an attribution of either 1890 or, assuming the photo of the original date plaque had been misread, 1893.

A review of the documentation associated with the Maryland Historical Trust form for the bridge shows that this theory about misreading the photo of the original date plaque was correct. That documentation includes the original photo, showing the post-1893 style plaque, but the date is not legible on the photo. To assist readers in understanding the photo, the 1994 researchers wrote in the margin in parentheses "1883 Wrought Iron Bridge Company"—even though there was no way of extracting the 1883 date from the photo itself. Separately, on the previous page, the documentation also includes an earlier schematic drawing of the bridge, including a sketch of its date plaque. That drawing has the date of 1893. The 1976 Maryland Historical Trust form, combined for Noble's Mill and the adjacent bridge, also correctly identifies the date of 1893 for the bridge.

Although the documentation includes both a drawing of the plaque and the 1976 form with the correct date, the remainder of the documentation and the Maryland Historical Trust form reiterate and support the 1883 date. The documentation even includes a page from the Wrought Iron Bridge Company's 1885 catalog, presumably to support the 1883 date of attribution. If the 1883 date were correct, then the Noble's Mill Road Bridge should have been listed in the 1885 catalog. However, it is not listed. There is a bridge crossing Deer Creek in Harford County listed, but it refers to The Rocks of Deer Creek. The Rocks is now a state park, ten miles away from Noble's Mill. There is a bridge at The Rocks, the Cherry Hill Road Bridge, with a pre-1893 Wrought Iron Bridge Company plaque, and it is almost certainly this bridge which is referred to in the 1885 catalog.

The "9" mistaken for an "8" is just one of the documentation errors found on a handful of Wrought Iron Bridge Company bridges in the mid-Atlantic area. Some of these errors are minor, but they are errors, nonetheless. For instance, many sources provide a date of either 1876 or circa 1876 for the Four Points Bridge in Maryland, based on the date on its plaque. The plaque clearly states "Patented Nov. 21st 1876." This may seem nit-picky, but referring to the construction date as "circa" 1876 is imprecise, because it implies that the date is somewhere close to 1876, but could be before or after. It leaves no constraint on the date in either direction. The phrase "Patented Nov. 21st 1876" contains a certitude that "circa" does not include. With the exact patent date on the plaque, we know for a fact that the bridge was completed sometime after Nov. 21st, 1876. Based only on the plaque, it may have been completed five or ten years after 1876. However, it cannot have been completed before Nov 21st, 1876, because there is no way they could have produced the cast-iron plaque and attached it to the bridge before they knew what the patent date was going to be.

For some reason, this imprecision regarding the Four Points Bridge became embroiled in the historical documentation for the Poffenberger Road Bridge, also in Maryland, just a few miles from Four Points. The Poffenberger Road Bridge does not have a builder plaque attached, but these are often missing after more than 100 years, and the lack of a plaque does not indicate anything definitive. The National Register of Historic Places Inventory Nomination Form for the Poffenberger Road Bridge lists a probable date of 1878 but does not explain the source of this date. The form also states that it is a Wrought Iron Bridge Company bridge, without any qualification or explanation.

This information has then been adopted by multiple later sources. Bridgehunter.com lists the Poffenberger Road Bridge as Wrought Iron Bridge Company, with a date of 1878. The Wikipedia page for the bridge lists the builder as Wrought Iron Bridge Company and provides a date of circa 1878. The 2002 book by Legler and Highsmith states that the ornate nameplate and decorations in the corners of the Four Points Bridge portal are reminiscent of those on the Poffenberger Road Bridge, suggesting that it also was constructed by the Wrought Iron Bridge Company at about the same time. This statement is problematic because, although both bridges have ornate decoration on the corners of their portals, that was true of many different bridge designers, and there is really no similarity between the portals of Four Points and Poffenberger Road. Legler and Highsmith go further than the Wrought Iron Bridge Company attribution by stating that the Poffenberger Road Bridge may have been constructed by the Penn Bridge Company.

As with the Noble's Mill Road Bridge, only historicbridges.org appears to have looked deeper into the situation and made a correct attribution for the Poffenberger Road Bridge. The website noted that the portal ornamentation of the Poffenberger Road Bridge was distinctive, consisting of an intricate, hand-cut geometric design that exactly matches the portal on the Bauer Road Bridge in the Calhoun County Historic Bridge Park in Michigan. Because the Bauer Road Bridge has legible cast-iron buttons inscribed with "PENN" on its lattice joints, the Poffenberger Road Bridge can confidently be attributed to the Penn Bridge Company. This means that all of the historic documentation attributing this bridge to the Wrought Iron Bridge Company is incorrect.

An interesting mystery, still unresolved, involves the builder plaque on the Lower Toddsville Road Bridge crossing Oaks Creek in Cooperstown, New York. An Existing Conditions Survey from 2007, available on historicbridges.org, shows a photo of the eastern portal with an ornate grill and a white house in the background, but with no builder plaque. There is no mention of a plaque either in the summary of the inspection, nor in the recommendations for restoration. Similarly, the listing for this bridge on bridgehunter.com has a clear, clean photo of the portal, taken in 2010. That photo clearly shows that there is no plaque on the bridge, although it does show the same ornate grill and white house.

Then, both historicbridges.org and bridgehunter.com show 2018 photos. The photo on bridgehunter.com was taken from the opposite direction and is not clear, but it appears to show the backside of a plaque in place across the ornate grill. Historicbridges.org shows detailed photos of the front of this plaque, revealing it to be a Wrought Iron Bridge Company plaque. During a 2021 site visit conducted by the author, with photos, this Wrought Iron Bridge Company plaque was still in place, centered above the portal. The 2021 photos also show the ornate grill and the white house in the background, confirming that the 2007, 2010, 2018, and 2021 photos are all of the same bridge.

This would not seem to be a problem. Many of the plaques on these bridges have fallen off or been removed over the years. Restoration projects on these bridges often involve the attachment of replacement plaques, so it would not seem too unusual for a new plaque to have been attached between 2010 and 2018. The problem, though, is that there is no suggestion or indication of any restoration or rehabilitation activity during this timeframe. In fact, quite the opposite—this bridge has not been restored and returned to the road network, nor preserved in a park or connected to a trail system. Instead, it has been left to rust to pieces.

A commenter on bridgehunter.com noted that there had been a limited 2006-2007 restoration effort that involved replacing the wooden plank deck and placing traffic barriers on the ends. This effort clearly had nothing to do with preserving the bridge. Instead, it was done for safety reasons only, and therefore would likely not have inspired anyone to go to the expense and trouble to create and attach a replacement builder plaque. Also, the comment, posted in 2019, makes no mention of any restoration efforts between 2010 and 2018. The 2010 photos show the wooden deck in good shape, which is consistent with a 2006-2007 deck replacement. By 2021, the deck was so degraded that it was unsafe to walk over it. In between, someone attached a new, or reattached the old, builder plaque. Either way, they expended time and money to attach a plaque on a bridge that was otherwise left to the elements. It seems there is an untold story here somewhere.

The Pumpkin Run Road Bridge in Greene County, Pennsylvania, is reported on bridgehunter.com and historicbridges.org to be dated 1895, citing the Pennsylvania Historic Bridge Inventory. However, the Wrought Iron Bridge Company builder plaque is of the type usually only found on pre-1893 bridges. Although they also list the 1895 date, historicbridges.org notes that the bridge uses the type of bracing used by the Wrought Iron Bridge Company in the 1880s, suggesting an error with the 1895 attribution, although they do not go so far as to question its validity.

The Higginsville Road South Bridge in Hunterdon County, New Jersey, has a builder plaque that identifies the construction date as 1893. Both bridgehunter.com and historicbridges.org adopt the 1893 date. The New Jersey Historic Bridge Inventory discussion of this bridge, quoted on historicbridges.org, refers to this bridge as being one of ten New Jersey bridges listed in the Wrought Iron Bridge Company's 1885 trade catalog. This would be a neat trick for the bridge to be listed in the 1885 catalog, given that it was not constructed until 1893.

Interestingly, the historical bridges cited here to demonstrate the complications of studying their origins and context reflect only a tiny corner of the world of just one bridge construction company. That fact alone gives an idea of how frequently these errors occur. Even more disconcerting is the lack of a reliable mechanism for correcting errors. Print sources are rarely reprinted with corrected information and internet sources are rarely updated—the authors of the original material have moved on to other projects. Even official records, such as Maryland Historical Trust documentation, can continue to misinform researchers for decades. The good news is that these are academic questions with no real-world consequences, mostly providing entertainment to bridgespotters. However, based on the large number of errors found on this limited set of bridges, there is likely to be enough material out there to keep bridgespotters entertained for a long time into the future.

MILFORD SWING BRIDGE, MILFORD, NEW HAMPSHIRE, AND KEESEVILLE SUSPENSION BRIDGE, KEESEVILLE, NEW YORK

Chapter 3 of *Bridgespotting: Part 1* discussed the concept of mill and factory bridges, specifically that these were small-scale suspension bridges known as swinging bridges and were intended to provide pedestrian access for mill or factory workers. Because these were inexpensive to construct and usually provided access to a single mill, they were often privately constructed by the mill company itself as opposed to the city or community. As a result, they were not constructed by well established companies and were not necessarily designed to last. Few of the original mill and factory bridges remain, although reproductions are popular.

Separately, Chapter 2 of *Bridgespotting: Part 1* also discussed the extensive reach of the iconic Berlin Iron Bridge Company of East Berlin, Connecticut, in the late 1800s, with hundreds of bridges to their credit, yet only a handful remain to be visited by bridgespotters in the twenty-first century. The best known of these historic treasures are the lenticular through-truss bridges, of which approximately 15 remain. Most of the other remaining Berlin Iron Bridge Company examples are lenticular pony truss bridges. Pony truss bridges tend to have little or no visible superstructure, so they are not as photogenic as the lenticular through-trusses, and are generally not the focus of conservation efforts or the creation of historic bridge parks.

In addition to the lenticular through-trusses and pony trusses, the Berlin Iron Bridge Company is reported to have constructed an estimated ten swinging suspension bridges. There is no readily available information on eight of them, which no longer exist, but two of them still serve their communities and are popular tourist attractions. One is in Milford, New Hampshire, and the other is in Keeseville, New York. Similar to privately constructed mill and factory bridges, these are small, pedestrian-only bridges that were used to provide access from worker housing on one side of a river to the mills and factories on the other side. In both cases, these bridges served a group of factories and mills, rather than just a single operation. This may be why these bridges were constructed by a more established, even prominent, bridge company, and why they have both lasted for more than 130 years.

The Milford Swing Bridge crosses the Souhegan River a few hundred feet upstream of the historic McLane Dam, which powered numerous mills and factories in Milford in the second half of the 1800s. The bridge provides access from residential areas into the Milford Oval, the historic town green that forms downtown Milford. As with any small-scale suspension bridge, it is a historic and visual novelty that serves as a local symbol and attracts visitors to the town.

More than most other small-scale suspension bridges, which are usually just functional, the Milford Swing Bridge is ornately decorated. The 25-foot-tall suspension towers are constructed of a pyramidal iron bar lattice on each side of the deck, connected by a matching crosspiece over the portal. The crosspiece is topped by an ornate grill consisting of a series of circles and then a row of fleur-de-lys. Where the suspension cable crosses the saddle over the end posts, the workings are hidden underneath a finial. In the middle of the grill is an ornate Berlin Iron Bridge Company date plaque. The bridge is only about 200 feet long and ten feet wide and does swing when people walk across it. There is even a handful of love padlocks attached to the chain-link fence lining the railing, which demonstrates the prominence of the bridge to local residents.

The Keeseville Suspension Bridge crosses the AuSable River in downtown Keeseville, and is just one of several important historic bridges crossing the AuSable Chasm, also known as the Grand Canyon of the Adirondacks. Because of its setting above dramatic bedrock rapids, its location is more scenic than that of the Milford Swing Bridge. However, the bridge lacks all of the decorative elements that are included on the

Milford bridge. The structure of the suspension towers and portals, with the iron lattice pyramids connected by a matching crosspiece, is the same as the Milford bridge, but the crosspiece is not topped by a decorative grill.

Another difference is that the saddles on Keeseville are not topped by a finial or any other covering. This is unusual for suspension bridges of all sizes. Most frequently, the suspension cables disappear into the structure of the tower or are otherwise covered by a housing or decorative covering. As a result, bridge enthusiasts cannot actually see the manner in which the cables cross the saddle. This may seem to be a minor issue, but for specialized bridgespotters interested in the bridge structure, the spot where the suspension cables cross the saddle is where the rubber hits the road. It is this specific location where the weight of the entire bridge is borne. Therefore, although Keeseville is not decorative, it is interesting in that it provides a rare opportunity to observe the saddle.

Unfortunately, only these two examples of a Berlin Iron Bridge Company suspension bridge remain, so any attempt to learn more about each bridge by comparing and contrasting each to similar contemporary examples by the same company is limited. However, just comparing these two bridges, one dated 1888 and one dated 1889, raises a series of historical mysteries for further exploration.

Although the construction of the towers appears to be similar, the suspension systems on the two bridges are quite different. Milford uses a single suspension cable, which is anchored into a large metal bracket in the ground and crosses a single groove in the saddle above the tower. In contrast, Keeseville is supported by five suspension cables on each side. In the central, suspended portion of the bridge, these are braided into a single cable. As it nears the saddle, the braided cable splays into five separate cables, which cross through five separate grooves in the saddle and are then anchored into the ground several inches apart. In addition, the nuts closing the suspender connections on Milford have square ends, while those on Keeseville have rounded ends.

The most unexpected difference between the bridges is the type of date plaque present on each. Chapter 2 of *Bridgespotting: Part 1* discussed how the size and ornate shape of the date plaques of the Berlin Iron Bridge Company's lenticular through-truss bridges followed a uniform style.

This included plaques on seven bridges with dates ranging from 1886 to 1896. The 1889 Milford Swing Bridge falls squarely within this date range, and has the exact same style of date plaque as the lenticular through-truss bridges. The 1888 Keeseville Suspension Bridge is also within this date range, but has a completely different style of date plaque. The plaque on the Keeseville Bridge is almost entirely rectangular, with concave corners, but no other embellishments. It does not look similar to that on any remaining bridge by the Berlin Iron Bridge Company. Even the phrasing on the plaque is different. The text on all of the lenticular through-truss bridges, including the Milford Swing Bridge, refers to "Built By The Berlin Iron Bridge Company," while that on Keeseville states the bridge was "Erected by Berlin Iron Bridge Company."

Given that only two suspension bridges by this company remain to be visited and examined, there is no ability to conduct a weight-of-evidence study that could provide a likely explanation by comparing and contrasting a large number of similar bridges. Of course, no two bridges are alike and small differences are not unexpected. However, these bridges were constructed by the same company only one year apart, so the meaning of these differences is another little mystery awaiting some enterprising bridgespotter.

COLUMBIA-WRIGHTSVILLE BRIDGE, PENNSYLVANIA

The Columbia-Wrightsville Bridge crosses the Susquehanna River between York and Lancaster, Pennsylvania, approximately 50 miles west of Philadelphia and 50 miles north of Baltimore. The current bridge was opened in 1930, and it is the fifth generation bridge at what is one of the most important and eventful river crossings in the early United States.

The Susquehanna River is not necessarily a household name except to locals who live in central Pennsylvania. There are no large cities or famous tourist centers on the river. The river is unusual in that it is both wide and shallow, flowing in rapids over bedrock for much of its length, and therefore was never navigable for commercial shipping. Because the river did not support shipping, no major cities developed. Another unusual feature is that the river is long, flowing more than 400 miles from central New York in the north to the Chesapeake Bay in the south. Despite not being as well-known as the Hudson, Potomac, Connecticut, or Delaware, all of which are home to major cities, the Susquehanna is the longest river in the eastern United States.

One of the most important factors in the early political and economic development of the United States was the settlement of the west. This settlement occurred through the migration of populations either living in, or newly arriving in, the major port cities of New York and Philadelphia. These migrants, traveling on foot, horse, or cart, needed to cross the Susquehanna River on their way west. Because the river is wide and not navigable, it created a formidable obstacle to this migration, as well as to trade and communications between the major port cities and the western settlements. A ferry service was established between Columbia and Wrightsville as early as 1726, but after a substantial increase in westward migration following the Louisiana Purchase in 1803, construction of an early bridge became important not to ease local traffic, but to support the creation of a nation.

The first bridge at this location, a wooden covered bridge on stone piers, opened in 1814 but was destroyed by ice floes in 1832. The second bridge, also a wooden covered bridge, opened in 1834. The second bridge was later modified in 1846 to add a railway to complete a link between the Northern Central Railway in York and the railway between Columbia and Philadelphia. Through the Northern Central Railway, this completed the early railroad link between Philadelphia and Baltimore and, through the B&O Railroad, west to Ohio. The Susquehanna River is more than 5,000 feet wide at Columbia, so both the first and second bridges were the longest wooden covered bridges in the world at the time. For a sense of scale, the longest covered bridge in the world in 2022 is Hartland in New Brunswick, at about 1,200 feet long.

In 1863, the second bridge was the focus of one of the most consequential events in United States history. One common misconception of the Battle of Gettysburg is that the town of Gettysburg marked the deepest penetration of the Confederate Army into Union territory during the Civil War. This is not accurate. The primary purpose of the Confederacy's Pennsylvania campaign was to capture Harrisburg, which was the capital of the second-most populous state in the Union. The capture of Harrisburg would have accomplished multiple logistical and psychological objectives that could have ended the Civil War and changed the future course of American history.

The problem, though, was that Harrisburg was on the east side of the Susquehanna River, and the Confederate Army was on the west side. Because the river was a full mile wide and not navigable, capture of the Columbia-Wrightsville Bridge to allow a crossing of the river by the Confederate Army was necessary. While the full Army was moving eastward into Gettysburg, detachments were sent further forward to secure the bridge. These detachments cut the Northern Central Railway line at Hanover Junction 30 miles east of Gettysburg, captured the town of York, and then on June 28, 1863, reached the shore of the Susquehanna an additional 13 miles further east at Wrightsville.

They were too late. The wooden bridge was burned by Union troops, foiling the Confederate advance, and giving the Union's Army of the Potomac time to reach Gettysburg and begin the battle three days later. While Gettysburg is the famous name as the site of the battle, it was not the furthest advance of the Confederacy. The furthest advance was actually a short distance onto the bridge, where mounted Confederate soldiers pursued retreating Federal defenders until they reached the burning sixth span. If the Confederate Army had succeeded in capturing the bridge, they likely would have continued on to Harrisburg and threatened Philadelphia, possibly resulting in a different outcome of the Civil War.

The third bridge at this location, constructed by the Pennsylvania Railroad in 1868, was made of wood and steel, and used the same stone piers as the second bridge. It carried carriages, trains, and pedestrians but was destroyed by flooding in 1896. The fourth bridge, also constructed by the railroad, was a steel bridge placed on the same stone piers and completed in 1897. The rail bridge continued to carry trains until the 1950s, at which time it was scrapped. The stone piers used by the second, third, and fourth bridges, now almost 200 years old, remain visible on the north side of the current bridge.

The roadway carried by the fourth bridge was included as part of the Lincoln Highway, designated in 1913 as the nation's first coast-to-coast roadway between New York City and San Francisco. It was then redesignated as US Route 30, the main east-west highway crossing southern Pennsylvania, in 1926. The resulting increase in traffic created conflicts with the rail traffic on the fourth bridge. As a result, the current bridge was planned as a traffic-only bridge and was constructed parallel to and just a few feet south of the rail bridge, opening in 1930. Although the current bridge still carries local traffic between downtown Columbia and downtown Wrightsville, a modern concrete and steel bridge, the Wright's Ferry Bridge, was constructed less than a mile to the north in 1972. The Wright's Ferry Bridge carries the current alignment of US Route 30.

This historic location should be enough to attract history buffs to Columbia and Wrightsville, but it is probably the bridge's size, construction type, and decoration that are the main attractions for bridgespotters. Almost unknown except to locals, no longer carrying a major highway, not located near any big city or major tourist sites, the Columbia-Wrightsville Bridge is a hidden gem. The bridge is constructed of 28 concrete arches sitting on concrete piers. Each arch, individually, is 185 feet long, making the overall length, not counting approaches, about a mile long. The bridge is also quite high, about 40 feet above the river.

Because the bridge is constructed of arches sitting on piers, it has no superstructure. The bridge carries one lane of traffic each way and has a sidewalk on its southern side. Therefore, the view of the bridge while driving across, or even walking across, is not particularly impressive. Much of the Susquehanna River upstream of Harrisburg flows through mountains and has beautiful landscape views. Below Harrisburg, at Columbia, the river flows across relatively flat Piedmont, so it does not provide landscape views except of the river itself.

The bridge has monuments at the four corners, each topped with large, cement, ornamental obelisks with cast-bronze bases and bronze decorations about halfway to the top. The cement parapets of the bridge are lined with ornamental cement monuments, each about ten feet high. These are the tips of the piers that project above the roadway, and each is a stepped, geometric art deco design. There is one on each side of the roadway, so there are more than 50 of these monuments along the length of the bridge. During a visit to the bridge in 2013, every second monument was topped by a boring, modern streetlight. However, by the time of a visit in 2022, these had been removed and replaced with low decorative iron and glass lamps that blend beautifully with the 1930s theme of the bridge's art deco architecture.

The fronts of the monuments facing the roadway include a series of bronze plaque dedications and memorials. There is a memorial to John Wright, who operated the first ferry here across the Susquehanna, creating Columbia as the gateway for migration to the west. An original plaque from the opening of the bridge on Armistice Day in 1930 dedicates the bridge to the Sons and Daughters of York and Lancaster County who served in the wars of their country. Another 1930 plaque lists the York and Lancaster County Commissioners responsible for the bridge. A plaque was placed in 1980, as part of the rededication of the bridge as Veterans Memorial Bridge.

Although there are nice views of the river itself, some interesting monuments, and the replacement of the modern streetlights with period lampposts is a major improvement, the limited views and decorations may not entice you to walk across, especially knowing it is a full mile long, and you then have to walk back. However, it is highly recommended you visit and view the bridge from the side, because it is stunning.

The first impression is of the enormous size which was, at the time, the largest concrete arch bridge in the world. Each arch, on its own, is quite large at 40 feet high and 185 feet long. Even more remarkable is that the bridge consists of a string of 28 of these arches. To provide another sense of scale, there were many memorial-type cement arch bridges constructed in the northeast and midwest United States in the years following World War I. Some of these are large-scale bridges that are still impressive structures today. For example, Hanover Street Bridge, in Baltimore, is ten cement spans long. Arlington Memorial, in Washington, DC, has nine cement spans. Several others, such as Springfield Memorial in Massachusetts, the Market Street Bridge in Wilkes-Barre, Pennsylvania, and Key Bridge, in Washington, DC, are large bridges, but have only six to eight spans. The largest, Market Street Bridge in Harrisburg, has 16 spans, but note that this bridge also crosses the Susquehanna River and is only 40 miles upstream of Columbia-Wrightsville. In comparison to these other large bridges, the Columbia-Wrightsville Bridge is 28 spans long. Viewed from the riverbank, the sight of these arches, gigantic near the bank and then diminishing in size as they disappear into the distance across the river, is impressive.

Columbia-Wrightsville Bridge, Pennsylvania

Contributing to the aesthetics is the decorative form of the arches and piers. Each span is constructed of three side-by-side arches, and each of these has an open spandrel filled by four smaller arches. These give the bridge, for all of its massive size, a light and airy appearance. Then, the piers are faced with a decorative, stepped art deco design, beginning near the base of the arch and then extending upward to become the small art deco monuments along the roadway.

The eastern end of the bridge is at Columbia Rotary Park, in downtown Columbia. A roadside historical plaque on the south side of the road, large enough to be read by people in passing cars, explains that the original name of the town was Wright's Ferry, settled by John Wright in 1726, and that the first bridge was constructed in 1812. A similar plaque on the north side of the road discusses the role of the bridge in supporting the Lincoln Highway. A more detailed plaque, meant to be read by pedestrians, describes the history of Columbia, how it came within one vote of being designated as the capital of the new United States in 1790, and showing a detailed aerial view of the city in its heyday. The plaque also describes the events of June 28, 1863.

There are riverfront parks with excellent views on the south side of the bridge on both the Wrightsville and Columbia ends. On the riverfront in Columbia is the Columbia River Park, the best place to view the entire bridge. In 2014, a lovely visitor center called the Columbia Crossing River Trails Center was opened here. The center is operated by Susquehanna

Heritage, for the Borough of Columbia, as an educational and recreational center for the lower Susquehanna River Valley. The park has benches and provides parking for the Northwest Lancaster County River Trail. The center includes a roofed picnic area, has historical displays, sells books and bridge-related items, and provides information on historic, recreational, and tourist attractions in the area.

BENJAMIN FRANKLIN BRIDGE, PHILADELPHIA

For a city as large as Philadelphia, and one so closely associated with a major river, you would assume that there are numerous major bridges to visit and walk. From any given location near the rivers in London or Paris, for example, you can see eight or ten bridges to walk over. Even crossing the Potomac River into downtown Washington, DC, there are six or eight nearby bridges visible, including highway bridges, railroad bridges, subway bridges, and bridges that appear to be abandoned and crumbling.

On the Delaware River in downtown Philadelphia, there is just one bridge. Not just one walkable bridge. Just one bridge, period. That bridge is the Benjamin Franklin Bridge. Philadelphia does have other bridges over the Delaware, but they do not lead into the downtown area. There are a large number of ugly, industrial-looking bridges, but they generally cross the Schuylkill River to the south and are not visible from downtown. From the sidewalk of the Franklin Bridge, only one other bridge is visible—the Walt Whitman Bridge, which is almost three miles away, nowhere near downtown, and without pedestrian access. In contrast, the Franklin Bridge connects the center of downtown Philadelphia to the center of downtown Camden. Fortunately for bridge walkers, the bridge has a beautiful pedestrian walkway that provides great views of all of it.

The Franklin Bridge is a steel suspension bridge constructed in 1926. When it was first built, it was the longest single suspension span in the world for a few years. The bridge is more than a mile long and rises more than 130 feet above the Delaware River. The bridge carries six lanes of Interstate 676 traffic in the center of the lower deck, and a railroad line on the outside of the lower deck on each side. Elevated above the rail lines and overlooking the traffic lanes below is a pedestrian walkway on either side.

HISTORIC BRIDGES

With the need for a massive, highly visible superstructure rising above the deck, the central towers and anchors at the ends of suspension bridges become a blank canvas for decorative architectural flourishes. On this bridge, the steel girders bracing the central towers were designed in a geometric "X" motif. The lower portion of each tower is braced with a row of six small square panels, each filled in with wide steel girder supports in an X pattern. Then, the middle of each tower is braced with three large, stacked rectangular X panels. This motif is then topped with another row of six small X panels. The appearance is one of solidity. The railings also follow this motif, being made of thick steel panels with small openings. The geometric design is even carried into the rivets on the girders, which are deliberately arranged to accentuate the edges and the connecting plates of the X-shaped girders. The whole structure is painted a lovely, complementary blue, a few shades darker than the sky but a few shades lighter than the water of the Delaware River.

The anchor towers at the end of the bridge are of smooth-faced white granite. Each of the anchor towers serves as the focus for a small plaza. The small plaza consists of a widened part of the cement walkway, an elevated granite platform shaped to provide seating, and a granite parapet serving as a railing. On the outside of each walkway are the anchor towers, which from the walkway appear to be simple, small granite buildings rising about 30 feet above the level of the walkway. Each tower has a door framed by a granite portico and decorative sconces for lighting. On the western end, one door is topped with "Philadelphia" inscribed in the stone, and the other door with "Pennsylvania" inscribed. Similarly, the inscriptions over the doorways on the eastern end read "Camden" and "New Jersey." Over the doorway, each tower is topped by a row of four windows.

The appearance of these cute granite anchor towers from the walkway is deceiving. The substructure of the bridge cannot be seen from the walkway but, after walking over the bridge, you have an opportunity to view it from a different angle from Race Street Pier and Columbus Boulevard, which pass underneath the western end of the bridge. Race Street Pier is a beautiful small city park, developed on a pier in the shadow of the bridge, and it provides a perfect place to view the bridge from underneath. From this vantage point, the anchor towers can be seen for what they are: gigantic, 100-foot-tall massive stone towers. The cute little granite buildings that nicely frame the bridge's walkway are just the surface expressions, like the tip of an iceberg, of the enormous pile of stone supporting the bridge and holding the anchor cables from underneath. The remainder of the tower, below the deck, is rough-faced white granite with a carved, decorative coat of arms facing outwards, and the date 1926 is inscribed in Roman numerals above the portico of the door.

The walk across the Franklin Bridge has pleasant views, but it does provide a challenge to those with vertigo. The bridge is more than 130 feet high and, although it has solid steel railings, the pedestrian walkway is situated outside of the supporting cables, rather than inside. This makes the walkway seem to be suspended directly above the water, with little support. By being elevated above the roadway and railroad tracks, the pedestrian walkway seems semi-isolated on this enormous bridge. For much of the length, the roadway and tracks are not even visible, unless you specifically look over the edge to find them. They are still audible, though, and the bridge shakes a little when trains pass.

Although only one walkway, that on the south side, is open to pedestrians, it is fortunate that the skyline of downtown Philadelphia, the Walt Whitman Bridge over the Delaware, and, for what it is worth, downtown Camden are also on the south side of the bridge. Thus, the bridge walk provides excellent views of all three. The most impressive of these is the magnificent view of the skyline of downtown Philadelphia, sitting right off the end of the bridge. The view of Walt Whitman Bridge is mostly just a silhouette, but the distal view may be beneficial since the bridge looks sleek and clean from a distance.

Even the views of downtown Camden are pleasant enough. For all of Camden's bad press, the riverfront, at least as seen from above on the bridge, appears to be nicely done. Downtown Philadelphia does not have a riverfront promenade along the Delaware River, as the waterfront is instead lined with marinas and old warehouses converted to condos. However, Camden has constructed a nice red brick promenade, beginning at the bridge and extending south past the former New Jersey State Aquarium (now called the Adventure Aquarium) to the moored battleship, USS New Jersey.

HISTORIC BRIDGES

The walkway can be accessed from surface streets on either end. On the Camden end, the walkway ends at a stairway leading down to surface streets on the campus of Rutgers University—Camden. On the Philadelphia end, the walkway continues down to street level at a large traffic circle with an enormous aluminum sculpture serving as a grand entrance into the city. One warning needs to be made for being out on the walkway: way up there, on a narrow sidewalk so far from the surface streets, the last thing you are looking for is to avoid being hit by traffic. There is traffic, though, in the form of a police jeep used to patrol the walkway. It is good to know that the bridge is being patrolled, but your first encounter with the jeep coming from behind you on the sidewalk, in the middle of the river, is unexpected and can be alarming.

As with many bridge walks, this one should be combined with other nearby activities. On the Camden end, this can include the aquarium or the battleship, each within easy walking distance of the bridge. The more obvious recommendation, though, is the historical sites surrounding Independence Hall in Philadelphia. The western entrance to the bridge is only a few blocks from these sites. In fact, the best way to access the bridge is probably to park at the National Constitution Center on Race Street, just one block from the entrance to the bridge walkway. If you plan to visit Independence Hall, you will need to acquire tickets (free, but specifying an entrance time) from the visitor center. Since tickets run out early, consider obtaining tickets at the visitor center first, then go for a bridge walk and see the other sites, and then return at your appointed time to see Independence Hall.

Other important sites located within a few blocks include the Philadelphia Mint, the Betsy Ross House, Ben Franklin's gravesite, the Liberty Bell, the historic neighborhood of Penn's Landing, and the Independence Hall complex itself. Most everyone knows the history of the signing of the Declaration of Independence here in 1776. What is not as well-known is that this complex of buildings was also the location of the signing of the Articles of Confederation and the Constitution. The buildings also served as the US Capitol from 1790 to 1800 during the administrations of George Washington and John Adams, before the capital was finally moved to Washington, DC. Although Washington, DC is the home to a large number of memorials to the nation's founders, this small area of Philadelphia, a few steps off the end of the Franklin Bridge, is where they did the things for which they would later be memorialized.

BURNSIDE BRIDGE, ANTIETAM, MARYLAND

The Burnside Bridge in Antietam, Maryland, is a small, seemingly innocuous bridge that only became important when it stood between one army and another. The 1836 bridge, originally called Rohrbach Bridge, was one of almost 20 stone arch bridges built in Washington County in the early part of the 1800s, and is one of three that crossed Antietam Creek in this area.

There was never much question as to the ultimate outcome of the Battle of Antietam on September 17, 1862. The Confederate Army under Robert E. Lee was in retreat from the Battle of South Mountain a few days before, being chased back toward Virginia by the Union Army under George McClellan. The Union Army had an overwhelming superiority in numbers, with something on the order of 80,000 Union soldiers facing about 40,000 Confederates. However, the Confederate Army was in place first and occupied all of the key defensive positions. Antietam Creek is only about 100 feet wide and a couple feet deep, but it is wide and deep enough to make an unpleasant crossing if someone on the other side is shooting at you. Therefore, Lee chose the narrow strip of land between the Potomac River on the west and Antietam Creek on the east as the battleground.

The way to attack an army holding defensive positions, especially if you have superior numbers, is to go around them and attack them on their flank or rear. This was the role played by the Burnside Bridge. As the "Lower Bridge" furthest away from the main fighting in the cornfields a mile or two to the north, the bridge offered the Union Army a chance to cross the creek to the south of the Confederate positions, and then come up and attack them from behind. However, the bridge was in a position that was advantageous to the Confederate defenders. The terrain occupied by the Union Army east of the bridge is flat, but there is a steep hill on the western side of the creek, right at the base of the bridge. The hill was occupied by 500 soldiers from Georgia. The 9th Corps under Ambrose Burnside had more than 5,000 soldiers. Having thousands of soldiers available does not help much if they can only cross the narrow bridge four or five abreast. Anyone trying to cross the bridge was easy pickings for the Georgians. Union attacks on the bridge began at about 9:30 a.m., more than three hours after the main battle began. Three separate attacks were repulsed by the Georgians, bodies of Union soldiers piling up on and near the bridge. Ultimately, by 1:00 p.m., the Union soldiers were able to take the bridge, but only because the Georgians began to run out of ammunition and retreated.

The Burnside Bridge that was fought over so heavily can be visited today. The bridge crosses the creek on three stone arches and is only about 200 feet long. The bridge was still actively used as a roadway up through 1966, so it had been modified to accommodate cars. The National Park Service purchased the bridge in 1966 and restored it to its 1862 appearance, which was possible because of numerous photographs taken a few days after the battle. Antietam was the first battlefield ever to be photographed immediately after the battle, with the dead still lying in piles. The National Park Service has posted many of the photographs, including some of the bridge, in the exact locations from which they were taken. It is one thing to stand on a battlefield and know, generally, that men died here. It is quite another to stand in a spot and look at a photograph of that same spot covered with bodies or fresh graves, recognizing the hill slopes, the width of the creek, and the bridge.

The bridge is Stop Number 9 on the car tour of the Antietam Battlefield. There is a parking lot on the top of the hill, near the position of the Georgian soldiers. Hiking paths lead down the hill from two separate parts of the parking lot. One of these passes a monument to William McKinley, who was a soldier here at Antietam almost 40 years before he became president. The other pathway stops at an overlook of the entire bridge area and has interpretive panels. Both paths lead down to the southern end of the bridge. On the north side of the bridge, a series of bronze plaques describe the battle for the bridge, and there are five or six carved granite monuments honoring specific military units that fought here. The bridge is connected on both ends to hiking paths that wind through the battlefield, all of them passing historical exhibits and monuments.

The bloodiest day in United States history was not at Gettysburg. It was not Pearl Harbor, D-Day, or 9/11. It was the bloodbath at Antietam on September 17, 1862. The fighting at the Burnside Bridge was not decisive in terms of which army won the battle, but it did contribute to enormous Union casualties. This bought time and allowed the Confederate Army to slip back into Virginia intact under cover of darkness the following night. The high casualty rate and the exhaustion of the Union Army and its supplies were the reasons given by McClellan in resisting Abraham Lincoln's orders to pursue the Confederates into Virginia and finish them off. Instead of turning the battle into a complete defeat for the Confederacy, the war continued for another two and a half years.

LUDENDORFF BRIDGE, REMAGEN, GERMANY

The story of the Bridge at Remagen is familiar, but most people only know its general outlines. World War II, 1945, Europe, the Allies' manpower and armament production had finally matched and then exceeded that of the Germans. The battle for air supremacy had been fought and won. The primary factor allowing the war to even continue was the ability of the German Army to dig into defensive positions behind geographic barriers. First the English Channel, then the Ardennes, and then the Rhine. There was no longer any question whether these barriers could be overcome. That question was answered on D-Day, but there was a major question about how many lives would still need to be lost on both sides to finish the job. The better the defensive positions, the more difficult it would be.

The Rhine River was the last of the barriers, the only thing stopping the Allied Armies from being able to break out across Germany. From the Swiss frontier at Basel to the river mouth at Rotterdam, the Germans had the intention and capability to destroy every bridge on 600 miles of river to stop, or at least slow, the Allied advance. To cross the river, the Allied Armies would have had to use boats and other equipment in full view and range of the German guns on the right bank. Hitler ordered all of the bridges destroyed, and they all were—except for one. When the US Army reached Remagen on March 7, 1945, they found that the Ludendorff Bridge still stood. It was damaged from several German attempts to blow it up, but was still intact. After a battle to clear the German defenders in the bridge towers and on the opposite shore, it could be crossed by tanks and troops. The lives of thousands of soldiers, on both sides, had been saved.

This story is well-known. It was taught in history class, books were written, and movies were filmed. The phrase "Bridge at Remagen" is world-famous. When taking the scenic train ride along the Rhine between Cologne and Bonn to the north, and toward Koblenz and the Rhine Gorge to the south, tourists are likely to perk up a little bit when they hear that the next stop is Remagen. They might jump off the train and take the short walk to the riverfront to at least see the famous bridge. They will look upstream, look downstream, and then look upstream again. They may blink a few times. No bridge. They have a good view of the river for a long way in both directions, but there is certainly no bridge. Nothing that could remotely have "at Remagen" as part of its famous name.

This is a little stunning when you contemplate that the reason they are looking for it in the first place is because the Germans failed to destroy it! It is only famous because it was the one bridge that was *not* destroyed. Given its fame and historical importance, it is inconceivable that it was casually dismantled sometime after the war. It simply has to be there.

This scenario happens because people only know the generalities of the story, and not the specific details. The critical, important detail for someone wanting to visit the Bridge at Remagen, or at least see it from a distance, is that the bridge collapsed into the river ten days after the US Army first crossed it. Having failed with explosives, the Germans continued to try to destroy the bridge with air strikes, frogmen in the river, and even V-2 rockets. Meanwhile, Hitler, enraged at the failure to destroy the bridge, held kangaroo court-type trials of five army officers, sentencing them to death, which was carried out by firing squad the next day. The continued attempts to destroy the bridge were unsuccessful, at least in terms of it taking a direct hit, but the attempts to destroy it did weaken it. On March 17, as hundreds of Americans were on the bridge making repairs, it collapsed, killing 28 US soldiers. By then, the bridge was no longer critical, militarily. In the intervening ten day period, the US Army had established other nearby crossings on pontoon bridges. When the bridge collapsed, it was just never reconstructed.

So how does the Ludendorff Bridge, which ceased to exist more than 65 years ago and was never rebuilt, merit mention in a book describing tourist bridges? The answer is that a prominent part of the bridge was left in place. The remaining feature of the bridge, that which allows it to be visited by tourists today, is two fortress-like towers, built of large blocks of black basalt. The towers served as abutments to hold the eastern and western ends of the bridge's steel trusses, and also housed defensive positions allowing the bridge to be protected during the war. A small section of the bridge's stone arches also still remains on the Remagen end of the bridge. Although the bridge itself is long gone, the towers not only remain as a visual reminder of the historical role of the bridge, but the tower on the Remagen bank has been converted into the Friedensmuseum, or Peace Museum.

The museum is worth the admission charge, but mostly just for the ability to wander around inside the interesting tower. In the 1970s, the stone piers in the middle of the river were finally removed because they were interfering with river traffic. The stones of the piers were dredged out of the river, and were broken up and sold as souvenirs. The proceeds were used to establish the museum. The displays are mostly just photographs and text (including English translations) but with few artifacts. The photographs and text are heavily focused on the events of the capture of the bridge and provide little information on the earlier history of the bridge prior to the war, or on the events of March 17, when it collapsed. However, the inside of the tower is interesting on its own. It is really two octagonal, castle-like towers, connected at the base, with the bridge deck having passed in the space between them.

More important than the exhibits in the museum is the ability to sit on a bench at a small plaza overlooking the river, contemplating the historical importance of the events that occurred here. The wall of the tower at the plaza includes plaques installed to commemorate the armies that fought here, including the US Army 9th Infantry Division, 9th Armored Division, 78th Infantry Division, and 99th Infantry Division.

An interesting question still remains: why was the bridge not reconstructed? After all, rail transport was still needed in post-war Germany. Most of the infrastructure for the rail system, including the right-of-way, rails, and tunnels were still in place, making reconstruction at the same location an obvious choice. Tour books and websites describe the reason as local opposition to disturbance of the visual appeal of the Rhine Valley which, sitting on a bench at the small plaza, seems to be an excellent reason.

Another reason may possibly be found in the history of the planning of the bridge. The bridge was built in 1916, two years after the beginning of World War I, to move troops and war materiel to the western front. This seems understandable, given the nature of the warfare occurring at that time. What is a little harder to grasp is that the bridge was planned and designed for this purpose in 1912. This was two years *before* the war began. This perspective, suddenly, is chilling. Then, to make it worse, a quick look at a map shows that Remagen is not anywhere near the German-French border. It is close to the German-Belgian border, making the planning for the bridge in 1912 even more diabolical. This is because the bridge was designed as part of Germany's Schlieffen Plan for making war on France. The Schlieffen Plan was developed to bypass strong French defenses by simply marching German troops through Belgium and Luxembourg, violating their neutrality. If these countries allowed foreign troops to pass through unharmed, fine. If not, they would be crushed. Which, of course, is what happened. Twice.

The Peace Museum is dedicated to peace, but does not display much information or have many exhibits associated with this dedication. Given the legendary status of the bridge, it is easy to assume that the dedication is associated with the end of World War II, which was expedited at this location. However, the more significant dedication may lie in the deliberate choice not to rebuild the bridge. The primary purpose of the bridge was to support the German Empire's invasion of adjoining neutral countries. Hopefully, the choice to not rebuild the bridge reflects, in some small way, the fact that bridges for this purpose are no longer needed.

CHAPTER 3
COMMUNITY BRIDGES

MITTLEREBRÜCKE, BASEL, SWITZERLAND

The Mittlerebrücke, or Middle Bridge, in Basel is the location of the oldest permanent bridge crossing of the Rhine River. The Romans had built a few bridges over the Rhine, including temporary wooden bridges constructed by Caesar near Koblenz, but the location that has been continuously occupied by a bridge for the longest period of time is the site of the Mittlerebrücke. The original bridge was built in 1225 to support traffic on the Gotthard Pass route between Germany and Italy, and then it remained the only bridge crossing the Rhine over its 600 mile length between the North Sea and the Bodensee for many centuries. This historical significance is not obvious, though, because the current Mittlerebrücke is only about 100 years old.

In addition to its historic location, the Mittlerebrücke has also played a prominent role in the centuries-long rivalry between the Old Town sections of Grossbasel and Kleinbasel. The Mittlerebrücke has connected the two parts of the city since the thirteenth century. As the name suggests, Grossbasel is the larger part of the city, situated on the south bank of the Rhine, and home to the Munster, Rathaus, train station, and other more prominent municipal, cultural, and religious institutions. Kleinbasel, on the other hand, is much smaller, serving mostly as a bedroom community for Grossbasel. Located on the northern bank of the Rhine, Kleinbasel is one of those unusual quirks of geography in which the Rhine does not form the border between Switzerland and Germany. Grossbasel is located on the "normal" side of the river, with respect to the German-Swiss border, while Kleinbasel is an anomaly, on the "wrong" side of the river, which is only part of Switzerland because it is a suburb of the largest city in Switzerland. Kleinbasel is the red headed stepchild. Thus, there is a rivalry between the two parts of the city.

For centuries, the residents of Grossbasel demonstrated their attitude toward the Kleinbaselers through their display of the Lällekönig. This is a small bust of a bearded man that stood at the gate of the bridge on the Grossbasel side and greeted visitors from the Kleinbasel side by sticking out its tongue and rolling its eyes. Although the original Lällekönig is now in the Historical Museum, a copy still overlooks the bridge. The residents of Kleinbasel responded with their famous Vogel Gryff festival every January. In this event, dancers from Kleinbasel wearing symbolic costumes perform a dance in the middle of the bridge, making sure the entire time to keep their backs turned toward Grossbasel and the Lällekönig.

The Mittlerebrücke is central to any tourist visit to Basel today. Although there are not many tourist sights in Kleinbasel, there are riverfront hotels located a short walking distance from the Marktplatz in Grossbasel, and the bridge serves as more than a connection between them. The bridge is the best place to see riverfront views of the skyline of Basel, dominated by the Munster on top of a high bluff. The central spot to take in this view is from the Käppelijoch in the middle of the bridge, a prominent tourist sight on its own, with its grate doors covered with love padlocks.

CHARLES RIVER BRIDGES, BOSTON, AND KENNETH F. BURNS BRIDGE, WORCESTER, MASSACHUSETTS

While it may seem redundant to include profiles of two different sets of bridges used as spectator seating for rowing competitions, each offers unique attractions and are located close enough to each other that they both deserve mention. The bridges cross the Charles River between Boston and Cambridge, and Lake Quinsigamond in nearby Worcester. The events are the annual Head of the Charles rowing competition in Cambridge and various regattas in Worcester.

The Charles River between Boston and Cambridge was substantially reengineered in the nineteenth century. Originally a wide, marshy estuary, the area was dammed, backfilled, and channelized to make the quiet, narrow ribbon of a river that exists today. This, plus its location near several prominent universities, makes it a world-class destination for rowing competitions.

The historic center of the Boston-Cambridge connection is at the Lars Anderson Bridge and Weeks Footbridge. Although the Anderson Bridge is not particularly old, dating from 1915, it is just a few steps away from John F. Kennedy Street, the main historic street through downtown Cambridge. This street is the location of homes built in the mid-1700s and is a few blocks from the historic Harvard University campus. Weeks Footbridge, constructed in 1926 and located just about a quarter-mile to the east, connects the main part of Harvard University to the business school across the river. Further downstream are Western Avenue, River Street, Boston University, Harvard, and Longfellow Bridge.

An excellent time to visit this area is near the end of October, not only for the foliage displays, but for the annual Head of the Charles River rowing competition. This event attracts rowers not only from universities but from all age groups, for two full days of racing between and under the bridges. More than 200,000 spectators attend the event. The riverwalks on both sides of the river are lined with vendors selling food and spectators pack the bridges, which provide a unique, overhead viewing angle for the races.

While viewing rowing events from the Boston bridges is an important bridge tourism destination, it is not without issues. The bridges are historic, constructed to carry traffic in a major city long before the rowing competitions became popular, and only incidentally hijacked by rowing spectators later. Except for the pedestrian-only Weeks Footbridge, the bridges still carry traffic throughout the competitions, but their narrow sidewalks limit viewing access.

In contrast, the Kenneth Burns Bridge in Worcester, opened in 2015, was designed to accommodate rowing spectators from its inception. Rowing is popular in Boston, but with its larger population, universities, baseball team, and tourists visiting the city for its history, the Head of the

Charles event is just one more activity among dozens. Worcester, on the other hand, is a smaller city situated on a lake that is considered one of the best natural bodies of water for competitions in the world. Rowing is not merely an event in Worcester—it is almost a religion. The Quinsigamond Rowing Association (QRA) website describes the history of rowing on the lake. With the first races having occurred in 1857, the lake has hosted US Olympic trials, as well as numerous regional and national championship events. The QRA hosts six events on their own and supports numerous others on the lake throughout the season. There are races every weekend for three months in the spring.

When the existing Route 9 bridge across the lake between the towns of Worcester and Shrewsbury was being replaced, celebration of rowing was one of the major objectives of the local community. The most obvious need was to incorporate wide sidewalks and benches to provide dedicated viewing locations for the numerous rowing events. However, the consideration of rowing did not stop there. The designers needed to plan the construction, as well as the demolition of the existing bridge, in a way that did not interfere with ongoing rowing events on the lake. Also, boating-related decoration was provided through the installation of large modern sculptures, in the shape of sails, on the four corners of the bridge. Even the name of the bridge celebrates rowing. Kenneth Burns was a local rowing hero who founded and served as coach of the Shrewsbury High School rowing team. He was responsible for bringing the US Olympic rowing trials to the lake in 1952 and also served as chief of police in Shrewsbury for more than 20 years. Not necessarily related to rowing, the bridge and sail-sculptures are pleasantly bathed in colored lights with color-changing capability, allowing the bridge to be used for light shows visible from the state and city parks on the shorelines.

ASHTABULA COUNTY COVERED BRIDGE FESTIVAL, OHIO

When studying regional clusters of objects such as covered bridges, it is rarely obvious why a cluster exists. Is it because more were constructed here than in other locations? Is it because the bridges in other locations were lost in greater numbers? Was a prominent local construction company being patronized? Is it coincidence, or just random?

In the case of the cluster of wooden covered bridges in Ashtabula County, Ohio, the reason is well-documented. Ashtabula County is the center of a prominent cluster of covered bridges because a single individual, in the early 1980s, decided that the community should protect, cultivate, and expand their covered bridge heritage to create a prominent tourist attraction. Then he spent much of the next 30 years making this vision a reality.

That individual was John Smolen, a lifelong Ashtabula County resident who was elected as county engineer in 1980. Ashtabula County was once home to 48 covered bridges but only 12 remained by 1980. Having grown up in the county and watched as the covered bridges disappeared one-by-one, Smolen's first act as county engineer was to develop a proposal for the county commissioners. He proposed that the 12 remaining bridges should be rehabilitated, one each year. Of the 12, all but one still carry traffic in 2022, and the lone exception, Graham Road Covered Bridge, is the center of a Metropark, hosting events such as dinners, picnics, and weddings.

In addition to the rehabilitation of the old bridges, Smolen championed the construction of wooden covered bridges when new bridges were needed. The county now has six covered traffic bridges that have been constructed since 1983, including both the shortest and longest covered bridges in the world, as well as a gorgeous covered pedestrian bridge in one of the most scenic locations in the county. Smolen's argument in favor of wooden bridges was not just to create nostalgic replicas for tourists. He stressed that, if properly maintained, wooden bridges in areas with harsh winters would last longer than cement or steel, because road salt is corrosive to cement or steel but preserves wood.

The success of Smolen's program is celebrated every October with the Ashtabula County Covered Bridge Festival. The first annual festival was held in 1984 and was used as an opening and dedication ceremony for the completion of the rehabilitation for the Middle Road Covered Bridge. Since then, many of the festivals have included openings and dedications for both rehabilitation projects and new covered bridges.

The main festival events occur at Giddings Park in the town of Jefferson. The festival features vendors selling crafts from booths, craft demonstrations, games and rides for kids, a covered bridge photo contest, live music, and plenty of food options, with an emphasis on bean soup served from giant kettles. A major attraction is the mini-bridge on wheels, carried to Giddings Park as part of a parade. The parade features traditional items such as a grand marshal, bands, baton-twirlers, and the Covered Bridge Queen and her court. While at Giddings Park, visitors can inspect the former law office of Joshua Giddings, a prominent congressman and abolitionist in the 1830s to 1850s. The office is packed with Giddings' original furniture and books.

The festival publishes an official souvenir program that includes a map with recommended routes to all of the bridges, as well as the locations of other spots of interest. These include numerous wineries located in the northwestern part of the county and dozens of barn quilt locations. Barn quilts are squares with large-scale geometric designs painted on the sides of barns, and Ashtabula County has more than 100 of them, including on four of the bridges. The southwest part of the county also has a large number of Amish farms.

Of course, the most important activity to pursue at the festival is to find and inspect each of the 19 covered bridges in the county. The bridges are in the northeast, northwest, and southwest parts of the county, with none in the southeast. As with any cluster of covered bridges, they encompass a range of old, new, large, small, clean, rustic, historic, tourist gimmicks, and other types of bridges. During the festival, community and charitable groups set up tables at most of the bridges and sell food, crafts, and bridge-related items.

Accessibility varies among the bridges. All are drivable except Riverview, which was constructed as a pedestrian bridge in a park, and Graham Road, bypassed and preserved in a park. Smolen-Gulf and Harpersfield are also in county parks and can be accessed by parking in lots at those parks. Mechanicsville and South Denmark are also bypassed by newer bridges but remain drivable. Both can be viewed easily from the side by walking across the bypass, and both have large barn quilt square designs painted on their sides. West Liberty Street Bridge is located in a downtown area, with ample parking along streets or at businesses. The other 12 bridges have space at one end, some more than others, to pull over your car to visit the bridge.

Smolen-Gulf Covered Bridge, Ashtabula County, Ohio

The gem of the collection is also one of the newest, which seems unexpected given that covered bridge tourism generally attracts history buffs. The Smolen-Gulf Bridge opened in 2008 and was constructed, of course, by John Smolen. The Gulf is a gorge, 90 feet deep, on the Ashtabula River. The steep-sided Gulf is an anomaly in what is otherwise relatively flat farmland in the county. Because its topography created severe floods within the Gulf, bridges at this location needed to be high, as well as long enough to span not just the river but the entire gorge. The bridge is more than 600 feet long, beating out the 450-foot-long Cornish-Windsor Bridge as the longest covered bridge in the United States.

What is most interesting and attractive about the Smolen-Gulf Bridge is not what it is, but what it is not. It is not a nostalgic gimmick that limits traffic, or will weather and look decrepit in a few years. It is actually a large, modern-looking bridge, constructed with modern equipment and design, which just happens to mostly be made of wood and be covered with a roof. The piers are cement as is the roadway. The roof is aluminum, and the wood truss is held together by galvanized steel reinforcement. The bridge easily carries two lanes of traffic, including large trucks, and also has a pedestrian sidewalk on both sides. The sides of the bridge are wide open, allowing the sidewalks to be used for viewing the river below that flows through Indian Trails Park. The bridge can be accessed by parking at Indian Trails Park, which has a kiosk with picnic benches and historical exhibits at the turnoff from Highway 25. After walking across, the bridge can be viewed from the side and from below by taking the roadway to another parking lot further down into the park, along the river.

An unexpected bonus lies almost directly beneath Smolen-Gulf Bridge. The newest wooden covered bridge in the county, opened in 2016, is the Riverview Bridge, a pedestrian-only bridge that carries hiking trails in Indian Trails Park. Constructed after Smolen retired as county engineer, he is still listed on the plaque as a consultant. Like Smolen-Gulf, Riverview is a modern bridge with an aluminum roof and asphalt deck and just happens to be of wooden truss construction.

Another of the newer bridges, West Liberty Street Bridge, was constructed in downtown Geneva in 2011, again designed by Smolen, and constructed by carpentry students at the local vocational school. At 18 feet long, Liberty Bridge is considered the shortest covered bridge in the nation. Upon first sight, you can see that it is basically nothing more than a cement culvert with a roof built over the top. However, once you get over the fact that the bridge is a gimmick intended to capitalize on the county's attempt to be the covered bridge capital, you can see that it is a complex, interesting, and attractive structure. It is open-sided, with a peaked, aluminum roof and barn quilt squares at each portal. The bridge carries one lane of traffic in each direction and also has a sidewalk on each side, making the bridge wider than it is long. The 18 foot length of the span is spelled out in brick on the roadway at each end. A small faux tollhouse is located at one end, and a kiosk on the opposite side of the road has an exhibition plaque describing the bridge and its construction.

The four other newer covered bridges are more conventional in size and shape, with no gimmicks or claims of records. These include Netcher Road built in 1999, State Road built in 1983, Caine Road built in 1986, and Giddings Road built in 1995. Netcher Road is decoratively painted red with white trim and has a cupola on the roof. State Road, Caine Road, and Giddings Road each look similar from the outside—plain with an unbroken line of windows and no extra ornamentation. However, there are differences in the color and construction type. State Road is a lovely, reddish brown, weathered color and has the distinctive diagonal beams of a

Town Lattice truss. There is a difference between "rustic" weathered and "neglected" weathered, and State Road is rustic. The color of Caine Road trends more toward "neglected" weathered, and the truss type is not as eye-catching. Giddings Road is painted dull gray and may be the plainest of all the bridges.

With the dozen older bridges, it is difficult to pin down many of the construction dates. Not only are the specific dates not necessarily documented, but in many cases the bridge is a hodge-podge of pieces of former bridges destroyed in floods and subjected to multiple subsequent renovations. The earliest of the bridges were constructed in 1867 and 1868, including Doyle Road, Harpersfield, Middle Road, Mechanicsville, Root Road, and Windsor Mill (also reported in some sources as Wiswell Road or Warner Hollow). Olins (1873) and Riverdale Road (1874) are almost as old. Of these, Harpersfield and Windsor Mill are listed on the National Register of Historic Places.

Three of the older bridges, Harpersfield, Middle Road, and Olins, have a cute "Century Bridge" plaque placed on the inside by the Ashtabula County Historical Society. These plaques are cast-bronze reliefs in the roughly rectangular shape of the county, showing a landscape with some trees, a small house, and a covered bridge crossing a stream. The plaques for Harpersfield and Middle Road have a date of 1868, while that for Olins has no date. Since it does not make sense that the historical society would have recognized these three bridges and not the others, it is apparent that some of the plaques have become souvenirs.

The most unusual bridge in the county is Harpersfield, crossing the Grand River. Consisting of two spans and more than 200 feet long, the bridge was the longest covered bridge in the state prior to the construction of Smolen-Gulf. The most unusual feature is the result of a flood on the Grand River in 1913, which cut a new channel on one end of the covered bridge. The covered bridge was not damaged, but a new section of bridge needed to be added to create a longer bridge. This section, an additional 140 feet long, is a steel through-truss span that joins to the wooden span in the middle of the river, creating a hybrid wood/steel crossing.

More than any other bridge in the county, the Harpersfield Bridge has been made into an accessible tourist attraction. The bridge is in a county

Metropark with plenty of parking, and the Covered Bridge Shoppe at the eastern end sells bridge-related items, art, crafts, and snacks. Both the steel and wooden spans have a pedestrian sidewalk, and there are even several love padlocks attached to a metal component on the wooden railing. There is an Ohio Historical Marker plaque at the western end and multiple plaques inside the covered span. These include a National Register of Historic Places plaque and the Century Bridge plaque.

Among the other bridges, there are a few highlights. Large, laminated wood arches characteristic of Burr arch construction are found in the Benetka Road, Olins, Mechanicsville, and Netcher Road bridges. Of these, the arch in Mechanicsville is original, Benetka Road and Olins are later additions for added strength, and Netcher Road is one of the new bridges. In addition to the Covered Bridge Shoppe at Harpersfield, there is a small covered bridge museum at Olins, and Mechanicsville is across the road from a pub and restaurant.

Finally, as with any cluster of covered bridges, several are plain looking, without any substantial decoration. Riverdale Road is distinctive for its green roof, and Windsor Mill is yellow with planks laid in a decorative radial pattern above the portal. Although they have some historic interest, Middle Road, Root Road, and Creek Road are mostly just gray, barn-like bridges.

KRÄMERBRÜCKE, ERFURT, GERMANY

Although the Ponte Vecchio is iconic, and Pulteney Bridge is located in one of the major tourist cities in England, they are not the only prominent examples of shops on bridges that attract tourists. Largely unknown to western tourists because it is in the formerly communist East Germany, Erfurt is a delightful tourist town with a largely intact medieval city center. There are many tourist attractions, including not one but two cathedral-sized churches sitting on a hill overlooking an enormous square. The city also has substantial connections to Martin Luther, who studied and became a monk in the city, and to Johann Sebastian Bach, whose parents were married there. However, the largest attraction, by far, is the Krämerbrücke.

The Krämerbrücke, or Merchant's Bridge, is in every way as visually interesting as the world-famous Ponte Vecchio. Both sides of the bridge are lined with three story-high houses that seem straight out of a Brothers Grimm fairy tale. Each of the 32 houses is brightly colored in shades of orange, red, yellow, and green, and most of them display the crossed wood beams that are characteristic of half-timbered construction. The exteriors of the houses, facing upstream and downstream on the River Gera, have balconies and window boxes decked with flowers. The city has accommodated and encouraged visitors to the bridge by placing viewing platforms on the western, downstream side, and by constructing a new cement bridge with wide pedestrian sidewalks, benches, and historical plaques engraved into the pavement on the eastern, upstream side.

Viewing and photographing the bridge from its sides is a popular activity, but the actual treat is the experience of walking across. From the outside of the bridge, the houses are pretty, but from the inside of the bridge, they are almost overwhelming. The roadway between the houses is extraordinarily narrow, only about 17 feet wide. This means you can walk out of one shop door and into another on the other side of the bridge in about four steps. Although the houses are only three stories high, the narrow distance between them means you have to crane your neck to view them. The claustrophobic effect is heightened by the configuration of the bridge. The roadway is sloped, curved on the southern end, and passes through an archway under a church on the northern end. There are no breaks between the buildings to see out of the sides. When walking across with medieval houses towering over you on both sides, there is no indication at all that you are on a bridge.

The shops on the bridge are touristy, but high-end touristy, selling art, glass, and jewelry, as well as food and drinks. The bridge is enormously popular, so you are sharing this experience shoulder-to-shoulder with dozens of other tourists at any time. Every June, the bridge is the focus of an annual festival, the Krämerbrückenfest.

Both the northern and southern ends lead into quaint old town squares with shops and restaurants. The square on the northern end looks like any other medieval town square, with a church and a prominent bell tower on one side. The church has a large arch leading underneath the tower, suggestive of a cloister or garden on the other side, but the arch actually leads out onto the bridge. This church, the Ägidienkirche, has been in place at least since 1110. Originally, there were shops on the ground floor, with the nave of the church on the second floor above the arch. The interior of the nave still functions as a church, although it is no longer original. The tower is accessible, and a platform at the top offers amazing views not only of Erfurt but of the narrow roadway, packed with people. There was originally a church at the southern end as well, but it has since been removed.

Not to be missed while shopping, people-watching, or admiring the architecture on the bridge is a small plaque on the wall of the arch underneath the Ägidienkirche that reads, without any additional explanation, "Via Regia." This may not be a familiar phrase, but its historical importance cannot be overstated. The Via Regia, or Royal Road, was the primary trade, transport, and pilgrimage route connecting western to eastern Europe for more than 2,000 years. Although it has many branches at its western end in Spain, France, and the Low Countries, and at its eastern end leaving Poland and into Ukraine and Belarus, the Via Regia was mostly limited to a single route as it passed directly east-west through central Germany.

The two primary north-south flowing rivers in Germany are the Rhine in the west, and the Elbe in the east. The Via Regia was the overland route connecting these two rivers, linking the waterways of the Rhine to those of the Elbe. Where the Via Regia connected with the River Main a short distance from the Main's confluence with the Rhine, the major trading center of Frankfurt grew. Where the Via Regia approached the Elbe, the major trading center of Leipzig grew. Where the road crossed smaller rivers in between, it crossed at fords, many of which were developed into bridges, and grew into settlements. The city of Erfurt, the capital of the German state of Thuringia, grew where the Via Regia crossed the River Gera at what was originally a ford, and then from 1117 was a wooden bridge, and then from 1325 was a stone bridge. The 1325 stone bridge is today known as the Krämerbrücke, and all of the traffic from eastern to western Europe for hundreds of years passed across this bridge and through this archway underneath the Ägidienkirche.

QUEENSBORO BRIDGE, NEW YORK CITY

One unusual interior space present on some bridges is known as the down-under space, where enclosed structures have been developed underneath the bridge approaches. There are two of these in New York City. In Brooklyn, an entire neighborhood exists in the shadow of bridge overpasses and is known as DUMBO, for "Down Under Manhattan Bridge Overpass." The other is underneath the Manhattan end of the Queensboro Bridge.

The space underneath the Queensboro Bridge overpass was walled in when the bridge was built in 1909 in order to create useable interior commercial space for a fruit and vegetable market. However, the Bridgemarket was more than just a store. It was designed by Spanish architect Rafael Guastavino, who specialized in designing interior spaces with tiled vaulted ceilings. Guastavino patented a method of using interlocking tiles to support vaulted ceilings and he designed decorative arcades for dozens of buildings in the northeastern United States from about 1881 to 1908. His work is found in many of the most prominent buildings in New York, including Grant's Tomb, the Cathedral of St. John the Divine, Grand Central Station, Carnegie Hall, and the Museum of Natural History. One of the better known examples is the Bridgemarket and Guastavino's Restaurant, built into the structure underneath the roadway approaches to Queensboro Bridge.

The use of the interior space and public access to it has varied over the years. The original Bridgemarket closed in the 1930s, and the space was sometimes unoccupied and sometimes used by the New York City Department of Transportation. In 1973, Queensboro Bridge, including the interior space designed by Guastavino, was designated a landmark by the New York City Landmarks Preservation Commission. It took until the late 1990s for the space to be reopened as a grocery store called the Food Emporium, a housewares store, and Guastavino's restaurant. In 2005, the restaurant was closed to the public, but it is still open for private events. The housewares store was moved to a different location in 2010 and the Food Emporium closed in 2015.

After being unoccupied for six years, the space was reopened as a Trader Joe's grocery store in December 2021. The white tiled vaults soar 40 feet high above the shelves. Although there is no shortage of restaurants and neighborhood grocery stores in midtown Manhattan, the new store attracts shoppers from large distances for this unique experience.

BRIDGE BETWEEN CONTINENTS, NEAR KEFLAVIK, ICELAND

There is one excellent example of a physical bridge that so embodies the symbolic meaning of the word "bridge" that it was built and named only for its symbolic purpose and serves literally no transportation function at all. This is the Bridge Between Continents on the Reykjanes Peninsula, about 60 miles southwest of the capital of Reykjavik, in Iceland.

The physical bridge is extremely underwhelming. It was built in 2002, so is not historic. It is only about 60 feet long and 20 feet high, so it is not large. It does not rise above the surrounding volcanic landscape, so there is no elevated platform that can be used for scenic views. In fact, there is little to view except the black, boulder-strewn lava field. There are no distant mountains, and no trees. There is a view of the ocean about a half-mile away, but you can get a much better view of the ocean by pulling off at one of the many roadside viewing areas along the highway that you used to get here. The structure of the bridge is boring and unremarkable, constructed of tubular steel with a wire-mesh rail and a metal grate deck. The deck is only about three feet wide, so only allows passage of one person at a time, on foot. The body of water crossed by the bridge . . . well, there is no water. There is only sand, derived from basalt lava flows. You can follow trails down though the boulders and wade through the thick, black sand beneath the bridge.

Yet, despite this innocuous location and appearance, the parking lot is full, and the area is crawling with tourists waiting their turn to walk across the bridge. Why? Because this is a very special location, both scientifically in terms of the earth's geologic processes at work and symbolically for friendship between peoples. This tiny canyon was not formed the way most other canyons on earth were formed. It was not eroded into the surrounding landscape by flowing water. Instead, the basalt lava flows on either side of the small canyon have been pulled apart, very slowly, by plate tectonics. Iceland is just a peak in the Mid-Atlantic Ridge, the boundary between the North American and Eurasian Plates. Thousands of miles long, the ridge is submerged beneath the Atlantic Ocean for almost its entire length, except for this one location where it peeps out above sea level, forming Iceland. The earth's crust is being ripped asunder along this ridge while magma from the mantle is continually rising, forming volcanoes and making new crust. This rift cuts right across the nation of Iceland, from the Reykjanes Peninsula on the southwest to the northeast.

At 60 feet wide and 20 feet deep, the size of the rift in this part of the Reykjanes Peninsula does not require bridges to be crossed. A bulldozer could knock down the walls of the ravine and build a road through here, with just a slight dip in it, within minutes. In fact, this is what was done about a half-mile away, on Route 425, which is the highway along the coast. There is no bridge on Route 425 where it crosses the rift. Instead, the uneven surface was simply smoothed out and paved over. Also, there is nothing on either side of the bridge to walk to. There is a parking lot for tourist cars and buses on the eastern side, but there are no buildings on either side.

The Bridge Between Continents has no functional purpose whatsoever. It was built entirely for tourists, with the symbolic purpose of linking the peoples of North America with those of Europe and Asia. The lava field on the eastern side, which includes the parking lot, is located on the Eurasian Plate. The lava field on the opposite side is on the North American Plate. This symbolic intent is reflected throughout the area with informational plaques on both ends of the bridge and in the large numbers of tourists who venture to this remote, relatively unattractive location, in order to leave their love padlocks on the wire railings.

DUNDAS AQUEDUCT, LIMPLEY STOKE, ENGLAND

Most of the largest canals constructed in England in the early nineteenth century during "canal mania" extended from shoreline ports to large inland cities such as Manchester and Birmingham, feeding coal in and moving industrial products out during the Industrial Revolution. Another subset was a large number of spur canals, which were shorter and narrower, and were usually intended to link small coal, building stone, or slate-producing districts to the larger-scale canal systems. These spur canals often made the difference between poverty and riches for communities in these districts.

The Kennet and Avon Canal was different in that it cut directly across the country, linking a major port on the east coast to another on the west coast. Sure, ships could carry goods between the ports by going out into the ocean, traversing hundreds of miles down one coast, through the English Channel, and then up the other coast. However, ocean travel involved a greater distance and is subject to the vagaries of weather. It is much more convenient to take a shorter, direct route from one side of the country to the other on flat, protected, quiescent canals.

The name of the River Kennet is not widely known but, importantly, it flows into the Thames at Reading. The name of the River Avon is familiar because of its association with Shakespeare, but the river at Stratford-upon-Avon is not associated with the Kennet and Avon Canal. Lots of rivers in England are the River Avon, and the River Avon at Stratford-upon-Avon is a different River Avon than the one that flows through Bradford-on-Avon, through Bath, and then empties into the sea at Bristol.

The Kennet and Avon Canal was constructed in stages. The River Avon from Bristol to Bath was originally tidal, so it was at least partially navigable. Locks were constructed on this stretch of the river to make it fully navigable by 1727, but this did not require construction of a separate canal. Upstream of Bath, a canal that was separate from the river was necessary. This waterway, extending all the way to Reading, was also navigable by 1727, but the connection to Bristol was not completed until the Dundas Aqueduct joined the individual segments in 1810. The completed waterway, 87 miles long, allowed goods to be shipped by barge from the Bristol Channel to London and the Thames Estuary without ever entering the ocean.

As with most of the major, large-scale canals, the Kennet and Avon Canal attracted a large number of spur canals. Small mining and industrial centers situated a few miles on either side of the main canal constructed spurs to link into the larger system, thus giving them easy access to markets in Bristol and London that were not available by horse and cart. One such mining center was the Somerset Coal District, located a few miles to the southwest of Bath. To improve access from the Somerset coal fields to markets in Bath, Bristol, and beyond, the Somerset Coal Canal was constructed beginning in 1792 and opened for business in 1801. The Somerset Coal Canal intersects with the Kennet and Avon Canal at Dundas Basin, a few miles southeast of Bath, at the western end of the Dundas Aqueduct carrying the Kennet and Avon Canal over the River Avon.

The Dundas Aqueduct and its surrounding area are much more than just a bridge that carries boats over a small river. The Somerset Coal Canal has an important connection to the history of geology, and attracts geologists from all over the world. One of the most famous geologists of all time—Bath surveyor William Smith—designed the route of the canal. In the process, he sliced open the earth, observed the fossils and correctly interpreted how they related to the rocks in which they were found, invented the science of stratigraphy, and drew the world's first geologic maps.

The aqueduct was also a great engineering achievement. It was designed by John Rennie, the prominent architect who designed numerous canals during canal mania, including the Kennet and Avon, and then proceeded to design multiple bridges crossing the Thames in London, including the London Bridge that you can now see in the Arizona desert. Dundas Aqueduct was completed in 1810, and is enormous. At almost 500 feet long, it is constructed of famous Bath Stone with ornate flourishes.

Like most canals constructed during canal mania, the entire canal system at Dundas Basin, including the Kennet and Avon Canal, Dundas Aqueduct, and the Somerset Coal Canal only operated for a short time before they became obsolete. The Great Western Railway linked London and Bristol by 1841 and although the Kennet and Avon Canal continued to carry minor levels of traffic, it was usually in some condition of disrepair. The Somerset Coal Canal closed in 1898. Dundas Aqueduct leaked, and, despite being designated as a Scheduled Ancient Monument in 1951, it was closed to boat traffic in 1954, although it remained open for pedestrians walking along the towpath. The rest of the Kennet and Avon Canal was closed by the early 1960s, and the entire canal system at Dundas Basin was abandoned and allowed to fall into ruins.

Fortunately, large portions of this system have been restored and rewatered and are now a substantial tourist and recreational attraction. Dundas Aqueduct was restored and reopened by 1984. The easternmost

COMMUNITY BRIDGES

quarter-mile of the Somerset Coal Canal was restored and reopened in 1988, and the entire Kennet and Avon Canal was reconstructed as a recreational waterway and reopened in 1990.

Dundas Basin today attracts tourists and recreational users for a variety of reasons. Of course, the centerpiece is Dundas Aqueduct, which you can cross by foot, bicycle, or in a boat. The western end of the Kennet and Avon Canal at Bath is only about three miles to the north, and the lovely little Cotswolds town of Bradford-on-Avon is about five miles to the south, making the perfect distance for a day hike or bike ride in a scenic and historically important area.

The Dundas Basin, which is a wider pool of water within the canal, is situated at the intersection of the aqueduct and the Somerset Coal Canal. This basin housed a wharf and small iron crane that are still there, and were used to transfer coal from the small Somerset coal field barges to larger barges on the Kennet and Avon. The Somerset Coal Canal is lined with private longboats that are cute because they are so low and narrow, and many of which serve as residences.

The area can be accessed by car, as there is a car park at the western end of the Somerset Coal Canal a short walk from Dundas Basin and the aqueduct. There is also a bus stop—the Dundas Aqueduct stop accessible by a short bus ride from the central station in Bath.

BARRAGE VAUBAN AND PONTS COUVERTS, STRASBOURG, FRANCE

The old city of Strasbourg is located on an island called the Grand Île in the River Ill, resulting in dozens of historic bridges to visit. The most famous of them, the Ponts Couverts, or Covered Bridges, are part of an amalgamation of bridges, towers, walls, dams, locks, and mills in the Petite France neighborhood on the southern end of the Grand Île, where the river separates to flow around either side of the island.

The name of the Ponts Couverts has likely misled and confused a large number of tourists. The Ponts Couverts cross the River Ill only a short distance downstream of another structure crossing the river, the Barrage Vauban. The confusion is a result of the fact that the Ponts Couverts are not actually covered while the Barrage Vauban, which is not a covered bridge either, has the appearance of being a covered bridge from a distance.

The original bridges at this location, built around 1300, were covered, hence the name. The current bridges are an 1865 replacement, without covers. Meanwhile, the view of the nearby Barrage Vauban from the Ponts Couverts has an appearance similar to that of Ponte Vecchio or Pulteney Bridge, looking as if it has two levels of shops built across the tops of arches over the river. It looks like a covered bridge. Therefore, when you perform an internet search on Strasbourg, or on covered bridges in Europe, you are likely to find websites that incorrectly label photos of the Barrage Vauban as the "Covered Bridges." Tourists go to this location planning to see something that looks like covered bridges and they are immediately satisfied when they see the Barrage Vauban right there, having all the appearance of a covered bridge.

It is only when you actually explore the area that the complexity of the configuration of bridges, locks, and other structures begins to make sense. The location where the River Ill separates to flow around both sides of the Grand Île is also a substantial elevation drop that, before the area was re-engineered hundreds of years ago, was waterfalls. The waterfalls became the location of mills, to take advantage of the water power. The mills, in turn, produced jobs, leading to the settlement and development of a city, and thus leading to the need for walls to protect the residents. The city wall was built across the river at this location in 1300, and the portion of the wall that crossed the river on arches became the Ponts Couverts.

Another complication is that the river does not simply divide into two branches at this location. It divides into five branches, with one main branch flowing around the western side of the Grand Île, and four small finger-like branches splitting off into mill races, passing through mills, and then rejoining on the eastern side. The city wall and the Ponts Couverts cross these four small branches, and therefore are actually four separate bridges that make up the Ponts Couverts. Although the fourteenth century bridges were replaced in 1865, the original defensive towers situated between the bridges are still in place and are a prominent landmark for tourist photographs. The beauty and attraction of the views from these bridges are documented by the numerous love padlocks.

Although they were part of the city wall and connected to the towers, the Ponts Couverts were not the only component of the defenses of

Strasbourg. In the 1680s and 1690s, the Barrage Vauban was constructed just a few hundred feet upstream of the Ponts Couverts, and it is also complex and unusual. The view of the Barrage Vauban from inside the city fortifications looks like a series of two-story buildings with arched windows, crossing the river over 13 arches. The opposite side, facing away from the city, is different. Instead of a series of arched windows, people approaching the structure from the outside were greeted by a 25-foot-high blank wall pierced by narrow rifle slots that appear much less welcoming than the windows on the city-side.

Ponts Couverts at Strasbourg, France

Even then, the true defensive purpose of the Barrage Vauban is not obvious, because there is much more to it. The structure is not just a bridge because, in case of attack, it could easily be converted into a dam. The 13 arches were constructed with slots so that barriers could be lowered to block the openings. This had an obvious advantage in closing off the arches, so that attackers could not enter the openings. However, it also closed off the flow of the river, causing the water to back up, rise, and flood the fields south of the city. The dam not only stopped attackers from entering the city, but also made it impossible for them to encamp outside the city walls.

The manner in which the structure could be converted from bridge to dam was ingenious. Of the 13 arches, 11 are low, with an opening of only about six feet above river level. The open corridor on the first floor of the interior of the structure is at the level of these low arches, crossing over the top of them from one end to the other like the deck of a bridge. The low clearance provided by these arches would successfully stop armies from entering the city in ships, but it would also have interfered with everyday navigation and commercial shipping. Thus, the other two arches are much higher, at the level of the second story of the interior of the structure. This allowed large boats to deliver goods into and out of the city. The larger openings could also be closed off entirely, just like the smaller arches, to function as a dam.

The two higher arches had an inconvenient effect in that they were higher than the floor of the corridor that passed through the first floor of the interior of the building. To solve this problem, movable wooden bridges were built inside the structure at these two arches. During normal operation, the movable wooden bridges were lowered to floor level in the corridor, creating a continuous corridor. These wooden bridges could be raised, as needed, to allow passage of larger boats. This corridor is used as a bridge by pedestrians and bicyclists today. During times of crisis, the interior wooden bridges were drawn up, and a barrier was lowered to close off the arches. Defenders could still move along the full length of the structure along the corridor on the second floor, firing at attackers through the rifle slots.

This can all be seen when crossing the Barrage Vauban today. In most of the length of the first floor corridor, you are walking above the top level of the smaller arches, so you are walking on a stone floor, with stone walls on both sides and a stone ceiling. When you reach the sites of the two higher arches, you actually leave the stone structure and emerge into the opening of the arch. The floor is wooden and crosses the flowing river just beneath your feet. The sides of the bridge are open, with views along the axis of the river both upstream and downstream. Attached to the stone walls and short wooden bridge are the old chains and pulleys used to raise and lower the corridor floor and allow larger boats to pass through.

As interesting as this engineering achievement is, it is not the reason that the Barrage Vauban is today a major tourist attraction and symbol of the city of Strasbourg. The reason for that is the roof terrace, which was added in 1965. The roof terrace is one of the prime spots from which to see all of the landmarks of Strasbourg in one single, elevated view. The view to the south is uninspiring, but the view north into the city, which is a UNESCO World Heritage Site, is impressive. At your feet, between the Barrage Vauban and Ponts Couverts, is the basin through which the Strasbourg tour boats maneuver as they enter and exit the lock system on the river. On the other side of the basin, just a few hundred feet away, are the Ponts Couverts passing between their medieval towers. Immediately north of the Ponts Couverts are the picturesque Alsatian-style houses of the wildly popular Petite France district, jammed with tourists. In the background, about a half-mile away, is the enormous spire of the cathedral. This view makes the terrace on top of the Barrage Vauban one of the biggest tourist attractions in a city filled with tourist attractions.

FREDERICK DOUGLASS BRIDGE, WASHINGTON, DC

The idea of building ballparks at bridges has been maturing since 1992, and now in 2022 it is beginning to work in reverse. Instead of building ballparks at the end of important bridges, bridges are now being built at the locations of important ballparks.

Nationals Park, in Washington, DC, followed the model of the Cleveland Guardians (previously Indians), Cincinnati Reds, Pittsburgh Pirates, and multiple minor league teams by being constructed at the end of the old Frederick Douglass Bridge over the Anacostia River in what, at the time, was an industrial area adjacent to the closed Washington Navy Yard. The bridge, a steel-plate girder bridge constructed in 1950, was serviceable mostly as an exit ramp for commuters from Interstate 295 into Capitol Hill. It was not particularly attractive or special. It had sidewalks, but they were narrow, and nonresidents would rarely venture to the south side of the river on foot.

When the ballpark was constructed in 2008, the hope was that it would spur redevelopment in the area, similar to other downtown ballparks. However, 2008 was a bad time economically for real estate development, and attendance in the first few years suffered from a combination of losing baseball teams and having the ballpark surrounded by a less-than-affluent neighborhood. Both situations improved in the 2010s, and the Capitol Riverfront is now one of the most desirable neighborhoods in the city.

Once this success had taken hold, the old Douglass Bridge became a hindrance to further development. New, clean, glass-sided, high-rise condos provided spectacular views of the ballpark and the river, but that view included the unattractive bridge. Meanwhile, the lack of matching development on the south side of the river, the narrow sidewalks, and the inertia of a long-standing disreputable reputation made it unlikely that substantial numbers of people would walk across the bridge to attend baseball games, or for any other reason. In short, the bridge itself was partially responsible for holding back development in the hottest real estate market in town.

In 2012, planning began for the replacement of the bridge—and not just any replacement. The bridge was planned with two substantial goals in mind. The first was to provide a bridge that was not just aesthetically pleasing, but that served as a work of public art deserving of its prominent location just down the street from the US Capitol. The second objective was to facilitate the spread of redevelopment to the south side of the river by providing safe and inviting pedestrian access between the neighborhoods south of the river and the ballpark, with its surrounding bars and restaurants.

The new bridge opened to traffic in 2021, and it has already dramatically modified the viewscape along the Anacostia shoreline. This is because, in contrast to the existing bridges in the area, the new bridge has a prominent, modernistic superstructure, with the bridge deck suspended from three high arches that dominate the view along the river.

As of this writing in early 2022, the new Frederick Douglass Bridge is an interesting study in an examination of tourist bridges. The effect of the sculptural superstructure is complete, and it does decoratively dominate the skyline, especially when lit at night. Also, one of the bridge's sidewalks is open so walkers, joggers, and cyclists can use it to access the ballpark or workplaces on Capitol Hill.

In its current state of construction and development, its attractions and pedestrian-friendly features are still a work in progress. The bridge will ultimately have wide sidewalks for pedestrian and bicycle access and will eventually have redeveloped parks, with trails, on both shorelines. However, there are no condominiums, parks, or other developments on the south end of the bridge yet, so there is not much foot traffic. The viewing platforms on the western sidewalk are not yet open, and the eastern side sidewalk is not open yet at all. The areas at both ends of the bridge are a massive construction site and are likely to remain so for several years to come.

But that is the point. Bridges can serve as engines to spur development and become community centers in the twenty-first century, just as they did hundreds and thousands of years ago. They can be designed with tourist and recreation-friendly features in mind. They can be integrated not only into currently existing developments and park systems, but they can be centerpieces of planned developments and new park systems. All of this, and more, was done at the Frederick Douglass Bridge, largely due to the foresight to place the new ballpark on the riverfront more than ten years ago.

CHAPTER 4

DECORATED BRIDGES

HAMMERSMITH BRIDGE, LONDON

One of the most ornately decorated bridges you will find, the Hammersmith Bridge would almost certainly be on the list of the most visited and photographed tourist bridges in the world if it were located just about five miles east of where it is. Five miles east would put it in the middle of the busiest tourist district in London, and its unique engineering, historical importance, and over-the-top decorations would make it just as much of a landmark as Tower Bridge. As it is, located in a suburb off the beaten tourist path, the Hammersmith Bridge is a well-known image, but it is probably visited by very few London tourists.

The bridge crosses the Thames in the suburb of Hammersmith. It is located within walking distance of the Underground, so it can be reached by casual London tourists, if they wish to take a few hours out of their day to visit. The bridge was built in 1887, a few years before Tower Bridge. The construction of Hammersmith Bridge is similar to Tower Bridge in that it is an eyebar chain suspension bridge, and the internal framework of the suspension towers is hidden underneath layers of outer decoration. At Tower Bridge, the decoration is stonework. At Hammersmith, it is metal, forming a dark green ceremonial arch through which traffic passes. The arches are embellished with applied decorations in dark green scrolls and gold highlights, and then topped by green and gold cupolas with golden spires. A cartouche over the roadway bears the construction date of 1887

DECORATED BRIDGES

beneath the monogrammed letters "MBW." The monogram refers to the Metropolitan Board of Works, which constructed the bridge.

One unusual feature is the enormous, dark green anchor blocks holding the ends of the eyebar chains. The anchors of suspension bridges are not always visible. Often, they are underground or beneath the deck of a bridge. Some suspension bridges are anchored into bedrock, while others are anchored under massive stone towers. At Hammersmith, the eyebar chains are held under heavy metal anchor blocks, approximately 15 feet high. The green and gold decorative scheme on the anchor blocks matches that of the towers. The ends of the anchor blocks are decorated with large green and gold scrolls, and the cupola and spire on top of the suspension towers are repeated on top of the anchor blocks.

The final touch is on the sides of the anchor blocks facing into, and away from, the roadway. The sides are emblazoned with golden leaves surrounding coats of arms of the British monarchs. In the center is the 1887 version of the heraldic shield of the United Kingdom. The shield is divided into four quadrants, with the three English lions in the northwest and southeast quadrants, the Irish harp in the southwest quadrant, and the single rampant lion of Scotland in the northeast. The shield is surrounded by six escutcheons held within golden circles. The figures inside the six circles represent the arms of the six jurisdictions within the boundaries of the Metropolitan Board of Works, including the City of London, and Kent, Surrey, Westminster, Colchester, and Middlesex counties.

LOWER TRENTON BRIDGE, TRENTON, NEW JERSEY

It is likely that nobody deliberately goes to the Lower Trenton Bridge, which crosses the Delaware River in Trenton, New Jersey, as a tourist. The local population may use the sidewalk on the north side of the bridge for jogging and biking, as this bridge south of downtown and the Calhoun Street Bridge north of downtown both connect to riverfront trails, creating an accessible loop up one side of the river and then down the other, totaling about two miles. These recreational users cannot see, and probably do not care about, the most famous attraction of this bridge. However, for people traveling by train between Washington, Baltimore, and Philadelphia to the south and New York and Boston to the north, the bridge is a prominent, and somewhat amusing, landmark.

A bridge has been at this location since 1806, making it the earliest bridge crossing on the Delaware River. The original wooden bridge was demolished in 1875 and was replaced by an iron bridge. Beginning in 1917, the city's slogan "Trenton Makes, The World Takes" was emblazoned on the south side of the iron bridge in letters almost ten feet tall. The bridge was rebuilt in steel in 1928, and the slogan was reinstalled in 1935. Ever since, the slogan has greeted travelers on the nearby US Route 1 bridge and on passenger trains passing through Trenton. The three bridges are each within a short distance of each other, so the gigantic letters dominate the view toward downtown, and not just in daytime. Even as early as 1917, the letters have been illuminated at night, not by flood lights from the side, but through lights physically placed within the letters. These lights were originally incandescent bulbs that were replaced by neon in 1935, and then by LEDs with color changing capability in 2017.

The slogan has occasionally been mocked throughout the years, as the business of Trenton has transitioned away from manufacturing and toward state government. However, whether it is still accurate or not, it has now become a prominent landmark greeting visitors to Trenton.

CALVIN COOLIDGE MEMORIAL BRIDGE, NORTHAMPTON, MASSACHUSETTS

The Calvin Coolidge Memorial Bridge crossing the Connecticut River in Northampton, Massachusetts, is a good example of a bridge dedicated to a politician done in a manner both tasteful and informative. The bridge was constructed in 1939, just a few years after Coolidge died. The bridge has three large stone monuments, with one on either side of the roadway on the eastern end of the bridge, and a single monument on the southern side of the bridge on the western end. Each monument is constructed of white granite, and stands about 25 feet high and 30 feet long. The top corners of the monuments have stylistic eagles carved into the stone, framing the name of the bridge, which is inscribed in stone in large art deco style letters.

The main face of a monument on either end of the bridge is occupied by a large bronze plaque that bears a relief portrait of Coolidge, as well as an impressive list of the political offices he held. Of course, he is known as a president of the United States, but those who live outside of Massachusetts may be challenged to name any of his other accomplishments. Prior to being president, he was vice-president, governor of Massachusetts, lieutenant governor of Massachusetts, president of the Massachusetts Senate, a member of the State Senate, mayor of Northampton, and a member of the State House of Representatives. These accomplishments show that this is not just a memorial to a random president of the United States, but a monument to a local boy done good, having risen from mayor of Northampton to the White House in only 12 years.

MARKET STREET BRIDGE, WILKES-BARRE, PENNSYLVANIA

The Market Street Bridge across the Susquehanna River in Wilkes-Barre, Pennsylvania, is one of several memorial bridges built in the United States shortly after World War I. Like other memorial bridges of the same era, the bridge was designed to serve as a prominent, grand entrance to the city center by framing the view of the downtown buildings from the bridge through a series of enormous monuments.

The bridge itself is an attractive series of reinforced concrete open-spandrel arches, with six arches crossing the river and an additional six arches forming the approach on the northwestern end. The bridge is wide, considering that it was built in 1929. The roadway is five traffic lanes wide, and the sidewalks on each side are more than 15 feet wide.

The bridge connects downtown to a commercial and residential neighborhood on the northwest side of the river. Both sidewalks pass through ornately decorated, 40-foot-high monumental arches on each end of the bridge. Each monumental arch is constructed of a white granite base about four feet high, and then carved white sandstone to the top. The side of each monument uses sandstone blocks of different sizes in alternating layers for a decorative effect. The sides of the monuments facing traffic and pedestrians consist of flat columns topped by pilasters, a capital, and then a gigantic carved stone eagle with outstretched wings.

Monuments on Market Street Bridge, Wilkes-Barre, Pennsylvania

The open archway on each monument is only about 15 to 20 feet high, and then the remainder of the surface of the monument facing outwards toward travelers entering the bridge is used for dedicatory inscriptions honoring a variety of different groups and values. On the four monuments, above each arch on a long lintel, is carved a single word: Perseverance, Patriotism, Progress, and Prosperity. Above each word is a stone plaque, decoratively outlined in carved stone leaves, inscribed with a longer dedication. On the downtown end of the bridge, the Perseverance arch is dedicated to the Fortitude of the Early Settlers, and the Patriotism arch is dedicated to the Service of Our Heroes in Every War. On the northwestern end of the bridge, the Progress arch is dedicated to the Culture Begot by our Schools and Teachers, and the Prosperity arch is dedicated to the Industry Builded by Human Hand and Brain.

Interestingly, the back side of each monument facing inward toward the center of the bridge has the same lintel and stone plaque outlined in carved leaves, but these are blank, making the arch look incomplete. It appears the designers were making space available for adding future dedications, but none have been added in the past 100 years. Because the northwestern end of the bridge is so much longer due to the approaches, the sidewalk on that segment has also been decorated by 20-foot-high monumental obelisks in white sandstone. The entire length of the sidewalk on both sides of the bridge is flanked by ornate, light-gray, 20-foot-high lampposts.

The bridge carries traffic from Market Street directly into the diamond-shaped central square of downtown Wilkes-Barre, just a few steps off the end of the bridge. The riverfront on both banks of the river was recently redeveloped into lovely riverwalk promenades, with trails following the top of the levee on both sides of the river, and providing an elevated view of the bridge and downtown. The riverfront promenade on the western end of the bridge is Nesbitt Park, which is north of the bridge, and Kirby Park Natural Area to the south. On the eastern end of the bridge, the sidewalk is connected to a promenade along the top of the levee that crosses an attractive little modern pedestrian bridge and continues north a few blocks to the beautifully ornate Victorian-style Luzerne County Courthouse, which dates from 1909.

PANTHER HOLLOW BRIDGE, PITTSBURGH

Pittsburgh is an extremely hilly city, consisting of elevated plateau-like areas incised by deep, narrow ravines. The property that eventually became Schenley Park, the most visited of the urban parks within the city, is no exception. Residential neighborhoods were being established in this area about five miles east of downtown by the 1880s. However, the rough, rocky topography limited development and the property, now covering more than 450 acres, was donated to the city for use as a park in 1889.

The northwestern corner of the park includes complex topography, ravines, and several important Pittsburgh landmarks. The northern side of Schenley Park is bordered by the campuses of two major universities, Carnegie-Mellon University on the east and the University of Pittsburgh on the west. A deep ravine known as Junction Hollow separates the two campuses and also forms the northwestern boundary of the park. The hill within the park south of Junction Hollow is the home of the famous Phipps Conservatory and Botanical Gardens. The conservatory and gardens, in turn, are bordered on the south by the most prominent ravine in the park, Panther Hollow, named for the wild cats that once roamed there. More than 120 feet deep, Panther Hollow neatly slices through the park from east to west, separating the park into southern and northern halves. The only connection between the two halves is Panther Hollow Bridge.

Given that the bridge is best known for its use by college students walking to and from classes, it is larger than you might expect. Several hundred feet long, it carries one lane of traffic plus a bicycle lane each way and has a sidewalk on each side. Although you would not notice by driving over, pedestrians on the sidewalks can see that the bridge is quite high.

The stream that flows through Panther Hollow is small, but there is a dam almost directly underneath the bridge that creates Panther Hollow Lake, which is a small pond on the west side of the bridge. The pond is surrounded by walking trails, and there is a steep, rustic set of stone stairs from the sidewalk on the southwestern corner of the bridge down into the semi-remote underworld of the hollow. Just moments removed from the busy traffic and multitudes of college students crossing the bridge into the universities, the hollow is quiet, with no cars and just a few hikers and sunbathers, and the enormous steel arch of the bridge looming overhead.

From the hollow, you can inspect and photograph the structure of the bridge. The central portion of the bridge consists of a single steel arch, painted yellow, crossing the hollow. The steel arch is anchored into stone arches on either side, and the stone arches are anchored into the bedrock walls of the gorge. The stone of the arches is an attractive, cross-bedded sandstone.

The most well-known attraction of the bridge is the large bronze sculptures of panthers found at each corner. The four panthers each sit on sandstone pedestals about seven feet high, and each panther is life-sized, about four feet high and six feet long. The panthers stand on bronze rocks and are crouched to attack, frozen in a roar and showing their big bronze teeth. The signature of the sculptor, G. Moretti (for Giuseppe Moretti), is inscribed into the bronze rock at the back end of each panther.

DECORATED BRIDGES

The stone pedestal holding the panther on the northeastern corner has an information plaque and a historic landmark plaque on the yellow, ornate steel railing. There can be some confusion regarding the name of the bridge, including which names are "official" versus those that are just descriptive. The historic landmark plaque on the northeastern corner looks official and was installed by the Pittsburgh History and Landmarks Foundation. This plaque identifies the bridge as "Schenley Park Bridge over Panther Hollow," with Henry B. Rust as the engineer and a construction date of 1897. However, a short walk away is another bridge commonly referred to as Schenley Bridge, on the north side of the conservatory and gardens. The Schenley Bridge is a twin to the Panther Hollow Bridge, similar in construction and size. It crosses Junction Hollow and Boundary Street and has a similar historic plaque citing its name as "Schenley Park Bridge over Boundary Street," also identifying Henry B. Rust as the engineer and 1897 as the construction date. Schenley Bridge leads into the small greenspace of Schenley Plaza, which is surrounded by the Carnegie Museum and Library, Frick Fine Arts Building, and one of the most prominent landmarks of the Pittsburgh skyline, the 42-story Late Gothic Revival Cathedral of Learning. The names of the two bridges are often confused, but only one of the bridges is famous for its sculptures.

It is often assumed that the sculptures on the bridge were developed as an homage to the mascot for the University of Pittsburgh sports teams, the Pitt Panthers. The chronology of the park, bridges, and universities is revealing, and the opposite happened. The park was established in 1889, and the large Victorian-style Glasshouse of the Botanical Gardens was constructed in 1893. Both Panther Hollow Bridge and Schenley Bridge were constructed in 1897 to facilitate access to the conservatory and Botanical Gardens from the main part of the park to the south and the developing neighborhoods to the north. The Phipps Hall of Botany, housed in an ornate stone building, was constructed just on the northern end of Panther Hollow Bridge, as an addition to the Botanical Gardens, in 1901. It was not until 1909 that the scattered buildings of the University of Pittsburgh were consolidated into a new campus on the northwestern side of Junction Hollow, when the university adopted the bridge's panthers as its mascot.

Visiting the bridge as a non-resident is a little difficult, because any location bounding two major universities is going to have parking restrictions. There is parking for the conservatory and gardens available along Schenley Drive, but the number of spaces is limited. Before trying to visit, review the conservatory website for directions to visitor parking garages at the universities.

DUMBARTON (Q STREET) BRIDGE, WASHINGTON, DC

As discussed in Chapter 4 of *Bridgespotting: Part 1*, decorations usually have some meaning behind them, based on a memorial, commemoration, allegory, or other concept. On those bridges, there is a thematic connection between the various sculptures, plaques, and inscriptions, even if that connection is difficult to decipher. However, decoration is sometimes done just for aesthetic purposes, without any substantial hidden meaning.

The City Beautiful Movement, which called for integration of aesthetics and function, was a major force in city planning and architecture in the United States from 1893 through the 1920s, and its effect can be seen on hundreds of bridges built during that time. One of the weirder examples is found on the 1915 Dumbarton Bridge, also known as Q Street Bridge, crossing Rock Creek and the Rock Creek Parkway in Washington, DC. Dumbarton Bridge displays a mish-mash of different, and apparently unrelated, decorative motifs. Somehow, this bridge managed to combine an ancient Roman architecture theme with an American Wild West theme.

The bridge structure consists of five stone arches in the Romanesque Revival style, based on the designer's review of photographs of Roman aqueducts and a bridge in the mountains of Italy. The theme of Roman aqueducts is repeated, in miniature, in the upper frieze of the spandrel on the side of the bridge, facing traffic. The base of each arcade in the aqueduct, though, is formed with a corbel that is carved in a distinctly non-Roman theme. Each corbel is a small, carved Native American head, complete with full headdress. Dozens of them!

The model for the sculpted heads was a life mask of the Oglala Lakota Sioux Chief, Kicking Bear. Kicking Bear was one of the most prominent natives in the western United States from the 1870s through the 1890s. He fought at the Battle of the Little Bighorn, and was instrumental in

DECORATED BRIDGES

spreading the Ghost Dance religion, which was opposed by the US government and led to the massacre at Wounded Knee in 1890. He was arrested and later released on condition that he join a European tour of Buffalo Bill's Wild West Show. In 1896, he traveled to Washington, DC as part of a delegation presenting grievances to the Bureau of Indian Affairs. During that time, agreed to have a life mask made to be used as the example of a Sioux warrior for display in the Smithsonian Museum of Natural History. It was this mask that the sculptor, Alexander Phimister Proctor, used to create the dozens of sculpted heads used as corbels on the spandrel of the bridge.

One of Dozens of Carved Masks of Kicking Bear
Lining Dumbarton Bridge, Washington, DC

Because of the configuration of the creek and road crossed by the bridge, the Roman and Native American-themed decorations are seen only by drivers along Rock Creek Parkway, most of whom do not live in the neighborhood. The decorations on the side of the bridge are not seen by people driving by or walking across. Instead, local residents are confronted by a completely different decoration—an enormous, life-sized bronze buffalo guarding each of the four corners of the bridge. These have resulted in the popular local nickname for the bridge, Buffalo Bridge.

CHAPTER 5

DECORATIVE BRIDGES

LIBERTY BRIDGE, GREENVILLE, SOUTH CAROLINA

The small Liberty Bridge in Greenville, South Carolina, is difficult to describe. When trying to find an appropriate adjective, the word "unnecessary" comes to mind. This is because this bridge, which spans the Reedy River in Falls Park in downtown Greenville, serves no functional purpose in providing access from Point A to Point B. Yes, you can use it to cross from one side of Falls Park to the other, if you wish. You could also do that on the Main Street Bridge located only a few hundred feet away.

This lack of functionality is part of the appeal of Liberty Bridge. It serves a different purpose in providing a spectacular viewing platform from which to see the Falls of the Reedy River. The Reedy is not a large river. It is only about 300 feet wide and shallow as it flows over bedrock outcrops. Therefore, the Falls are not enormous, only about 30 feet high, but they are an impressive sight. They also have historical significance as the location of the first European settlement in Greenville, in 1768, when a mill was established to take advantage of the elevation drop.

Another purpose of the bridge is to serve as an amazing piece of urban art because it is not as much a bridge as it is a gigantic sculpture. The bridge appears to be a work of art, and then only incidentally also happens to have a deck that connects to both banks of the river.

A third apparent purpose of the bridge speaks to the status of Greenville as home to many national and international engineering and manufacturing companies. The city has one of the highest per capita populations of engineers in the country and takes great civic pride in having this highly educated and nationally important workforce. It is no accident that the city chose to use a clever and unique design, one that has won numerous engineering awards, in constructing this bridge.

Constructed in 2004, the Liberty Bridge is unusual even for cable-stayed bridges. One desirable engineering and artistic characteristic of cable-stayed bridges is that you can put the cable anchors anywhere you want. You are not constrained by the need for the cables to be vertical, or for the anchor towers to be directly over the center of the bridge. At the Liberty Bridge, the designers took full advantage of this freedom.

To develop a straight cable-stayed bridge, designers have two choices for anchor locations and cable angles. The easiest, and most common, is for the anchor towers to be located within the longitudinal axis of the straight bridge deck. This can be done with one or more towers located anywhere along the length of the bridge, from either end or in the middle. However, they must be located directly in line with the deck, to pull the deck straight up instead of pulling it over to one side. Alternatively, the anchor towers can be located on the sides of the bridge, outside of the axis. To do this, you have to balance the lateral pull of the cables by placing the same number of cables on both sides of the bridge, spreading the lateral forces equally. Even though one set of cables is pulling the bridge deck out in one direction, the other set exerts an equal pull in the other direction, and the end result is that the bridge deck remains straight.

But what if you want a curved bridge? That cannot be done with a normal suspension bridge or with a cable-stayed bridge with anchor towers within the bridge axis. A curved bridge can only be achieved by anchoring the ends of the deck to the bank, and then pulling the deck out in one direction by using an anchor tower off to the side of the bridge. This describes the design of the Liberty Bridge.

Why was it designed to be curved? Apparently, the city just wanted an artistic viewing platform to act as an urban showpiece, while also demonstrating their engineering ingenuity. The effect is very successful. The curve in the bridge serves as a perfect viewing platform for the Falls in terms of height, distance, and angle of view. The concave side of the curve faces the Falls, while the needle-like supporting towers lean at weird angles away from the opposite side that overhangs the park. With all of the cables and anchor towers located on the convex, downstream side of the bridge, there are no visual obstructions at all on the upstream side facing the Falls.

From the deck of the bridge facing the Falls, the sense is that of being in an amphitheater suspended in mid-air, in a perfect position to view the scenery. The fact that you can enter the platform on either side or cross without looking at the Falls at all, if you prefer, is a secondary consideration. The result is that the bridge looks and feels different from other bridges. Although the deck bounces up and down when people walk on it, as expected for any bridge suspended by cables, it also sways a little from side to side. This side-to-side movement is outside of our normal range of experience, and is very disconcerting, but it makes sense because the deck is held in place by forces pulling on it from the sides.

Another interesting but unsatisfying feature is the inability to capture the uniqueness of this bridge in photographs. More than any other bridge you have ever seen, this bridge is completely three-dimensional and asymmetrical. Other suspension and cable-stayed bridges are effectively two-dimensional. They have substantial length and height, but their width is narrow compared to the length and height. Also, they are symmetrical, with the exact same configuration of supporting cables on one side as the other. Because these bridges are two-dimensional in shape, they can be easily captured in two-dimensional photographs.

The feeling of the curve on the Liberty Bridge cannot be captured in pictures. The pictures look like pieces of the bridge are falling over, and there is no sense of how the angles and curves are working together to hold the thing up. The problem is made worse by the city's decision to use a silhouette image of the bridge as a sort of city trademark on their road signs. While the desire to capitalize on this unique landmark is understandable, it does not work well. Unless you have actually walked the bridge and understand how it is balanced, the image used on the signs is extremely confusing. In fact, it is not all that clear that it is even a bridge. It could be some other complex jumble of cables and towers.

It is unlikely that anyone is going to visit Greenville just for the pleasure of walking this bridge but the bridge is mandatory if you happen to be in town on business. In fact, all of downtown Greenville is delightful, and the Liberty Bridge and Falls Park are just two of many reasons to hang out for an evening. The city has done an amazing job of revitalizing its beautiful Main Street with shops, restaurants, and bars. The river area on both banks has been the focus of new apartment, condo, hotel, and office building developments. The riverfront is lined with cafes, as well as promenades integrated into and under the bridges. Liberty Bridge is just part of this new, comprehensive redevelopment scheme, all within a small, easily walkable area. The best time to visit the area is at night, maybe for dinner, and then take an after-dinner walk along the beautifully lit bridge and Falls.

GATESHEAD MILLENNIUM BRIDGE, NEWCASTLE-UPON-TYNE, ENGLAND

There are a few features of the Gateshead Millennium Bridge that attract tourists and recreational users. As a newer bridge constructed in 2001, it contributes to the walkability of the redeveloped former dock areas, allowing pedestrian and bicycle access to new office buildings and condominiums on both sides of the river. By day, it is also a prominent work of public art, and by night, it is beautifully lit with saturated, ever-changing colors. However, the biggest attraction is that, once or twice each day, the bridge is both an engineering marvel and a kinetic sculpture.

At first glance, Gateshead Millennium appears to be a modern cable-stayed bridge similar in appearance to the Clyde Arc in Glasgow. The dominant visual feature is a high, white metallic arch extending from one bank to the other, with angled white cables from the arch connecting to a curved deck, but the similarity to Clyde Arc stops there. The connecting cables on Gateshead Millennium are actually not cables at all, but rods. The deck is not so much suspended from the arch as it is rigidly connected to it. This rigidity is necessary because, unlike Clyde Arc, both the deck and the arch of Gateshead Millennium move together as a single unit. The ends of the deck and the arch on either end of the bridge connect in a single point, which is a gigantic axle on which the bridge rotates.

DECORATIVE BRIDGES

In its normal position, the curved deck sits low over the water, blocking the passage of boats, while the arch rises high over the surrounding quayside buildings. When needed to allow boats to pass, motors pivot the axle, lowering the arch on one side and raising the deck on the other side. The motion continues until the deck and the arch are each about the same height over the water, at which point they are both high enough for large boats to pass underneath. The openings, which generally last about ten minutes, occur once per day in the summer and only on an as needed basis during other seasons. The times are posted on a placard at the south end of the bridge, and tourists gather, cell phone cameras held aloft, in the best viewing areas to capture selfies with the Tilting Bridge, as it is locally known.

Note that if you are visiting Gateshead Millennium due to an interest in unusual movable bridges, the 1876 Swing Bridge is just a short walk away. The movement mechanism on Swing Bridge is by rotation upon a central axis, which is not extremely rare for rail bridges, but is somewhat unusual for roadway bridges. While the bridge is not a modernistic kinetic sculpture, the rotation mechanism is done in a nicely decorative manner. Instead of being placed off to the side, the control room for the bridge is located within a small cupola, designed to look like the cap of a lighthouse, directly above the central axis.

IOWA WOMEN OF ACHIEVEMENT BRIDGE, DES MOINES, IOWA

A prominent feature of the Des Moines skyline on the north side of downtown is the high white arch of the sculptural Iowa Women of Achievement Bridge, also known as the Center Street Bridge. At the time of its construction in 2010, downtown Des Moines already had two old bridges—the Red Bridge and Riverside Park Drive Bridge—that had been rehabilitated and converted for pedestrian and bicycle use to connect the downtown Riverwalk trail systems to other trails on the opposite bank of the Des Moines River and the Raccoon River. Center Street Bridge was constructed in 2010 as a third pedestrian and bicycle-only bridge connecting these trail systems. Considering this seemingly limited purpose, and the fact that the Red Bridge a short distance away also offers a pedestrian-only connection between these trails, construction of the Center Street Bridge seems unnecessary. It is somewhat surprising, then, that it was constructed on a monumental scale.

From the side, the bridge appears to be a normal cable-stayed bridge, similar to the Clyde Arc in Glasgow in that it crosses the entire river on a single, high, white steel arch, with crisscrossing suspender cables filling the middle of the arch. There is a difference, however, in the structure. On Clyde Arc, the single deck passes through the arch and the suspension cables connect, at increasing angles, to either side of the deck, resulting in a honeycombed appearance of the cables when viewed from the side. The cables on the Center Street Bridge also appear to be honeycombed, but this is not because they connect to opposite sides of a single deck. Instead, this bridge has a deck that splits into two separate pedestrian decks, one passing on each side of the arch. The cables connect diagonally to the inside of each deck, leaving the outside of each deck seemingly hanging off the side with no visible means of support. As with Clyde Arc, Lowry Avenue, Gateshead Millennium, and other new cable-stayed bridges, the white arch serves as a blank canvas to capture colored LED lighting, mostly in white and shades of blue.

GRAY'S LAKE PARK BRIDGE, DES MOINES, IOWA

Gray's Lake is a small park on the southern fringes of downtown Des Moines. The lake was originally an oxbow on the Raccoon River, but it was expanded to about 100 acres in size by the removal of sand and gravel in a quarrying operation that ended in the 1950s. The property was purchased by the city and converted into a park in 1970. Following a major flood in 1993, a local couple named Kruidenier donated funds for improvement of the park infrastructure, including a playground, beach, boat rentals, and trails, all with an attractive view of downtown skyscrapers less than two miles away. On the southern edge of the lake, a narrow bridge approximately 1,400 feet long was constructed across a small embayment in the lake to complete a hiking and biking trail circuit.

The construction type and size of this bridge is unremarkable. The bridge is constructed of steel girders sitting on cement piers, with a 15-foot-wide cement deck. The bridge is not lighted from the sides, and does not have normal lampposts to provide white light for walking or biking at

DECORATIVE BRIDGES

night. In fact, the lack of "normal" lighting fixtures to allow use of the bridge for hiking and biking at night was entirely deliberate. A critical concept in the use of dramatic, deeply-colored lighting is that it can only be accomplished in the absence of white light. Any uncontrolled intermixing of white and colored light will result in washing out the colored light, eliminating any decorative effect it might have had. Because the decorative attraction of the Gray's Lake Park Bridge is its deeply-colored lighting scheme, there are no other sources of normal white light provided.

Instead of lampposts, halogen lighting fixtures are embedded behind the support posts along the railing. Each support post is specially designed to hold gradationally-colored stained glass plates, about two feet high and a few inches wide. Passing white light through the stained glass plates, the fixtures project geometric prisms of deep color onto the white cement deck. The halogen lights are strategically placed so that the support posts and narrow railing wires are used to cast shadows separating white triangles of light from the gradationally-colored prisms. Enough light is cast by the decorative system to illuminate the pathway for hikers, runners, and bikers at night, but the white and colored shapes were intentionally designed to prevent the white light from washing out the colors. The result is a series of prisms of deep yellow grading into orange grading into red, and deep purple grading into dark blue into dark green.

The colored designs cannot be seen from a distance, but only by pedestrians walking across the bridge. This would not be unusual, except that city parks in most cities are typically closed after dark. To be appreciated, the Gray's Lake Park Bridge must not only remain open but must also attract visitors to walk the bridge after sunset. Although the park can be reached by walking from downtown, there are also ample parking lots available, allowing the park to attract visitors from throughout the metro area.

HIGH TRESTLE TRAIL BRIDGE, MADRID, IOWA

One of the most famous lighted bridges in the entire United States is located in Iowa between the towns of Madrid and Woodward, approximately 30 miles northwest of Des Moines. The High Trestle Trail extends 25 miles from Ankeny to Woodward. It is a rail trail, meaning it is an abandoned railroad bed that has been converted to a bike trail. When this is done, it usually involves removal of the rails and ties, regrading of the railbed to a flat surface, either paving or packing of gravel to make a ridable surface, and installation of trail facilities such as trailheads, parking lots, and rest areas with benches, water, and restrooms. The process also often involves rehabilitation of former railroad bridges to provide bike access across rivers and highways.

The feature that makes the High Trestle Trail Bridge a major attraction is not the bridge structure itself, nor its length of about a mile, nor its height of almost 150 feet, nor its conversion into a bike trail. It is a long and high bridge, but there are many longer, higher rail trail bridges. Instead, the unusual feature is a sculptural artwork consisting of a series of steel squares through which the deck of the bridge passes. Each square is about ten feet long on each side, and each successive square is rotated a slight angle farther than the last.

The squares represent the supports used to avoid cave-ins in coal mines, and the stylized streaks of brown stone on the large, cement entry towers on the four corners of the bridge represent coal deposits found within the local limestones. The deck has been expanded at intervals, providing viewing platforms with historic and informational plaques. There is also a convenient viewing platform set off to the side of the bridge on the western end which allows for a side view of the bridge's piers and square sculptures.

When viewed along the axis through the squares, the effect is that of a spiral design, rotating as it becomes smaller and smaller before disappearing into the distance. In an odd way, the design is not just a static sculpture but is kinetic. A kinetic sculpture has movement, usually achieved through moving pieces of the sculpture. In the case of the High Trestle Bridge, the movement is not supplied by the sculpture itself. Instead, the sculpture is intended to be viewed from the viewpoint of a bicycle rider, and it is the bicycle that supplies the movement by moving the observer of the sculpture instead of parts of the sculpture. The effect is that the spiral unwinds in front of you as you proceed and, of course, it is more intense the faster you ride. If you cannot visit, the effect can be seen on multiple YouTube videos. When walking across, or just standing and observing, the movement stops, and the squares return to being just an interesting sculpture.

While the kinetic sculptural effect is interesting, it would likely not attract casual visitors other than cyclists, except for its most amazing feature: after dark, the squares along a lengthy segment of the bridge come alive, outlined in blue neon lights. The resulting image of the bright blue spiral design has turned an interesting bike ride into a statewide, and even nationwide, tourist attraction. The spirals are rusty reddish-brown during the daytime, then an attractive mix of rust red outlined in neon blue at dusk, and then fully blue at night. This is probably the only bike trail that specifically attracts riders at night.

The image has become so iconic that it is now a local, and even statewide, symbol, similar to how the New River Gorge Bridge has become a symbol of the state of West Virginia. If you drive to Madrid from Des Moines, your first hint that you are approaching the vicinity of the bridge comes when driving into Madrid on State Route 17. The large "Welcome to Madrid" sign is constructed of rust red steel girders, and the words are displayed against a background of a spiral series of rotating rust red squares. The road crosses the bike trail just before entering downtown, and there is a trailhead parking lot on the east side of Route 17. You may have to do a double take before you realize that the bike racks at the trailhead, and also those at the bridge itself, are in the form of rust red steel squares, each one rotated a bit farther than the next.

All road signs indicating the location of the trail and direction to the bridge, which is about two miles west of town, display the image of the spiral. Then, turning west from Route 17 to drive toward the bridge, the most prominent sight will be, as in many small midwestern towns, the large water tower. In many of these towns the water tower is used to display a town motto, or the names of famous individuals who hail from the area. In Madrid, the water tower displays the rust red spiral square design of the bridge sculptures. If you decide to stop at the local convenience store to buy a snack or soda before proceeding to the bridge, you might notice, on the small newspaper rack by the front door, a copy of the local paper, the *Madrid Register-News*. The banner head of the paper displays, of course, the spiral square design.

Water Tower in Madrid, Iowa, Showing Image of Bridge Sculptures

The image is not only used to attract visitors to tiny Boone County. You will also see many images of the bridge inside the Des Moines airport. Prominent photos of the blue squares are on display in some of the artwork in the gate areas. At the Hudson News shop, you will see that the frieze above the shop's entrance is a series of white silhouettes of downtown Des Moines skyscrapers, among which are a series of the spiral squares. Although the bridge itself does not have a gift shop, refrigerator magnets showing the blue spiral design are available at Hudson News.

The final confirmation that the image has gone national is a television commercial developed to encourage post-COVID tourism to Iowa in 2021. The 30-second commercial shows images of downtown Des Moines and many other statewide attractions. However, the final image, the coda on this appeal to Americans to make Iowa their first vacation destination after escaping quarantine, is a scene of cyclists traveling through the blue spiral squares at dusk.

The only respectable way to access the bridge, of course, is by bicycle. The bridge is located about two miles from both Madrid and Woodward, so it is an easy bike ride—in spring, summer, and fall. In winter, though, not so much. The best car access is to use West North Street/State Route 210 west out of downtown Madrid for about a mile, and then follow road signs to the south to a parking lot at the Grant's Woods Conservation Trail. This is a hiking trail through the woods and leads about another half-mile west to meet the biking trail. Once on the biking trail, it is about another half-mile to the bridge itself, and another half-mile from the end of the bridge to the blue-lit segment. Although the entire bridge is lined with the steel squares, only about one-third of the length has the blue neon lights, and these are at the Woodward end of the bridge.

PUBLIC GARDEN FOOTBRIDGE, BOSTON

From the beginning, the Public Garden Footbridge was nothing more than a cute decoration in a completely artificial garden. The Public Garden was constructed in 1837 and, although adjacent to the more famous Boston Common, it is not part of the Boston Common. It is a separate park specially designed as a botanical garden, the first in the United States. The garden is small, covering only 24 acres of flowers, walking paths, statues and other public art, with a small lake crossed by a tiny bridge.

The bridge was built in 1867 as a decorative suspension bridge. It never served a functional purpose because the lake it crosses is artificial, and is small enough that you can walk around it in just a few minutes. Also, being situated in the middle of the garden with nothing but flower beds and lawns on either end, the bridge pretty much does not lead from one place to another. Finally, the structure of the bridge is completely unnecessary for its size. It was clearly designed only to be a visual attraction.

While many bridge designers have competed to construct the world's longest suspension bridge, the designers in Boston succeeded in building the world's shortest suspension bridge, only about 50 feet long. The suspension towers are only 20 feet high and are constructed of textured stonework and topped by light blue, frosted glass globe lampposts. The suspension structure consists of iron eyebar chains and these, along with the ornate railings, are the same light blue color.

The bridge was reconstructed in 1921 with steel girders supporting the deck, eliminating the utility of the suspension system. Functionally, adding steel-girder supports was not necessary. The bridge was constructed as a true suspension bridge in the 1800s and stood as a suspension bridge for 54 years. Because technology does not move backward, it could have been reconstructed as a true suspension bridge. However, suspension bridges hanging from above by cables or chains are, generally, less stable in the long term than bridges sitting on modern steel girders. While another small suspension bridge could have been built at this location in 1921, providing modern supports does result in a bridge that is less costly, requires less maintenance, and will probably last longer. Also, the designer of the reconstructed bridge added the steel-girder supports in as inconspicuous a manner as possible. The steel girders are hidden behind a façade along the deck girder and can only be seen if you deliberately go underneath the bridge looking for them.

The effect of the bridge is very successful. Even though crossing it is unnecessary to enjoy the Public Garden, it is a major landmark, frequently makes cameo appearances in movies set in Boston, and you will find plenty of tourists and locals on it and near it, taking pictures, at any given time.

VALLEY DRIVE SUSPENSION BRIDGE, YOUNGSTOWN, OHIO

The Valley Drive Suspension Bridge carries traffic within Mill Creek Park near downtown Youngstown, Ohio. The bridge was constructed in 1895 by the Youngstown Bridge Company, and it is easy to assume that, once given the commission to construct a prominent bridge in the most important park in their hometown, the company went all out to make it a special bridge. Only about 100 feet long and wide enough for one car to pass at a time, this is one of the most ornate and decorative bridges you will ever see.

The construction type is unusual, even for suspension bridges. The suspension chains are held up by open steel lattice towers, about 25 feet high, and each topped by a decorative finial. The crosspiece over the portal is also an open trellis, topped with a geometric diamond with curled tips at its corners. Almost every piece of steel used as a structural support within the bridge ends in a curlicue, leading to this bridge having more nicknames known to the locals than any other bridge. Formally reported to be named either Valley Drive Suspension Bridge or Mill Creek Park Suspension Bridge, the structure is also fondly known to locals as the Silver Bridge, Cinderella Bridge, Disney Bridge, and Castle Bridge.

DECORATIVE BRIDGES

The bridge can be accessed at a small parking lot at the East Cohasset Trailhead at the southern end of Lake Cohasset. There are also good views of the bridge from the trail. The bridge has sidewalks that can be used to access the West Cohasset and other trails on the opposite side of Mill Creek.

Valley Drive Bridge in Mill Creek Park, Youngstown, Ohio

Like the Public Garden Bridge, the Valley Drive Bridge is no longer a true suspension bridge. Viewed from the side, you can see an incongruous feature: a modern cement pier in the center of the bridge. The pier was added during a rehabilitation in 2007 to provide additional support. Also similar to the Public Garden, the designer was careful to avoid too much alteration of the appearance. The cement pier was deliberately designed so that it is not as wide as the bridge deck itself. As a result, it is largely hidden in the shadows underneath the bridge and can only be seen when viewing from the sides, and there are almost no viewing positions on the sides. The main attraction is the ornate decorations, which are best viewed by walking across the bridge, from which you would never know there is a cement pier beneath the deck.

As a side note, there are several other interesting attractions in Mill Creek Park that should not be missed, including three additional bridges.

Mill Creek Park encompasses a series of three artificial lakes along Mill Creek, so there are scenic drives, recreational facilities, and historic attractions throughout the park.

At the northern end of the park, where Mill Creek flows into the Mahoning River, a short stone arch bridge carries East Glacier Drive across a small creek. Some sources report a construction date for this bridge to be 1900 and others 1913. This bridge resembles one of thousands of other semi-interesting stone arch bridges and would be mostly unremarkable except for its extremely unusual parapets. The stone arch itself is constructed of light beige and tan blocks that appear to be sandstone. However, both sides of the roadway are lined with large, upright, angular chunks of black basalt.

There is no dedicated parking and no sidewalks, but the bridge gets little traffic, so visitors can park on the side of the road near the ends of the bridge to inspect the basalt columns up close. Alternatively, there are parking areas on the opposite side of Lake Glacier, allowing a full view of the bridge from a distance. The striking appearance of the jagged black blocks lining the bridge has led to several nicknames: Parapet Bridge, Dragon Bridge, and Prehistoric Bridge. While the bridge is unusual and interesting, Mill Creek Park's website somehow claims that this is the "most photographed bridge in Mill Creek Park." This would be difficult to achieve in any park that includes the Valley Drive Bridge.

The southern part of the park includes Lanterman's Mill, dating from 1846. The mill was restored in the 1980s and is once again operational as it was in the 1800s. You can tour the interior with its operating machinery, and purchase cornmeal, buckwheat, and whole grain flour in the gift shop or local stores.

Just downstream from the mill, the creek is crossed by the Lanterman's Falls Bridge. This is a lovely, open-spandrel single cement arch bridge dating from 1920. This bridge has sidewalks, so consider walking across to get an amazing aerial view of the mill adjacent to the impressive Lanterman's Falls.

A short distance upstream of the mill is the Lanterman's Falls Covered Bridge. This bridge sports a curved wood arch and has a covered sidewalk on the downstream side facing toward the falls, mill, and cement

DECORATIVE BRIDGES

arch bridge. Built in 1988, it serves to provide a connection between hiking trails on either side of the creek. Since a bridge was needed to connect the trails, a wooden covered bridge was clearly selected because its nostalgic theme fits in well with the historic mill.

RIVER NESS BRIDGES, INVERNESS, SCOTLAND

The topographic valley created by the Great Glen Fault provides relatively flat terrain, allowing the Glen to serve as a major transportation pathway between Scotland's east and west coasts in the Highlands area. The elongated lochs within the Glen were connected by the Caledonian Canal in the early 1800s, providing a means of boat transport between the North Sea and Atlantic Ocean. The easternmost stretch of the Canal, covering the final few miles between Loch Ness and the North Sea, is the River Ness. Inverness sits on both sides of the River Ness and serves as the regional tourist center for visitors to the popular Scottish Highlands and Loch Ness areas.

Inverness has several early, small-scale suspension bridges that are both decorated and decorative. Starting at the downstream end of the old town area, Greig Street Bridge is a gorgeous small-scale suspension bridge built in 1881. The suspension towers each consist of an open interlaced iron lattice about 30 feet high, topped by decorative finials. The corner bracing of the portals is a decorative series of circles and curlicues, and the entire bridge is painted sparkling white. A date plaque on the wall of one of the towers reads "Rose Street Foundry, Inverness, 1881."

The bridge is only about 100 feet long and about ten feet wide, and carries pedestrians only. The quaint bridge offers a prominent view of the historic and attractive Inverness Castle. As a result, this is probably the most romantic setting in Inverness, documented by the attachment of multiple padlocks. On the south bank, the bridge terminates at the Old High Church, a small but appealing church that dates to the 1100s and which served an important role during the Jacobite Rebellion. It has an interesting old cemetery, complete with historical plaques, which is worth a visit.

In the center of the old town area, where the city's High Street reaches the Ness River and becomes Bridge Street, the Ness Bridge crosses the river at the foot of Inverness Castle. The Ness Bridge is the oldest bridge location in Inverness, but the current bridge is at least the third bridge at this location. A bridge dating from 1685, sketched by artist J.M.W. Turner in 1831, was replaced after being destroyed in a flood in 1849. The current bridge, dating from 1961, is an innocuous cement bridge, but its historic location and proximity to the Castle make it an important starting point for exploring the history of the city.

Visible a short distance upstream of the Castle, Infirmary Bridge is almost an identical twin of Greig Street Bridge but on a slightly reduced scale. The white iron lattice towers, use of decorative circles in the corner bracing, and finials on top of the end posts are all similar to those on the Greig Street Bridge. The deck is only about five feet wide, and, like Greig Street Bridge, it is pedestrian-only. Constructed in 1879, the plaque on the suspension tower reads "W. Smith & Son, Ness Iron Works, Inverness." On its south end, Infirmary Bridge links into the Great Glen Way at the Inverness War Memorial and Cavell Gardens.

About a mile south of the city center, the Great Glen Way crosses the River Ness by hopping across a series of islands known as the Ness Islands. The Ness Islands are an urban park in an area where the river is narrow and winds through this series of wooded islands connected by footbridges. The footbridges are not spectacular or historical and, to most visitors, they only provide a nice location for a day hike if you are settled into Inverness for the day. The islands are intertwined with walking paths and various benches provide a place to sit and watch the river. A little further research provides another interesting historical tidbit related to the Ness Islands. Although Nessie, the Loch Ness Monster, is suspected to inhabit the depths of Loch Ness a few miles away, its earliest reported sighting, by St. Columba in AD 565, was actually in the area of the Ness Islands, not in the Loch itself.

A carved and painted wooden post at the entrance to the first bridge to the Ness Islands provides a schematic map covering the area from Infirmary Bridge to the southern end of the islands, including depictions of white suspension bridges at Infirmary Bridge and at two locations within the islands. The first bridge, only about ten feet long, is a small, modern footbridge with a decorative wrought-iron railing designed to look like

DECORATIVE BRIDGES

waves in water. This bridge carries the Great Glen Way across a narrow channel to the first of the islands.

The next bridge is the first of the two tiny, white suspension bridges constructed in 1988. Although the white suspension bridge motif appears to have been chosen to complement the larger Greig Street and Infirmary bridges a short distance downstream, the opposite appears to be true. Although the current bridges were constructed in 1988, original suspension bridges were constructed at these two locations in 1853. This suggests it was the tiny, white suspension bridges at these two locations that established the unifying theme, and the larger bridges, constructed 30 years later, were designed to follow that example. Instead of full-blown suspension towers, the portal on each end consists of two steel poles as end posts, and another steel pole crossing between them. Each end post, though, is topped by a decorative finial. Each bridge is only five feet wide and has a wood deck.

In between the two suspension bridges in the Ness Islands, a modern girder pedestrian bridge with decorative, dark green railings connects the two main islands in the park. It does this by connecting across the corner of a third island, with bends from island to island.

CHAPTER 6

CULTURAL BRIDGES

ALCÁNTARA BRIDGE, TOLEDO, SPAIN

With a history spanning more than 2,000 years, Toledo's architecture, much of it in an intact city center that is designated as a UNESCO World Heritage Site, captures periods of Roman, Visigoth, Moorish, Jewish, and Catholic influences. However, out of this extensive history, Toledo's most famous resident, and one of its most prominent tourist draws, was a painter. This painter, El Greco, was not even a native but had traveled from Crete through Rome to arrive in Toledo at the age of 35 in 1576.

A major attraction of the town to day tripping tourists from Madrid is its iconic skyline of medieval palaces and churches climbing the sides and perched on top of a rocky promontory above a curve in the Tagus River. A primary reason the skyline is so familiar and attractive is due to the fame of two paintings by El Greco: the 1599 painting of the skyline in the *View of Toledo* and the 1610 *View and Plan of Toledo*. Considered the earliest landscape painting in Spanish art, the *View of Toledo* is one of the more iconic scenes painted by El Greco, and the stone arches and towers of the Alcántara Bridge are shown prominently in the foreground. Today, many of the landmarks that El Greco painted in the late 1500s, including the bridge, are still there. The bridge is also shown in the *View and Plan of Toledo*, but it is not as prominent.

The *View of Toledo*, which is today in the Metropolitan Museum in New York, is actually famous for more than just presenting a view of the city

CULTURAL BRIDGES

400 years ago. El Greco used artistic license to manipulate the locations of specific buildings in order to generate a more appealing viewscape. The best view of the promontory, showing the bridge, the Alcázar, and the Castle of San Servando, was a view of the eastern side of the city from the north. However, the cathedral was not visible from that viewpoint, so El Greco simply filled in the cathedral to the left of the Alcázar. More important to many viewers is the manner in which the sky is shown in the painting. Instead of a blue or cloudy daytime sky, the city skyline is shown under dark, impressionistic storm clouds, bathing the buildings and the bridge in a ghostly blue light. The treatment of the sky implies that the painting is more of a psychological statement than a portrait of the city, and it is considered a forerunner of Van Gogh's depiction of the night sky in *The Starry Night*.

For art history fans and admirers of El Greco, Toledo has multiple attractions. Because El Greco lived and worked in the city for the final 38 years of his life, Toledo is the place to visit to become immersed in his paintings. The intact buildings and original road network provide the chance to walk the same city streets that El Greco walked, and to visit the same churches and buildings that he frequented. In most cities, this link between a city and a famous former resident is only academic. We know that Michelangelo lived in Rome, that Rembrandt lived in Amsterdam, because the history books tell us so. However, the *View of Toledo* gives us a more tangible link between the artist and the city. We can stand on the northern bank of the Tagus, walk across the bridge, compare the actual view to the one provided in the painting, and receive direct proof of El Greco's presence.

The Alcántara Bridge would probably be an important tourist bridge even if it had not been painted by El Greco. It is a large stone arch bridge more than 2,000 years old. The tower on the eastern end depicted by El Greco was replaced by a Baroque-style arch in 1721 but otherwise, the bridge looks as El Greco painted it. More importantly, it sits directly between the train station and the city center, meaning that thousands of tourists walk across on their day trips from Madrid. While in Toledo, make sure to also see St. Martin's Bridge, which was constructed on the western, opposite side of the city center in the late 1300s, as a complement to the Alcántara Bridge.

LONGFELLOW BRIDGE, BOSTON

In many cases where a bridge is named after a prominent local resident, that resident never saw the bridge and has no tangible link to the bridge or its location. The resident may have lived in a different part of the city or lived long before the bridge was ever built. Therefore, it may initially appear that the only literary connection of Henry Wadsworth Longfellow to his namesake bridge in Boston is the naming of the bridge after a prominent local poet. However, a little research reveals a few more links that probably attract a few tourists.

After moving to Cambridge to become a professor at Harvard College in 1836, Longfellow was a prominent citizen and landowner, with holdings on both sides of the Charles River, until his death in 1882. Longfellow's house, on the west side of Cambridge about a mile from the bridge, is today a National Historic Site, attracting Longfellow enthusiasts. Both Longfellow and his descendants donated land in the area, forming today's Longfellow Park on the north side of the river, and Harvard's athletic fields, called Soldier's Fields, on the south side. During Longfellow's lifetime, the West Boston Bridge, constructed in 1793, was the major bridge connecting Cambridge to Boston. Longfellow wrote his poem, *The Bridge*, about his midnight thoughts on the West Boston Bridge, in 1845. The West Boston Bridge was replaced in 1907 by the Cambridge Bridge, but the name was changed in 1927 to honor Longfellow.

Another connection to Longfellow is associated with one of his most well-known works, *The Midnight Ride of Paul Revere*, based on events which took place close to this location. The entire text of that poem is written, both as a reminder of these events and as a monument to the author, in paint on the sidewalk of the bridge.

BRIDGE OF SIGHS, VENICE

The entire plot of *A Little Romance* centers on the legend associated with the Bridge of Sighs in Venice, in which everlasting love can be ensured by kissing in a gondola passing under the bridge at sunset, at the time the

CULTURAL BRIDGES

bells of the campanile toll. The legend is documented in papers left by Elizabeth Barrett Browning in a crawl space underneath her former villa in Venice, as found by the distinguished diplomat Julius (played by Laurence Olivier), a later resident. Julius describes the legend to two young lovers, Lauren (played by Diane Lane) and Daniel (played by Thelonius Bernard), who have met in Paris.

Torn apart by Lauren's impending return to the United States and her mother's disapproval, Lauren and Daniel decide to ensure that they will meet again by arranging to kiss in a gondola under the Bridge of Sighs at sunset. This plan has complications, such as the fact that they are in Paris with no money to get to Venice, they cannot cross the Italian border alone as unaccompanied minors, and Julius is really a pickpocket who has completely fabricated the story. For his part, Julius comes to find that he has not been helping Lauren and Daniel visit her sick mother in Venice as he had been told, but has instead been assisting them in running away, an act that would likely be viewed by the police as kidnapping.

The charm of the film is that Lauren and Daniel discover Julius made up the story of the legend long before they reach Venice, but the three of them decide to proceed anyway, not because they believe the legend, but because they believe in creating new legends. The movie is just one of many examples of a story in which a bridge has magical romantic powers. For Lauren and Daniel, the bridge symbolizes the ability of young people to shape their own future rather than following the bad examples provided by their bumbling parents. In addition, after Julius is exposed as a pickpocket, the bridge comes to symbolize redemption for his previous life of crime as he risks capture to assist the young people in a race against the police to get to the bridge in time.

The artistry of the climax, with the orange glow of the sunset reflecting off the bridges as the gondola floats toward the Bridge of Sighs, and the tolling of the bells from across the city, is spectacular. The movie attracts many Venetian tourists to reenact the scene, causing gondola-jams at the bridge near sunset.

RIP VAN WINKLE BRIDGE, CATSKILL, NEW YORK

Among the bridges that have some association with famous works of art, literature, or music, the Rip Van Winkle Bridge crossing the Hudson River in Catskill, New York, gives you two connections for the price of one. It is both a literary bridge named after one of the most iconic characters in American literature, and an artistic bridge situated in the middle of one of the most important landscapes that influenced American painting.

The first association comes from Washington Irving's famous henpecked husband who fell asleep for 20 years. Although it is not a long story, almost every paragraph of Rip Van Winkle exudes the spirit of the Catskill Mountains, and especially the highest peaks of the range that, in the words of Irving, "are seen away to the west of the river, swelling up to a noble height, and lording it over the surrounding country." Because the mountains dominated the horizon viewed by the early Dutch settlers along the Hudson, legends arose about Henry Hudson and the crew of his ship, the Half-moon, visiting the mountains every 20 years and playing at nine-pins, which explained the faraway sound of thunder in the mysterious mountain ravines. It was while watching these bowlers, and sneaking tastes of their keg of gin, that Rip drifted off to sleep. By placing the scene of his story at the location where the peaks are seen from the Hudson River, Irving is identifying Rip Van Winkle's hometown as the village of Catskill, where his namesake bridge was constructed more than 100 years after his story was written.

The artistic connection of the bridge comes from the painters of the Hudson River School, the earliest association of painters in the United States. While the Hudson is a long river and passes through many scenic areas, the Hudson River School is specifically linked with the short segment of the river between Kingston and Hudson, where it forms the eastern border of the Catskill Mountains. The founder of the movement was the painter Thomas Cole, who first visited the Catskills and founded the school in 1825. Another of the better known painters of the Hudson River School is Frederick Edwin Church, who was a student of Cole's.

Although the bridge was named for Irving's fictional character who lived nearby, it links the actual homes of Cole and Church on opposite sides of the river. Cole made his permanent move to a cottage called Cedar

Grove, in Catskill, in 1832. Cedar Grove is now the Thomas Cole National Historic Site, located about a quarter-mile from the western end of the bridge. Church began studying with Cole in 1844, and purchased the land he used to build his mansion, Olana, in 1860. Olana, now a State Historic Site, is located about one-half mile from the eastern end of the bridge. Cedar Grove is a relatively modest home in the middle of the village of Catskill, so is not visible from the bridge. However, Olana is a large, ornate mansion with a combination of Victorian and middle eastern architectural elements, sitting prominently on top of a hill overlooking the bridge. Because the bridge has a sidewalk, and adding in a bridge length of about a mile, this puts the historic homes of the two most prominent members of the Hudson River School within a three-mile hike from each other.

Not to miss such a perfect opportunity for marketing, a partnership of the Thomas Cole National Historic Site, the Olana Partnership, the New York State Bridge Authority, and the New York State Department of Parks, Recreation, and Historic Preservation joined forces to form the Hudson River Skywalk that crosses the bridge. The Hudson River Skywalk manages the hiking route, operates the website, markets the experience to tourists, and hosts events and art exhibitions. The Skywalk promotes visits to experience the history and view art exhibits in both homes, and to enjoy the amazing view of the Hudson and the high peaks of the Catskills from the bridge.

Without its association with Rip Van Winkle and the Skywalk, the bridge would probably not be a substantial tourist attraction. Opened in 1935, it is a cantilever bridge that, although it is of large scale, is not particularly attractive. The bridge only carries one lane of traffic in each direction and, although the narrow sidewalk is mostly separated from the traffic lanes by a cement parapet, the traffic can be heavy, loud, and just a few feet away. Bicycles can be ridden in the traffic lanes, but must be walked if you wish to take them on the sidewalk. The sidewalk is expanded in some areas with exhibition plaques to allow pedestrians to step out of the way and enjoy the view. The bridge offers an amazing view of the Catskills, but similar views are available from the surrounding hilltops, including Olana, on the eastern side of the Hudson, without standing next to traffic.

CHAPTER 7
RECREATIONAL BRIDGES

WOODROW WILSON BRIDGE, WASHINGTON, DC

Woodrow Wilson Bridge was originally opened in 1961 as part of the construction of the Washington Beltway, which at the time was a six lane highway. Later in the 1960s and 1970s, the rest of the Beltway was quickly expanded to eight lanes, making the six lane bridge a major choke point by the 1980s. This was made worse by the bridge having a drawspan, resulting in major traffic backups when it was opened. The design of its replacement was highly controversial, with the transportation agencies wanting to construct a high bridge so that a drawspan was not needed, and the local residents wanting a low bridge that would not affect scenic views. The compromise was a bridge that still had a drawspan, but one that was about 20 feet higher than the original bridge, thus reducing the frequency at which the drawspan needed to be opened.

The result, opened to traffic in 2006, is a gorgeous bridge that is sleek, modern, and unique in appearance, crossing the river on open, curved V-shaped piers. Its most appealing feature is how its planners incorporated recreational uses by adding parks on both ends, as well as on the bridge's sidewalk itself. The two-mile-long sidewalk is about 15 feet wide, much wider than would be needed if it were designed just for pedestrians to cross from one side to the other. Instead, it was deliberately designed to support recreation, including cyclists, roller-bladers, joggers, and hikers. At intervals, the sidewalk is even wider to form park-like gathering places in the middle of the Potomac River, including benches, historical plaques, and observation telescopes with views of the monuments in downtown Washington.

The western end of the bridge crosses over Jones Point Park, a new urban park right on the river. The eastern end of the sidewalk ramps up to an overpass that crosses the Beltway to the National Harbor development on the south side of the bridge. The overpass is pedestrian-only, and it is a pleasant surprise to cross onto it and find that it is extensively landscaped as yet another recreational park space. The one drawback to the park experience on the bridge is that, with 60 mile-per-hour traffic whizzing by and the flight path for planes from Reagan National Airport directly overhead, the bridge experience can get loud. The sidewalk is lined with sound reduction panels to address this problem, but the panels cannot fix the noise from the planes.

When the bridge was planned, there were no major pedestrian destinations on either end. Instead, both ends were just a maze of highway on and off ramps in unappealing suburbs. A look at this area in the 1990s would have given no suggestion that recreational use should be a consideration in the design of the bridge.

The fact that the planners incorporated recreation has turned out to be a good thing. Downtown Alexandria, not far from the western end of the bridge, has since boomed, becoming one of the more desirable inner suburb areas for young professionals. National Harbor, a hotel, shopping, casino, and convention center resort complex on the riverfront, has been developed from scratch just off the eastern end of the bridge, and is connected to the bridge by the landscaped overpass. In addition to serving as a park and hiking trail in the middle of the river, the sidewalk connects on both ends into an extensive regional system of bike and jogging trails. The Mt. Vernon Bike Trail, which parallels the Potomac River for more than 17 miles, passes through Jones Point Park directly under the bridge. The trail leads to historic Mt. Vernon a few miles to the south, and along the river all the way to Key Bridge to the north, passing under Arlington Memorial Bridge on the way. The trail can be used to cross Key Bridge and join with the C&O Canal Towpath Trail, which continues about 180 miles to Cumberland, Maryland.

RECREATIONAL BRIDGES

O'CALLAGHAN-TILLMAN BRIDGE, BOULDER CITY, NEVADA

To the casual observer, the construction of the new Hoover Dam Bypass Bridge, opened in October 2010, appeared to be a direct response to the terrorist attacks on September 11, 2001. For more than 60 years, Hoover Dam served as the only road crossing of the Colorado River over a stretch of hundreds of miles. This came to a screeching halt on the morning of 9/11. Although passenger cars were eventually allowed back on the dam, commercial trucks were banned forever, requiring a diversion to a crossing at Laughlin, 75 miles to the south.

This greatly affected commercial traffic between most of the state of Arizona and all of Nevada and central California to the northwest. Construction on the bypass bridge began a few years later, and thus appeared to be a direct response to the ban on commercial traffic on the dam. Instead, the bridge had been conceived of for years, and its construction had been approved by the Federal Highway Administration just a few months before in March 2001. Unrelated to terrorism concerns, the dam had already become a major bottleneck on US Highway 93 between Arizona and Las Vegas, largely due to the status of the dam itself as an attraction.

Built in the 1930s when the area was sparsely populated, Highway 93 in the area of the dam was a picturesque, winding two-lane road leading through the side canyons of Black Canyon and down to the level of the dam. Sufficient for commercial traffic in the days before Las Vegas and the dam itself had become major tourist attractions, the volume of traffic had become unmanageable by the 1980s. Adding to the enormous traffic volumes and the obvious safety hazards of hairpin turns was the presence of pedestrians on the sidewalks and crosswalks, as well as attempts by drivers to do some sightseeing and photography while driving to the other side of the canyon. What could normally be a 15 minute drive became a routine hour, and could take two to three hours on weekends. Even before traffic was diverted after 9/11, a voluntary diversion south to cross the Colorado at Laughlin was common, as the extra distance was less of a restriction than the slowdown at the dam. The bypass bridge was going to be built anyway, but it is likely that the 9/11 traffic diversion served to expedite the process.

The area is accessed from Las Vegas by taking Highway 93 through Boulder City. As the road begins to descend down into the canyon, the road splits, with the main route continuing across the bridge into Arizona and the smaller route, which used to be the main route, winding further down into the canyon toward the dam. Less than a mile past a security checkpoint, a sign indicates the way to the Mike O'Callaghan—Pat Tillman Memorial Bridge Plaza on the right. Just up the hill, a large parking lot includes restroom facilities and a small memorial to Mike O'Callaghan, a Korean War veteran and former Nevada governor who passed away in 2004, and to Pat Tillman, the football player who joined the Army and was killed in Afghanistan in 2004.

From the parking lot, a short series of steps leads up a hill toward the bridge. The hillside is also terraced to provide a smooth zig-zag ramp that provides easier access for anyone with mobility issues. Both the steps and ramp end at another small memorial area, where space for the pathway was blasted through the hill's pink bedrock. This memorial area, decorated with curved concrete walls, includes benches, more memorial plaques, and plaques describing the construction of the bridge. Just past the memorial area, the pathway joins the main highway and becomes the bridge's pedestrian sidewalk.

The most important feature of the bridge walk is the amazing view it provides of Hoover Dam, more than 800 feet directly below. Being on the downstream side of the dam, the view includes a complex of buildings, transmission lines, and other facilities that are part of the power plant at the base, where the Colorado River exits the dam.

The open steel railing along the sidewalk is punctuated with more memorial, historical, and construction-description panels. Additional plaques on the sidewalk show the locations of the Nevada-Arizona state line and, although you cannot see it beneath the roadway, the apex of the arch. The sky is always full of tour helicopters, four or five at any given time, hired in Las Vegas for aerial tours of the dam, Lake Mead, and the bridge.

The bridge has no superstructure, so there is no obvious visible indication that you are even on a bridge. The sidewalk is separated from the traffic lanes by a concrete wall, so you can only see the tops of larger vehicles passing by and nothing of the view on the south side of the bridge. The bridge sits on cement pillars, so it does not move when traffic passes by as much as a suspension or cable-stay bridge does. The odd result is that, even at 800 feet high, the walk is not nearly as scary or thrilling as you would expect. While the view is great, there are no bridge structures above your head to add to your vertigo, the traffic is not whizzing by two feet from you, and the deck does not shake beneath your feet. One weird feature is that the pedestrian sidewalk ends abruptly at a barrier wall at the Arizona end of the bridge. The sidewalk was included only as an additional tourist attraction, providing yet another way to enjoy the dam, but it does not lead anywhere. It does not connect to a parking lot or even hiking and biking trails on the Arizona side. In fact, the sidewalk is narrow at about seven feet wide, and bicycles are not allowed.

The best way to admire the architectural beauty of the bridge is from the dam. The bridge consists of a gigantic, single concrete arch spanning from one canyon wall to the other. The bridge is the highest and longest arched-concrete bridge in the western hemisphere and the second highest bridge in the United States. The concrete arches support the highest concrete pillars in the world, and the pillars support the road surface. From a distance the deck appears perfectly flat, although you can see a slight convexity to it when you are actually walking it. Unfortunately, the view of the bridge suffers, as do all views on and around Hoover Dam, due to the ubiquitous transmission towers, electrical substations, and transmission lines throughout the canyon. One must not forget that, in addition to impounding water for water supply and recreation purposes, Hoover Dam is one of the largest power plants in the United States.

A visit to the dam itself would not be complete without visiting the numerous exhibits, memorials, and guided tours available. One of the fascinations of Hoover Dam is its history, how its construction in the early 1930s was a major source of jobs during the Great Depression, and how it led to the development of Las Vegas as a major city. There are books, documentaries, websites, and many other sources available to get whatever information you need to enhance your visit. In fact, the area abounds with information and tourist centers, including those on the dam itself, a Nevada State Welcome Center and Lake Mead National Recreation Area

Visitor Center on Highway 93, and another visitor center located in downtown Boulder City. Parking at the bridge is free, but there is a charge for parking at the dam. The parking garage at the dam is located adjacent to a large gift shop, cafeteria, and visitor center. There are also fees for entry to the visitor center and a tour of the power plant within the dam. Even without paying for the tours, a walk across the dam is enticing. The dam itself, and the other structures, were designed with a beautiful art deco touch.

SYDNEY HARBOUR BRIDGE, SYDNEY, NEW SOUTH WALES, AUSTRALIA

When viewing a photograph of the Sydney Harbour Bridge in Australia alone, without its surroundings, the profile of the bridge may not seem particularly special. It may easily be confused with other bridges of the same steel-through arch construction type such as the Tyne Bridge in Newcastle-upon-Tyne in England or Hells Gate in New York, or with other high, industrial-looking bridges with large superstructures of the same era, like Jacques-Cartier in Montreal. While still under construction in 1932, it was considered an iconic landmark in Australia due to its large size and importance in the expansion of the nation's largest city, but its image may not be easily recognizable to most people in the United States and Europe. However, when the photo is zoomed out and shows the bridge within its surroundings, it instantly becomes recognizable as one of the most photographed bridges in the world. This is because the bridge is close to, and much larger than, its more famous neighbor, the Sydney Opera House. The broader view of the bridge with the Opera House is an iconic image worldwide, but it is possible that only bridge enthusiasts and Australians would recognize the bridge on its own without the help of the Opera House.

The Sydney Harbour Bridge checks many different tourist-interest boxes. In addition to being a prominent feature of the skyline in the largest city in Australia, especially when coupled with the iconic profile of the Opera House, it is also known worldwide for its New Year's fireworks display—the first in the world every year due to its position near the international date line. It is also pedestrian friendly, with dedicated pedestrian and bicycle lanes offering amazing views of the surrounding cityscape.

It is lit with color-changing LED lights at night, beautifully contrasting the cool dark blue of the steel superstructure with the warm amber of the granite pylons. It also attracts tourists for being historic, not only almost 100 years old itself, but having been the scene of an important political protest during its opening ceremony.

Any one of these would be a reason to visit, but they are not the tourist attractions for which the bridge is most famous. More importantly, the bridge offers not one, but two completely separate tours of interior spaces, including access inside of and to the top of one of the anchor pylons and access to catwalks on the arch itself.

Access to the interior and viewing platform of one of the anchor pylons was made available to tourists almost immediately upon completion of the bridge. The pylons were added to the anchors as a strictly decorative item. There are four pylons, one on each corner, and interior access is available within the South East Pylon. Each pylon is constructed of granite quarried more than 100 miles away, and transported to Sydney on barges. The pylons are high at 270 feet above sea level, and the tour to the platform on top of the South East Pylon requires climbing 200 steps. Uses of the South East Pylon have changed since 1934, with different museums, exhibits, and other attractions having been housed there through the years. During World War II, parapets were put on top and the pylons were used as anti-aircraft positions.

The current attraction within the South East Pylon is known as Pylon Lookout, which opened in 2003. Although the base of the pylon is at ground level in a park, there is no entrance at the base. Instead, you have to take either the bridge stairs or a pedestrian lift from ground level on Cumberland Street up to the pedestrian walkway on the eastern side of the bridge. Then, walk along the pedestrian walkway toward the pylon and enter the pylon at this level. Walk up one level to the admissions counter, where you will find bridge artifacts on display. As of 2022, the Pylon Lookout hours are 10:00 a.m. to 5:00 p.m., entry fee is A$19, and the admissions desk accepts only credit or debit cards, no cash. Level 2 includes a souvenir shop and observation balconies on the east and west sides. Above level 2, a mezzanine displays historical information on the opening of the bridge. Above the mezzanine, the outdoor lookout platform on top of the pylon offers close-up views of the arch of the bridge and the Opera House to the east. Your trip can be planned with the help of the detailed, interactive Pylon Lookout website. The Pylon Lookout can be visited without an advance reservation, and your visit should include a walk across the bridge on the pedestrian sidewalk along the roadway.

Completely separate from the Pylon Lookout attraction, the Bridge Climb is probably one of the most famous bridge-based tourist attractions in the world, and is also one of the most prominent attractions of any kind in Australia. The Bridge Climb is exactly what its name implies—a climbing tour from the base to the apex of the arch, more than 1,300 steps and 440 feet above sea level.

The Bridge Climb headquarters is situated in the neighborhood known as The Rocks, within a building on Cumberland Street, accessible a short walk from ferry, bus, or train stops at Circular Quay. After checking in for your tour on the ground level, you can visit the museum exhibits, coffee shop, and restrooms. The gift shop offers the usual refrigerator magnets, coffee cups, T-shirts, and build-your-own Sydney Harbour Bridge kits, all sporting the stylized silhouette of the arch that serves as the logo for Bridgeclimb Sydney.

When the time for your tour arrives, you will climb to the second level, where your group of about ten people will congregate. Each person will undergo a breathalyzer test, sign a waiver, and be quizzed about potentially hazardous health conditions. You will be required to remove your watch, jewelry, cell phone, and camera, attach your glasses to a fixed strap, and, depending on the weather, either change into a one-piece jumpsuit or put the jumpsuit on over your clothes. Once dressed, you will go into a different room for training. You will be given a logoed hat, rag for wiping sweat, and headset so that you can listen to the guide on the tour. Each of these items will be clipped to your suit, so there is no way for anything to be dropped. Then, you will be given a harness that fits over your suit. Once out on the tour, the harness will be clipped onto a cable with carabiners, but before starting out, there is a practice cable and stairs in the training area so that you can become comfortable using these items while wearing the suit. Once everyone is suited up and practiced, the group will exit to the pathway at the base of the arch and immediately clip their harnesses to the cable. Then, the climb begins, one person at a time, handrails on both sides, everyone clipped in so each person moves in single file at the same pace as the other group members.

The climb occurs on the southeastern side of the arch, which is the side that overlooks the Opera House. If you have taken the full Summit tour, your group will climb along the top of the upper arch, with nothing above you. Once at the top, you will be given an opportunity to view the scenery, and the tour guide will take photographs, which will be available for purchase when you leave. At the top is a platform that connects the top of the eastern arch (the one you have been climbing) to the top of the western arch. Once your group is done viewing and taking photographs, you will cross to the western side in order to descend along the top of the western arch. Upon returning to the headquarters building and redressing, you are given a certificate of completion for the climb. You can then purchase photos of yourself at the top, and you will be allowed to keep your hat as a souvenir.

Unlike the Pylon Lookout, advance reservations are required for the Bridge Climb, and they are not inexpensive. The variety of available tours is remarkable. For example, a Sampler goes to the quarter point of the arch, the Summit Express takes the shortcut to the top of the arch by traversing up the curve of the lower arch and then stairs between the lower arch and the upper arch, and the full Summit goes to the summit along the top of the upper arch. The longest of the tours is the full Summit, which takes approximately three and a half hours. The general hours are 9:00 a.m. to 7:00 p.m. Then, there are climbs available at dawn (5:00 a.m.) a couple times a month (usually Saturdays), tours in Mandarin and Japanese, and special events such as karaoke, weddings, live music events, and packages that include dinner at local restaurants. Like the Pylon Lookout website, the Bridgeclimb website is user-friendly and detailed, allowing you to see what each tour involves and exactly when different tours are available. As of 2022, prices for a tour to the top started at A$248.

There are several ways a bridge can become attractive to tourists and recreationists. A bridge can be constructed with tourists in mind, so attractions are designed into the structure from its inception. Alternatively, a bridge can become attractive simply by aging gracefully, to the extent that the community chooses to preserve and celebrate it, resulting in tourism for its history. These are easy, but a bigger challenge is for an older bridge, one constructed without tourist access in mind, to have a veneer of tourist attraction retrofitted onto it 60 or more years after it was constructed.

In this respect, the Sydney Harbour Bridge has something in common with the Jacques-Cartier Bridge in Montreal. Both bridges opened in the early 1930s, at a time when bridges were entirely functional and serviceable, with little consideration of how they could be used as prominent local tourist attractions. Except for providing access within one of the pylons at Sydney Harbour, each bridge was mainly functional for almost 70 years. However, long after it was constructed the Jacques-Cartier Bridge became the focus of the Montreal International Fireworks Festival, and more recently the blank canvas used for nightly light shows. Similarly, the Sydney Harbour Bridgeclimb did not begin until 1998, when the bridge itself had been serving its primary, traffic-moving function, for more than 60 years. In both cases, these modifications have been enormously successful, and demonstrate how old bridges can be turned into tourist attractions and revenue generators for their cities.

PADLOCKED BRIDGES, PARIS

The number of padlocks in any location is almost a direct measurement of community and tourist interest in the city and its bridges. Many cities have a single, centrally-located bridge and, depending on the popularity of the town, that bridge may have a few padlocks or it may be overrun with padlocks. Paris is different. Paris does not have a single pedestrian bridge in a prominent tourist area that has been taken over by padlockers. A discussion of the love padlocks in Paris requires mention of no fewer than 12 bridges.

In researching this book, Paris was visited twice, in 2013 and 2016, and there were major changes in the love padlock situation between these two visits. The first visit, in 2013, was at the height of the craze. It was clear that Paris had completely embraced the practice, even to the extent of having installed railings deliberately designed to accommodate padlocks on at least three bridges: the Pont des Arts, Passerelle Senghor, and Pont de l'Archevêché. At that time, each of these three bridges was home to tens

RECREATIONAL BRIDGES

or hundreds of thousands of padlocks. The Pont des Arts and Passerelle Senghor are both pedestrian-only bridges providing incredibly romantic views of the Louvre. Both bridges had small-gauge wire-grid railings of the perfect size to accommodate the padlocks. Hucksters had set up shop on the bridges and did a brisk business selling padlocks right on the spot. On a nice day, you would have seen numerous couples huddled over their newly purchased padlock, debating what expression of love they should write on it with their borrowed Sharpie. The padlocking process on the Pont des Arts was even featured in a movie, *Now You See Me*, the camera following the thrown key down into the water until it settled among thousands of other keys at the bottom. Tourists would visit the Ponts des Arts just to see the padlocks.

Couple Purchasing Love Padlock on Passerelle Senghor, Paris, France

The prominence of the Pont de l'Archevêché was a little more difficult to understand. It is an old stone arch bridge that carries traffic. It is not nearly as picturesque, or pedestrian friendly, as the Pont des Arts and Passerelle Senghor, but the bridge offers an amazing view of the back side of Notre Dame Cathedral, with its flying buttresses. Perhaps it was this view, along with a railing constructed of perfectly-sized steel-mesh fence, which attracted tens of thousands of love padlocks. The locks were so densely packed that it seemed no more could fit, except couples were there all day, squeezing in more padlocks. For sheer density of application, the Pont de l'Archevêché may have been one of the most padlocked bridges in the world.

Not to be left behind, the Pont Neuf was also heavily padlocked. The Pont Neuf structure itself is stone, and therefore does not have padlocks directly on the bridge. However, there is a steel railing surrounding the Square du Vert-Gallant in the middle of the bridge, and this railing was taken over by padlockers. There is a similar fence surrounding the gardens on the western end of the Île de la Cité, at the base of the stairs below the Square du Vert-Gallant. This railing was not yet covered in 2013, but there were enough padlocks to show that it had been discovered, and it was only a matter of time before it became completely infested.

That was 2013. At that time, it was impossible to consider the tourist experience on the Parisian bridges without addressing the padlocks. Then, in 2014, a railing on Pont des Arts collapsed under the weight of the padlocks. The authorities had had enough. They famously, and controversially, removed the padlocks from the bridge, almost a million padlocks weighing more than 45 tons. They then replaced the padlockable wire railings with Plexiglas panels.

By 2016, the new watchword in Paris was #lovewithoutlocks. Many bridges in Paris have a sign reading "Nos ponts ne rèsisteront pas a votre amour," which translates as "our bridges can no longer withstand your gestures of love." There is now a nolovelocks.com website documenting the problems and a campaign for cities to ban the locks. All locks have been completely removed from Pont de l'Archevêché and Pont des Arts, and both now have Plexiglas panel railings. On three bridges, including Passerelle Senghor, Passerelle Simone de Beauvoir, and Passerelle Debilly, signs are posted showing a padlock covered by a red circle and a slash mark, with the slogan #lovewithoutlocks. Thousands of padlocks remain on Passerelle Senghor, but it is apparently legal because there are still hucksters openly selling locks directly on the bridge. The "no padlocks" sign has been plastered over with stickers, which advertise places that sell padlocks. However, most of the locks on that bridge have been removed, leaving the broken wire panels of the railings in place. In some locations where there are locks, you can see that the wire panel has become detached, and an unattractive plywood panel has been placed in front of it to protect passersby. There are also detached wire panels on the fence surrounding the statue of Henry IV in the Square du Vert-Gallant, where there are still tens of thousands of padlocks. There are thousands on the chain surrounding the replica of the Statue of Liberty torch at Pont de l'Alma, but at least one of the posts holding the chain is about to collapse under the weight.

In addition to these major padlock locations, smaller clusters of padlocks have popped up in a dozen other places. Where the bridges are made of stone and cannot be padlocked, the railing of the nearby staircase between the quay and river level has been attacked. This has happened on Pont Marie and Pont d'Iena, and Pont Notre Dame's narrow, ornate iron railing with intricate, curly leaves has invited even more padlocks.

The removal of the railings has stopped the padlock problem on Pont des Arts. Or has it? High up, on the lamppost's ornately curled arms, some very tall padlockers, or padlockers with a ladder, have been at work.

When a metal sign is attached to a bridge railing, it is usually secured with small metal ties, and it does not take much space to attach a padlock. Once one padlock is attached, other padlocks can be attached to it in a chain. The Pont d'Arcole has one such sign, with six metal ties holding it, and therefore six clusters of padlocks.

On Passerelle Simone de Beauvoir, the railing is constructed of a padlockable chain-link fence, but the fence is mostly empty except for a nice, clean version of the "no padlocks" sign, and near the sign, a few padlocks. Passerelle Debilly also has the no padlock sign, but because it is a steel superstructure arch bridge it is amenable to padlocks and has several hundred of them.

Finally, Pont Alexandre III is one of the most romantic locations in Paris, but without padlockable railings. It does, however, have allegorical cast-iron sculptures with relatively narrow components that are about the right size for a padlock. Like a small sculpture of a crab, with five padlocks attached to its legs.

In 2013, everything was clean and orderly, with a large number of people participating in this cute fad, but keeping it under control. By 2016, the overall sense was of a city sick of having to deal with the cursed padlocks. When yet another panel of padlocks collapses, they do not even fix it—they just put a plywood panel in front of it for safety.

RHINE FALLS BRIDGE, SCHAFFHAUSEN, SWITZERLAND

Like the Kleinbasel neighborhood of Basel, the city of Schaffhausen is a geographic anomaly on Switzerland's northern border with Germany. For most of the stretch of the Rhine River between the Bodensee (Lake Constance) and Basel, the river forms the international boundary, with Switzerland to the south of the river and Germany to the north. However, in a few isolated places, a small area north of the river is part of Switzerland, not Germany. Thus, the city of Schaffhausen and all of Schaffhausen Canton sit on the north bank of the river, and are the site of several bridges over the river. This anomaly was very inconvenient for Schaffhausen during World War II, when it was bombed twice by the Allies, having been mistaken for a part of Germany.

Schaffhausen came into being largely due to the presence of another geographic anomaly here, the Rhine Falls, which is the largest waterfall in Europe. The Rhine Falls consist of a series of spectacular cascades over sandstone bedrock about two miles west of Schaffhausen. Although the width and height of the Rhine Falls are small compared to Niagara Falls between the US and Canada, the falls are still dramatic and a major scenic attraction.

With a drop of about 75 feet in elevation, the falls serve as a barrier to boat traffic on the Rhine. During the Middle Ages, when the Rhine served as a superhighway for transporting goods throughout Europe, this barrier was inconvenient. The river has historically been navigable from its mouth at Rotterdam to the Rhine Falls, a distance of about 600 river miles, and again for a large distance upstream of the falls to the Bodensee. For centuries, all of the goods being transported through this area had to be offloaded at the base of the Rhine Falls, conveyed by cart about two miles upriver, and then reloaded onto different boats to continue their journey. As with other trade route locations where goods need to be loaded and unloaded, the activity requires substantial labor, leading to the development of a town to provide housing for the laborers and their families.

Schaffhausen itself has a few small bridges crossing the Rhine, which is about 1,000 feet wide in this area. There is little to see on the south bank, but the bridges do connect to the lovely Alt Stadt of Schaffhausen on the north bank. This includes a remarkable medieval fortification called the

Munot, sitting high on a hill overlooking the river. None of the bridges in the middle of town are particularly old or interesting, but they are worth walking because of the views they provide of the town and the Munot.

Despite the town's appeal, the highlight of the Schaffhausen area is the falls. These can be viewed from several vantage points designed for the purpose, including viewing platforms on both the north and south banks of the river. On the north bank are viewing platforms and a restaurant/gift shop complex located about a quarter-mile downstream at the base of the falls. This area is accessible by bus from Schaffhausen, or can be reached by foot or bicycle on the wanderweg, or Swiss hiking trail, from Schaffhausen.

Another great view can be obtained from a railroad bridge called the Rheinfall Brücke, which is situated over the rapids just upstream of the falls. The railroad, including the bridge, was constructed in 1857 to connect Schaffhausen to the Swiss town of Winterthur. In addition to providing a viewing location, the pedestrian sidewalks on the bridge are the only way for pedestrians to get from viewing areas on the north bank to viewing areas on the south bank.

Even aside from its spectacular location, the Rheinfall Brücke is interesting in itself. The bridge towers about 40 feet above the rapids on ten stone arches. The arches are pleasantly designed, using stone of different colors and textures to create an attractive visual effect. The piers themselves are made of a smooth gray stone, while the arches are outlined in a textured reddish stone. The spandrel between the arches and deck is then filled in with smooth-faced reddish and beige blocks.

The bridge is wide enough to support only a single railway track. The overhanging sidewalks are attached on either side of the bridge, no doubt inspired by the need to keep gawking bridge walkers off the narrow railroad tracks. The sidewalk on the upstream side of the bridge is accessible year round and can be accessed from the wanderweg on either side of the Rhine. The upstream side allows views of rapids on the Rhine but does not offer good views of the falls themselves. The bridge is close enough to hear the thunder and see the spray, so you can imagine how impressive the falls must be. However, because the view is toward upriver and the falls are downriver, it misses most of the view of the falls themselves, and you mostly just see water rushing toward the edge. The sidewalk on the downstream side is not open in winter, although the reason for this is not apparent.

Although the bridge does not provide a great view of the falls, it does have other amazing views. As if the falls needed assistance to be an incredible spectacle, the massive cliff face on the south side of the falls is topped by a dramatic castle, Schloss Laufen. Even without its position overlooking the falls, this castle, dating from the 1100s, would be a scenic and historic tourist attraction on its own. From the wanderweg on the north side of the river, the full scale of the engineering feat needed to complete the railroad bridge can be seen. This is because the bridge disappears straight into a tunnel bored into the cliff face about 40 feet above the river, but still 50 or more feet directly below the castle.

Having viewed the falls from the basin on the north side and from the bridge, you may feel that the views of the falls are actually a little disappointing, especially in winter. If you have just walked to the area without seeking information at the gift shops or tourist information center in Schaffhausen, you may think that the bridge is the best of the viewing areas, but it is not all that good. However, if you look carefully far off to the base of the cliff below Schloss Laufen, you will see, tiny in the distance and shrouded in mist, people. You will immediately realize that they are standing at the prime viewing spot, but it will not be obvious to you how to get there yourself.

The answer is that the best viewing area is only accessible by purchasing a ticket for entry into the castle and then descending the cliff face through the castle complex. The castle area can be accessed from the north bank viewing areas by crossing the railroad bridge, and then following the wanderweg to the top of the cliff. It can also be reached by car, city bus, or even train. After dramatically crossing the bridge over the falls and then plummeting directly into the cliff face, the Schaffhausen to Winterthur train stops immediately on the other side of the tunnel, at the base of the castle. From the small train platform (it cannot be called a station), stairs wind their way up to the castle. There is also a lift to the top, if needed. Once on top, the complex includes a lovely small church, a gift shop and snack bar area, and the castle itself, which has a restaurant. Access to the

RECREATIONAL BRIDGES

castle and, ultimately, to the best viewing platform, costs five Swiss francs in summer and three in winter. Tickets need to be purchased at the gift shop.

Unfortunately, the castle itself is not furnished or viewable as it was when it was a residence. Instead, it has been converted into a historical museum with exhibits on the falls. These exhibits are sparse for trying to fill a large space, and only provide some cursory information on historic persons who visited the falls, including Goethe and Austrian Emperor Joseph II. The castle is worth seeing only because you have to purchase the ticket to the falls viewing area anyway, so you might as well stop in, but you will not spend much time there. Instead, the reason to purchase the ticket is to get to the viewing area. This is a small platform at the base of the cliff face, elevated at an optimal position right above the falls. The platform is reachable by steps carved into the cliffs, leading down from the castle courtyard.

Even though the falls may not seem impressive to those accustomed to Niagara, the view from the platform is still spectacular. The noise of the falls is deafening, and you can feel the rock shake beneath your feet. To your left is the large open basin dug out by the falls as they eroded upstream after the retreat of the glaciers. To your right, and way above your head, is the railroad bridge, disappearing directly into the rock. One of the most amazing sights you will see, directly in front of you among the falls, is a gigantic erosional remnant of a rock towering over the falls, splitting the falls in two. Suitably called "The Rock," it just looks scenic until you notice a Swiss flag on top of it, and you will not be satisfied until you figure out how the heck it got there. Tracing backwards from the flag, you will see wooden stairs leading up the back side. Following these down to river level, it turns out that the rock creates an eddy of calm water on the downstream side of the falls. This area is just barely wide enough to allow boats within the basin to approach the falls and dock at the base of the rock. Ultimately, if you visit the falls in the summer, this is where you want to go for the most amazing experience possible.

As a major tourist attraction, the Rhine Falls may be reached by many methods, including by bus, car, or train, but since you are here for views of the river, it is highly recommended to approach the falls on foot. Crossing the river at Schaffhausen, the wanderweg on the south side of the river provides great views of the Schaffhausen Alt Stadt and the Munot. From there, the hike on the wanderweg, mostly through woods along the river, takes about an hour to reach Schloss Laufen. During this walk, the river transitions from flat, navigable water to rapids, and then rapids to waterfall. Before taking the left branch of the wanderweg up the hill to the castle, detour down the right branch to walk across the bridge. Even if it does not provide the best views of the falls, it is an amazing engineering achievement that needs to be walked. You can also walk down to the viewing areas on the north side of the falls from the bridge, and then double back across the bridge to climb up to the castle. Once you have completed your castle and falls visits, it is difficult to resist the train ride back under the castle and across the bridge you have just walked. After a few exhausting hours of hiking all over the falls area, you will be back in the Schaffhausen Alt Stadt having a fine beer within ten minutes.

MARIENBRÜCKE AT NEUSCHWANSTEIN, GERMANY

The Marienbrücke is not large or old and is hardly a household name, even for those who know about bridges. It is not even directly linked with the iconic castle. It is located about a mile away and is not located on the pathways that tourists use to access the castle. Even though the castle may be the most famous in the world and is therefore a magnet for tourists, it is likely that most of these tourists do not even know they are about to find themselves on a small bridge completely overrun by tourists. However, the Marienbrücke in Hohenschwangau, Germany, is probably one of the most photographed bridges in the world.

This status is almost entirely due to one important feature of the bridge, a feature unlike any other bridge: a captive audience, numbering in the thousands. All of them are standing, waiting, with plenty of time on their hands, all holding cameras, and all looking around for something dramatic and picturesque to serve as a backdrop for their selfies.

Every day of the year, thousands of tourists make the trek by train, bus, car, and bicycle to the ticket center in Hohenschwangau. They wait in the ticket line for an hour or more, frequently glancing behind them at the dramatic view of the castle rising among the cliffs. Once they have

RECREATIONAL BRIDGES 141

obtained their ticket with its printed reservation time, they immediately take the bus, or walk up the roadway, to the castle. Even if their reservation time is hours away, and the ticket office tells them the castle is only a 40-minute walk, they immediately head for the castle, having planned on arriving far in advance of their reserved time. If they miss their tour time, the chances of getting another the same day are slim, so they cannot risk missing their once in a lifetime opportunity by being late. Also, the castle is so much of an attraction that there is no reason to linger down in Hohenschwangau. Get to the castle as quickly as possible to find the entrance early, get oriented, stroll around to photograph the castle from all angles, and then wait another hour or more in the small courtyard of the castle with the other tourists. What is there to see from the courtyard? The Marienbrücke.

The dates reported for its construction vary. Some sources claim it was built as a wooden bridge in the 1850s but was then rebuilt as the current iron bridge in the 1880s, during the construction of Neuschwanstein. This makes it an early iron arch bridge, similar to dozens of others. It would be faintly interesting and would attract tens, maybe dozens, of visitors, if it were not so far away from everything. If it were located in central Munich, maybe a few bridge enthusiasts would visit it because of its age and engineering, but only if they did not have to go too far to see it. As it is in the mountains more than a hundred miles away, nobody would visit. The Marienbrücke would be a minor footnote of a tourist bridge. However, if you put the bridge on the opposite side of a picturesque gorge from the waiting area for one of the most popular tourist attractions in the world, the situation changes dramatically.

Knowing that the bridge is the only thing to look at while you are waiting, is it worthy of its prominent position? The answer is a definitive "yes," because it is among the most amazing settings for a bridge you will ever see. When looking out at the view from the castle courtyard, the Marienbrücke is the only man-made structure in sight. Even though it is a mile away, it is far more than just a tiny, old iron bridge framed against the trees in the distance. It is not an obstructed view blocked by trees; it is not a view down onto the top of it; and it is not an oblique view from an angle. Instead, the bridge is suspended in mid-space, at about the same elevation as the courtyard, directly across the gorge. In the far distance hovering above the bridge are snow-capped Alps. In the medium distance are the tree-covered hillslopes of the foothills. Then, these hillslopes are dramatically ripped open by a rock-walled chasm through which pours a narrow but enormously high waterfall. Spanning the chasm with a few gravity-defying iron bars is the bridge itself. While the bridge without a castle would not be visited by many people, those who did would be enchanted by the setting over a waterfall and the thrill of the enormous height. Although there are plenty of iron bridges from the 1880s around, this one suddenly becomes more impressive for the engineering feat that must have been required to place the bridge in this location.

Some bridges have a large number of photographs taken of them. Others have a large number of photographs taken of the view from them. The Marienbrücke is probably a record-setter in both categories, because for every picture taken of it by the captive audience waiting for entry into the castle, there are probably ten taken in the other direction, of the view of the castle from the bridge. Neuschwanstein is a castle famous for its appearance of being straight out of a fairy tale, but getting good photographs of it is problematic. The castle sits on a hilltop, so almost every view of it from a distance is oblique, looking up at it from below. Once you have climbed up to the entrance to be on the same level, you are now too close to be able to get the entire structure in your frame. There is only one place where you are at the perfect elevation, distance, and sun angle to capture the entirety of the castle in a single photograph. That is the view from the bridge, which is why a large proportion of the tourists make the 20-minute trek on the hiking path from the castle. Not because they are interested in old iron bridges, but for the perfect picture. Except for aerial photos that are obviously taken from helicopters or drones, almost every iconic photograph you have ever seen of Neuschwanstein was taken from the Marienbrücke.

BEAR MOUNTAIN BRIDGE, PEEKSKILL, NEW YORK

Because the barriers to travel have largely been conquered, we twenty-first century Americans, zipping around in our cars at 60 miles per hour, generally do not even know that they once existed. A river that once caused

RECREATIONAL BRIDGES

horse-and-buggy to make a two-day detour is now spanned by dozens of bridges, providing present-day travelers with multiple choices, and allowing the travelers to remain completely oblivious to how insurmountable a barrier once existed. However, there is one place where the barrier is so large, and the challenges to overcome it so enormous, that it still affects travel choices for hundreds of thousands of drivers every day. This barrier is the Hudson River.

The Hudson River Valley is one of the most scenic and historic areas of the eastern United States, celebrated in literature and art for more than two hundred years. The valley is also interesting geologically, with a recent geologic history that has had a large impact on the numbers and types of bridges there today. Even though the Delaware and Connecticut Rivers flow parallel to the Hudson, the Delaware on the west and the Connecticut on the east, the Hudson River Valley was subjected to a much different geologic history than the other two rivers, and this difference is reflected in their bridges.

The Delaware and Connecticut are what we think of as normal rivers. Most of the length of both rivers is free-flowing fresh water, and the rivers increase in size as they are entered by tributaries until they reach sea level, at which point they rapidly widen out into estuaries. In contrast, the Hudson River Valley was more deeply eroded by glaciers in the most recent glacial period that ended about 12,000 years ago, with most of the valley scoured to a depth below sea level. When the ice melted and sea level rose, seawater flooded the eroded channel, forming an estuary extending all the way to Troy, which is 160 miles inland from the ocean. Therefore, most of the length of the river is not free-flowing fresh water. The depth of the river and width of the valley are not governed by the size of the watershed or the tributaries, but by the erosive action of the ice sheet. As a result, the Hudson River between Troy and New York City is much wider and deeper than either the Delaware or Connecticut Rivers.

This difference has had a great effect on the construction of bridges. The type and size of bridges depends on several factors, including river width, depth, and use of the river for shipping. Shallow rivers, like the Connecticut above Hartford or the Delaware above Trenton, never had large ships sailing on them. Consequently, the small boats on these rivers did not need tall bridges to provide clearance. In addition, shipping was not a major commercial activity, so construction of bridges with piers was not disruptive to shipping.

The Hudson, on the other hand, being wide, deep, and tidal, supported a substantial shipping industry, with ocean-going vessels sailing as far north as Troy. These ships needed a large amount of clearance when they passed under bridges, and the shipping industry opposed the building of bridges because piers in the middle of the river posed a hazard. Finally, simply by being deeper and wider, it was technically more difficult to construct early bridges over the Hudson than it was for the Delaware and Connecticut.

The result of this difference was that the Delaware and Connecticut Rivers were the site of many bridges in the early and mid-1800s. These were mostly wooden covered bridges and early, small-scale, light-gauge steel through-truss bridges, all with low clearance. At many locations, there have been three or four generations of bridges as the older ones were destroyed by floods or became insufficient to handle growing transport needs.

On 160 miles of the Hudson River between Troy and New York Harbor, there were no early wooden or through-truss bridges. By the late 1880s, there were several bridges on the Delaware and the Connecticut, while there were still none over the Hudson. Any overland traffic, including railroads, traversing from south and west of New York City into New England had to either use ferries or go 160 miles to the north to cross the river at Troy. A traffic bridge was not constructed over the Hudson until 1924, a full hundred years after there were traffic bridges over the Delaware and Connecticut. There are still only eight highway bridges in this 160-mile stretch, while there are dozens on the Delaware and the Connecticut. The difficulty in bridging the Hudson is shown even today in Manhattan, where there are 15 bridges crossing the East and Harlem Rivers on the east side of the island, but only one bridge crossing the Hudson on the west side of the island.

Another factor affecting the magnitude and importance of the barrier formed by the Hudson is the number of people who want to cross it. The Hudson is found in the most densely populated part of the United

States. It is not in the middle of nowhere, presenting an inconvenience to a small number of people. It is, in fact, separating the entire population of the southeastern and mid-Atlantic United States from New York City, Long Island, Boston, and all of southern New England. Anyone wanting to drive between these two densely populated and industrial regions has to make a decision. Which of the crossings do I want to use? The wrong choice can easily lead to hours lost in detours and traffic jams.

For most traffic coming from the mid-Atlantic or southeastern states, the most direct route into New England is Interstate 95, across the George Washington Bridge. Based on an examination of a map and the distances involved to use other crossings, there is not even any competition. None of the other crossings are even remotely as convenient as the George Washington Bridge. This is why the George Washington Bridge is the most heavily used bridge in the world, and the traffic jam can easily last an hour or two to cross this bridge which is shorter than one mile in length. Depending on where you are coming from and where you are going, other reasonable choices are the Tappan Zee and Newburgh-Beacon bridges. Although they are not as convenient in terms of location, they at least carry 60 mile-per-hour interstate highways, and are not nearly as jammed as the George Washington.

Assuming you have extra time and are interested in scenic and historic bridges, the best choice is to cross at Bear Mountain, the first traffic bridge constructed over the Hudson. With the obvious need for a traffic bridge somewhere between Albany and New York Harbor, it is interesting to note that the main driving force behind the location of this first bridge was not primarily technical or logistical. The location was not selected because it was the easiest place to construct a bridge. It was not selected to link economically important communities together. It was not even selected as an optimal location to enhance long-distance traffic flow between New England and points south and west. Instead, the driving force behind the location was access to recreation.

The roads of the expanding metropolis of New York City in the late nineteenth and early twentieth centuries were built with crushed rock, and the easiest place to obtain rock was the cliffs of the Palisades on the west side of the Hudson. The destructive nature of the quarrying rapidly became a concern for the Englewood Women's Club of New Jersey. This concern grew into an interest in environmental conservation and preservation, which was funded by many of the leading industrialists and politicians in the area.

Most prominent among these was the Harriman family, which owned a large amount of property in the Hudson Highlands about 30 miles north of the city. By 1910, the Harriman family had acquired land in the Bear Mountain area and had donated it to the state for what eventually became Bear Mountain State Park. The park was immediately developed with hiking trails, ball fields, tennis courts, winter sports facilities, and the famous Bear Mountain Inn. The park became the prominent outdoor playground for well-heeled New Yorkers. It had one problem, though, which was that New York City was on the east side of the Hudson and the park was on the west side. This was no problem for the tens of thousands who visited the park by steamboats from New York City, but by the 1920s, more and more people wanted to access the park in their cars, resulting in enormous traffic backups at the ferry landings near the park. By 1923, a private company led by E. Roland Harriman began construction of the Bear Mountain Bridge, which opened in 1924.

The Bear Mountain Bridge is a suspension bridge, and it began an era in which a new record for longest suspension bridge in the world was set every few years in the United States. The record set by the Brooklyn Bridge lasted for 20 years from 1883 to 1903, and the record set by the Williamsburg Bridge just a mile or so away endured another 21 years until 1924. However, the record set at Bear Mountain lasted only for two years, until the opening of the Benjamin Franklin Bridge in 1926. The record would be reset again in 1929, 1931, and 1937.

The bridge design on Bear Mountain is somewhat unusual when compared with other suspension bridges of the same era. On what we envision as a "classical" suspension bridge design, there are three suspended spans: one between the two suspension towers, and one between each tower and the cable anchors on the shore. The two towers are constructed in the water body, and the main suspension cable is curved as it descends on both sides of each tower. On Bear Mountain, there is only one suspension span, the one between the towers. The towers are not in the Hudson, but are on the banks of the river. The deck sections between the towers and the roadway connections on either end are short enough that a deck-stiffening truss is all that is needed, and there are no vertical cables supporting the deck on the ends. The suspension cables on the ends of the bridge are not curved because they are not weight-bearing. Instead, they are straight, as they are pulled taut by the weight of the central section of the bridge. The bridge is also interesting in that it is narrow for such a high and long bridge. The bridge supports only one lane of traffic in each direction, with a bicycle lane and a narrow sidewalk on the northern side of the bridge.

The bridge is walkable, but not easily. The original purpose of the bridge was to support recreation in the state park. Bear Mountain State Park was the location of the first section of the Appalachian Trail, and the trail crossing of the Hudson is on this bridge. However, there are no designated parking lots on either end of the bridge to allow easy access by car to the bridge's sidewalk. You can drive your car over the bridge, but there is minimal space to stop, park, and take a quick walk. The best bet is to park at Fort Montgomery, or in the state park itself, and hike the portion of the Appalachian Trail out to the bridge.

The best features of the bridge walk are the views of the surrounding area, especially when leaves are changing in the fall. The Hudson Highlands is the first area of mountains to the north of New York City, and the view from the bridge includes almost nothing but spectacular wooded hillsides. The structures associated with the bridge, including the cable anchors on Anthony's Nose and the tollhouse and maintenance buildings at the western end, are constructed of rough brown stone, which matches the rustic theme of the buildings inside the state park, including gorgeous Bear Mountain Inn. Although the bridge can be walked on a hit-and-run drive up the Palisades Interstate Parkway, a better plan may be to see it on a full-day trip, combined with other sites and activities in the park.

CHAPTER 8
REPURPOSED BRIDGES

WALNUT STREET BRIDGE, CHATTANOOGA, TENNESSEE

The city of Chattanooga has two stunningly beautiful and historic bridges, right next to each other, crossing the Tennessee River. The Walnut Street and Market Street bridges are centered directly on downtown and sit only a few hundred feet from each other.

The Tennessee at this location is a large river, almost a half-mile wide, and it supports a variety of large commercial and tourism-related boats and ships. The area is hilly, so parts of the city overlook the river from high bluffs, especially on the southern, downtown side of the river. Finally, at the time of the construction of the bridges, the Tennessee River at this location was subject to enormous floods, with water levels reaching 58 feet above normal river level during the Great Flood of 1867. As a result of these factors, the bridges across the river must be high, soaring about 100 feet above river level. The height above river level, and the presence of a large superstructure sitting above the deck, makes these two bridges a prominent part of the Chattanooga skyline.

The main attraction is the Walnut Street Bridge, which consists of five enormous steel through-trusses resting on beautifully tapered piers. The piers are 100 feet high and made of white, rough-surfaced local stone. The tapering of the piers, with wide bases narrowing to only bridge-width at the top, makes the bridge appear to be gravity-defying. The five trusses are identical, each extending another 30 feet above the deck in an interlaced pattern and painted the same sky blue as the adjacent Market Street Bridge.

Walnut Street Bridge, Chattanooga, Tennessee

Included on the National Register of Historic Places, the history of the Walnut Street Bridge, both its early years and recent history, is fascinating. Constructed in 1890, the bridge served as a major traffic link between downtown and North Shore for more than 80 years. Then, one morning in 1978, bridge inspectors declared the bridge unsafe. The bridge was closed by noon, creating massive traffic jams for workers trying to get from downtown to their homes on the north side of the river. The bridge never opened to traffic again. It sat unused for more than ten years before plans were made to demolish it in the late 1980s.

Fortunately for bridge tourists, as well as for the residents of Chattanooga, public outcry stopped the demolition. Instead, the bridge was transformed into the second longest pedestrian-only bridge in the United States. The bridge is now part of the city park system, connecting running, walking, and bicycle trails in downtown and along the southern bank of the river with a city park and the North Shore neighborhood to the north. The bridge has many of the amenities expected of a city park, including park benches, historical plaques, decorative lighting, and plastic bag dispensers for dog walkers. The bridge is quite popular and any time of year you can expect to encounter families out for a stroll, as well as cyclists, joggers, roller-bladers, and dog walkers. About 30 feet wide, the bridge deck is now made of wood planks which, combined with the white wrought-iron railings and blue interlaced steel superstructure, make the bridge picturesque.

Not all of the history of the Walnut Street Bridge is so positive. The bridge was the site of two lynchings around the turn of the twentieth century, both black men accused of raping white women. The second of these, in 1906, became a landmark court case, the Shipp Trial, which was the only criminal contempt case ever tried by the US Supreme Court. Ed Johnson, the accused man, was clearly innocent, but convicted and condemned to death. Justice John Marshall Harlan heard the evidence, and the Supreme Court agreed to stay Johnson's planned execution so that an appeal could be filed. That night, the local sheriff, Joseph Shipp, removed the deputies guarding the prison and moved other prisoners off the floor where Johnson was being held. It took hours for an angry mob to break into the prison, but they succeeded in reaching Johnson and taking him to the bridge. He was hung from the second span north of downtown for several minutes, dangling 100 feet above the river. Then he was pulled up and shot five times. The Supreme Court, angry that their stay of execution had effectively been ignored, and that the lynching had apparently been aided and abetted by Shipp and his deputies, held a trial in which Shipp and five others were convicted of contempt of court and sentenced to prison terms ranging from 60 to 90 days.

Although not a repurposed bridge, the Market Street Bridge, located a few hundred feet to the west of the Walnut Street Bridge, is also a major part of the experience. This bridge is the newer of the two, having been completed in 1917, and it is also listed on the National Register of Historic Places. The bridge still carries traffic on Market Street from downtown to North Shore.

The unusual feature of the Market Street Bridge, which immediately draws attention, is the center between two arched sections. The center section is a drawbridge—the only drawbridge in the state of Tennessee. Specifically, the bridge is a double-leaf, rolling-lift bascule bridge, using gigantic concrete counterweights on either side to raise the two separate sections of the bridge deck. Each half of the center section consists of a central hinge, which sits directly on one of the large concrete piers. On the landward side of the hinge is the counterweight, held high in the air above the deck. On the river side of the hinge is the bridge deck and the supporting steel truss. When the bridge needs to be opened, small electric motors give each side a little push to begin raising the deck. Once lifted a little bit, the counterweights take over, moving downward on the landward side of the hinge while the bridge deck moves upward in the center. By using counterweights, this bridge construction technique requires only a little power to open and close the bridge.

The presence of the large-scale counterweights and steel truss mechanism above the bridge deck gives this bridge a distinct, early industrial-looking appearance. The appeal is further enhanced by the contrast of the white arches and counterweights with the sky blue of the steel truss. The bridge includes beautiful decorative elements on the deck. The decoration has an Egyptian theme, with large white cement obelisks guarding the approaches on both ends and smaller cement obelisks serving as lampposts.

As if their history and beauty were not enough, the Walnut Street and Market Street bridges have an even more attractive feature, which is the manner in which they are integrated into Chattanooga's redeveloped downtown area. In walking bridges, it is interesting to see how different cities have chosen to use or not use their waterfronts to enrich their urban environments. Few cities, maybe only Hartford, have done it as nicely as Chattanooga. On their southern ends, both bridges spill out directly into a large downtown area of shops, restaurants, museums, and new riverfront condos and apartments. The Market Street Bridge ends at the Tennessee Aquarium, which covers a large part of the riverfront with two large glass pyramid-topped buildings. Because the downtown area sits on bluffs elevated above river level, walkways are part of the riverfront promenade and connect the bridges at river level, along with additional walking paths higher up at street level, and then several curved staircases and pedestrian bridge complexes connecting the two levels. Every time you think there cannot possibly be any more interesting, intricate approaches to these bridges and museums, you find more.

Unless you live close by, Chattanooga is probably not high on your list of places to visit, and if it is, it is probably due to the nearby Civil War Battlefields and tourist areas associated with Lookout Mountain. However, what make a visit to Chattanooga necessary are not just the great bridges, but the way they have been integrated into the overall downtown redevelopment scheme. Chattanooga is definitely an unexpected treat, and the bridges are a big part of the reason why.

PURPLE PEOPLE BRIDGE, CINCINNATI

About a mile east of the Roebling Bridge in Cincinnati is the Newport-Southbank Bridge, also known as the Purple People Bridge. Dating from 1872, this bridge is a former railroad and traffic bridge that is more than a half-mile long. It consists of a series of four arched steel trusses on the southern end, then a much larger arched truss across the main channel of the Ohio River, and then a steel-girder section connecting the bridge to the north shore. Each truss is actually two separate side-by-side trusses, attached to each other by steel girders.

Railroad traffic on the bridge ceased in 1987 and, due to further deterioration and lack of maintenance, it was closed to vehicle traffic in 2001. The local communities and economic development organizations immediately moved to restore the bridge and convert it to pedestrian and bicycle use, and the bridge reopened in 2003. The restoration was accompanied by new developments on both riverbanks, including the massive Newport-on-the-Levee retail development and aquarium at the base of the bridge on the south shore.

The Newport-Southbank Bridge is a little unusual among converted railroad bridges in that it is still privately owned, by the Newport-Southbank Bridge Company. Although open to the public most of the time, it is also available to rent for private events. Because the bridge consists of side-by-side trusses, it actually has three separate components. The truss on the eastern side is not connected to the shore or the pedestrian lanes, and it has no deck. The truss on the western side is the main pedestrian area, flanked with benches and large cement planters with flowers. In between the two trusses, a completely separate sidewalk was built, about eight feet wide. This sidewalk has signs indicating that it is named Pagan's Path, dedicated to Wally Pagan, who was instrumental in the redevelopment. During private events, the main sidewalk on the western truss is closed to the public, but the public can still cross the bridge using Pagan's Path.

The purple color, actually more of a light lavender, has taken on a life of its own unlike the color of any other bridge. During the rehabilitation, the color was selected through testing of computer simulations by a dozen focus groups, all of them independently selecting purple as their choice. The bridge immediately became known as the Purple People Bridge even before it reopened, but the effect of the unusual choice did not stop at the paint color and the name. The bridge's signs, both on the bridge and on the riverwalk directing people to the bridge, are all in purple. None of these refers visitors to the Newport-Southbank Bridge but to the Purple People Bridge. PurplePeopleBridge.com is the bridge company's website, where you can get more information and reserve a private event. The website is mostly in purple.

Of course, these are decisions made by the bridge owners to help brand and market their product. Yet, it is interesting how much the community and tourists have embraced the purple theme. On any given day, it is surprising how many of the people on the bridge are dressed in purple! It is highly unlikely that anyone ever thought to wear a rust-orange shirt to walk across the Golden Gate, but you will see dozens of people wearing purple on the Newport-Southbank Bridge. As an added touch, the bridge has some love padlocks. Not thousands, but enough to be noticeable. These padlocks are inscribed with names or initials, as is customary on other bridges. However, what is not common on other bridges is that a large number of these padlocks have also been colored purple, by either paint or marker, before being attached.

Note that if you are combining this visit with the Roebling Bridge, you cannot easily walk along the riverfront on the Kentucky side of the river, between the Purple People Bridge in Newport and the Roebling Bridge in Covington, without some diversion, because Newport and Covington are separated by the Licking River. You can either walk further south into Newport to find the bridge over the Licking River, or you can cross the Taylor-Southgate Bridge back to Cincinnati, and then return to Covington by re-crossing the Roebling Bridge.

RED, GREEN, AND RIVERSIDE PARK DRIVE BRIDGES, DES MOINES, IOWA

As discussed with respect to the Center Street Bridge in Chapter 5, downtown Des Moines has multiple repurposed bridges that connect bike and pedestrian trails. The city was founded as Fort Des Moines at the confluence of two rivers, the Des Moines and Raccoon. This confluence is now the home of Principal Stadium, the ballpark for the Iowa Cubs, the AAA farm team of the Chicago Cubs. Both rivers have nicely developed Riverwalk trails that pass under and across three newly repurposed bridges, along with some uninteresting mid-century traffic bridges, and the amazing, modern, sculptural Center Street Bridge.

On the southern fringe of downtown, a short walk upstream on the Raccoon River from the stadium, is the Fifth Avenue Bridge, also called the Jackson Street Bridge, and more widely known in Des Moines as the Green Bridge. The Green Bridge was constructed in 1898 as a roadway bridge leading to southern suburbs of the city. The bridge was abandoned in the 1990s, rehabilitated, and then reopened as a pedestrian and bicycle-only bridge in 2016, becoming the fourth pedestrian bridge connecting trails in downtown Des Moines. It is a steel through-truss bridge, three spans long. Consistent with its name, the bridge is freshly painted dark green, with a black steel railing and wooden deck.

Directly at the confluence, crossing the Raccoon River on the back side of the baseball stadium, is the Riverside Park Drive Bridge, also known as the Southwest First Street Trail Bridge. This is a handsome open-spandrel cement arch bridge consisting of five arch spans and dating from 1937. This bridge was converted to pedestrian and bicycle-only use in 2006. The bridge is wide, with dedicated bike lanes in the middle of the bridge and sidewalks with comfortable benches and planter boxes on either side.

Directly opposite the main part of downtown, crossing the Des Moines River, is the Red Bridge. Constructed by the Des Moines Union Railway in 1891, the Red Bridge is a hybrid construction type that has been partially reconstructed a few times. The ends of the bridge are steel-plate girder construction, but the two spans in the middle of the river are the original steel through-truss spans. The bridge was abandoned in 1996, but it was rehabilitated and reopened as a pedestrian and bicycle-only bridge in 2004. The bridge is painted bright red and lined with a modern white railing. In the center of the bridge, between the two through-truss spans, a modern platform extending off both sides of the bridge has been added to the original structure. This modern platform is outfitted with benches and is designed to provide a relaxing park-like space in the middle of the river.

Many cities have rehabilitated a single abandoned bridge and set it aside for pedestrian use, providing links between the riverwalks and other park trails in the area. Des Moines has done this not with a single bridge but with three bridges within a short walking distance. More importantly, the conversions are not limited to blocking the ends to preclude car access and just allowing pedestrians to cross. Red Bridge had park-like platforms constructed on both sides, and both Red Bridge and Riverside Park Drive have benches added to develop the bridges into attractive park spaces in the middle of the river. Finally, both Red Bridge and Green Bridge are lighted at night. On both, the white lighting from the sides is relatively plain, although there is also lighting of the steel components from within the truss. Because the color of Green Bridge is a dark green shade, the lighting is attractive, but not attention-grabbing. However, the Red Bridge is a very bright shade of red, resulting in the bridge looking like it glows from within at night.

CALHOUN COUNTY HISTORIC BRIDGE PARK, BATTLE CREEK, MICHIGAN

There are many different ways in which the world of bridges can intersect with the world of parks. Bridges can be used within parks to provide access across water bodies or roads, to serve as viewing platforms for scenic vistas, or to be decorative works of public art. Park-like amenities, such as benches and landscaping, can be placed onto the sidewalk or deck of a bridge, especially if a historic bridge is being preserved and repurposed. Other obsolete bridges are closed to traffic, and new parks are developed around them by adding parking lots, some commemorative statues, and historical information plaques. Finally, in some rare cases, a bridge is either dismantled or disconnected from its abutments, placed on a truck, and transported to an existing park for both historic preservation and to connect areas of the park on opposite sides of a creek.

The Calhoun County Historic Bridge Park, in Michigan, has taken this latter concept to an extreme. Instead of preserving a single historic bridge by moving it and reconstructing it in an existing park, Calhoun County developed a new park solely for the purpose of preserving historic bridges. Between 1999 and 2007, five obsolete, historic bridges in Michigan were dismantled and reassembled on about 25 acres along the bank of the Kalamazoo River in Battle Creek.

The area has all of the normal amenities associated with a park, including trails through scenic wildflowers, boat and kayak launch ramps on the river, kiosks with picnic benches, multiple historical and environmental information plaques, and plentiful parking. Four of the bridges cross Dickinson Creek, which is a small tributary to the river. The fifth bridge crosses over the entrance road to the park, connecting the tops of hills on either end. All of the bridges are connected on both ends to wood-plank trails, and each has a sign indicating its name, construction date, and original location.

The first bridge you will see, and the largest of the group, is the Charlotte Highway Bridge, which crosses the park entrance road. This is a steel through-truss bridge, with a wood-plank deck, dating from 1886. Almost 200 feet long, the bridge is pleasingly painted in bright red. An appealing feature is the intricate, decorative casting on the date plaques over the portal entrance on both ends. The truss is quite high for such an old bridge, and the portal entrance has two top chords instead of the usual one. Originally, there was a date plaque on both top chords on both ends, so a total of four, but the uppermost of the plaques on the western end has been lost. The remaining plaque on the western end lists the names of the Commissioner, Supervisor, and Town Clerk, the date of 1886, and has floral, fan, geometric, and intertwined branch designs cast into the metal. On the eastern end, the lower plaque repeats the names, and the uppermost plaque lists the name of Buckeye Bridge Works of Cleveland as the constructor of the bridge. Close observation of the plaques reveals that they had been badly rusted and falling apart at one time, and the missing pieces of the plaques have been restored. This is apparent because the restored portions are only smooth-surfaced metal plate, but the intricate designs cast into the plaques are not recreated.

After exiting the eastern end of the Charlotte Highway Bridge, stairs lead back down to the level of Dickinson Creek. Signposts indicate that the trails through the park are part of the North Country National Scenic Trail. Extending from North Dakota to Vermont, this is the longest trail within the National Scenic Trail System.

The next two bridges, both set within a sea of purple wildflowers, are the 133rd Avenue Bridge and the 20 Mile Road Bridge. Both bridges are pony truss bridges, which is a common, early design for small-scale iron and steel bridges in the late 1800s and early 1900s. The 133rd Avenue Bridge, dating from 1897, was the first bridge moved to the park, in 1999. The 20 Mile Road Bridge dates from 1906, and was moved to the park in 2000. Pony truss bridges are usually of little interest to most people, because their low profile is not particularly picturesque. However, they are of great interest to maniacal bridgespotters, particularly those interested in studying early engineering and design.

Visible over the wildflowers from the 20 Mile Road Bridge is the Gale Road Bridge. This is another through-truss bridge, dating from 1897. The unusual feature here is that the bridge is skewed, and was designed to cross its stream at an angle. This means that all of the interlocking components and their connections meet at oblique angles, with no right angles to be found.

The final bridge is another unusual through-truss, the Bauer Road Bridge. This was originally constructed in 1880, and was moved to the park in 2005. As noted in Chapter 2, the Bauer Road Bridge is the key to identifying Penn Bridge Works as the construction company responsible for the Poffenberger Road Bridge in Maryland, due to the identical hand-cut, beautifully ornate portal bracings on each bridge. The historicbridges.org website makes this link by showing photos, taken in 2014, of the heavily-rusted lattice joint covers displaying the name "PENN" and the Liberty Bell logo. Unfortunately, during a site visit in 2022, the joint covers had rusted even further, and neither the "PENN" name nor the Bell logo was legible, making the photo documentation on the historicbridges.org website critically important in establishing the historical record.

Bridgespotters can, and often do, spend hours or days tracking down small pieces of bridge history, often separated by hundreds of miles from each other. The Calhoun County Historic Bridge Park gives you an opportunity to study five unique, historic bridges all in one place, and lovingly set into a well-maintained and landscaped park setting along a scenic river and trail.

NAVAJO BRIDGE, ARIZONA

One of the more scenic bridge locations in the United States is that of Navajo Bridge, which crosses the Colorado River in northern Arizona. The bridge crosses Marble Canyon, connecting the Navajo Nation on the east side of the river with the Glen Canyon National Recreation Area on the west. The bridge is sometimes referred to as the Grand Canyon Bridge by some sources, but this is a misnomer. Marble Canyon is a section of Colorado River, situated between Lake Powell and the Grand Canyon, where the river has cut a narrow canyon about 500 feet deep and 800 feet wide through flat-lying sedimentary rocks. The narrow width of the canyon, compared to the Grand Canyon itself, made this an obvious choice for an early bridge across the river.

There are actually two almost identical bridges at the location. The original bridge was constructed in 1929, and is a steel arch bridge that crosses the canyon on a single arch. Even today, the area is relatively remote and sparsely-populated, with the nearest city of any significant size being Flagstaff 120 miles away. The original bridge was only 18 feet wide and carried only one lane in each direction, and was the only bridge crossing a 600-mile stretch of the Colorado River for most of the twentieth century.

By the 1990s, traffic levels had increased, mostly due to the popularity of the scenery and outdoor recreational opportunities in the area. In addition to nearby Grand Canyon National Park and Glen Canyon National Recreation Area managed by the National Park Service, the bridge provides access to the Navajo Nation to the east, and to the Vermilion Cliffs National Monument to the west. The old bridge was no longer sufficient to handle the increased traffic, so the National Park Service constructed a second bridge, which opened in 1995.

REPURPOSED BRIDGES 159

While obsolete bridges are frequently supplemented or replaced by the construction of a new bridge, there are good and bad ways to do it. The *Bridgespotting* books document cases where a historic bridge that could have been preserved for pedestrian or bicycle use was torn down, such as at the Penobscot Narrows Observatory. They discuss situations where the replacement bridge was mismatched with the original bridge, disturbing the aesthetics of a scenic area, such as the Chesapeake Bay Bridge. At Navajo Bridge, the National Park Service clearly went out of their way to ensure that the new bridge enhanced the tourist and recreational attractions of the region.

The first requirement, more important than any other in this scenic location, was to maintain the aesthetics of Marble Canyon. The easiest way to preserve the aesthetics would be to construct a new bridge of the same style and size, creating a matching pair, such as was done at the Delaware Memorial Bridge. This was not entirely possible because the original bridge was to be closed to traffic, and the new bridge needed to be much wider to handle the increase in traffic. However, because both bridges are substructure arch bridges and there are few locations from which to view the bridges from the side, the difference in the width of the bridges is barely noticeable. Most photographs of the bridges must be taken from the side and, in these, it is not even obvious that there are two bridges because the substructure arches match perfectly, and the bridge in front blocks the view of the bridge behind.

The second objective in turning the original bridge into a tourist attraction would be to make it available for pedestrians, and this was done. In many cities, and even rural areas, where an obsolete bridge is closed to traffic but maintained for pedestrians, the bridge equally serves tourists, recreational users, and local residents commuting to home or work. At Navajo Bridge, there are no local residents, and there is no through-trail being served by the bridge. Instead, a parking lot and interpretive center was constructed on the western end, and the bridge serves only as a tourist attraction for viewing Marble Canyon from an elevated position, and to enjoy the bridge. In addition to views of the canyon, the bridge is known as a popular spot for watching California condors.

CHAPTER 9
MULTIPLE BRIDGE TOURS

VLTAVA BRIDGE TOUR, PRAGUE

Although the 630-year-old Charles Bridge is the only bridge in Prague that is a household name, it is just one of seven interesting bridges located within an easy walk of the amazing tourist areas in Prague's Old Town, Mala Strana, and Castle Hill. None of the other bridges are as old as Charles Bridge, as their construction dates range from the 1870s to the 1930s. They are all traffic or, in the case of Vyšehrad Bridge, railroad bridges. Nonetheless, the other bridges all have sidewalks on both sides, are not far away from Charles Bridge, and have some decoration or other attraction making a visit worthwhile. All of them offer amazing views of the city, Prague Castle, and Petrin Hill. Some of the views are closer in and some are farther away, but all of them have great views.

The bridges are on both the upstream and downstream sides of Charles Bridge. The first bridge downstream, Manesuv Bridge, connects the city's main concert hall, the Rudolfinum, with the Castle area and the Czech Parliament building on the west bank of the river. Dating from 1914, the Manesuv Bridge is four open-spandrel gray granite arches with subtle geometric patterns carved into the parapet.

About a half-mile further downstream is Čechuv Bridge, which would be a major bridge destination in any city that did not also have Charles Bridge. Čechuv Bridge dates from 1908 and is integrated into a pleasant river-level promenade on the northern side of the Josefov neighborhood near Old Town. This promenade is where Vltava River tour boats can be found. Stairs from the promenade lead up to Čechuv Bridge, which is composed of three open-spandrel steel-girder arches resting on ornate stone piers. The bridge has gigantic allegorical bronze statues on the piers facing upriver and decorative cast-iron railings and lampposts.

Čechuv Bridge defines a wide, central axis between the Old Town to the south and Lookout Point, a large city park on a hill to the north of the river. In the Communist era, the prominent Lookout Point was topped with an enormous statue of Stalin, making Čechuv Bridge the visual and pedestrian linkage between Stalin and the city. The Stalin statue is now gone, replaced with a large metronome sculpture which, given the prominence of its position off the end of the bridge, looks a little weird.

Walking in the opposite, upstream direction from Charles Bridge, the next bridge to the south is Legií Most, or Legion Bridge. Built in 1901, Legií Most crosses Strelecky Island, an urban park in the middle of the river. The sidewalk of the bridge has both a stairway and an elevator from the deck down to park level.

Legií Most consists of nine stone arches with elaborate decorative stonework throughout. The decoration is accomplished with stones of different colors, textures, and placement in either recessed or relief positions. The different colors include red, black, yellow, and multiple shades of white or tan. The decoration highlights the arch-rings, the piers, the spandrels, and the balustrades. On the four corners near the ends of the bridge are small stone towers with decorative domed roofs topped by elaborate copper metalwork. The ornate lampposts are large black iron posts topped with gilded lions. Like Čechuv Bridge, Legií Most would be a major bridge attraction in almost any other city.

The three bridges south of Legií Most are connected on the east bank of the river by an attractive riverwalk used for biking, jogging, and general tourist strolling. Jiraskuv Bridge, dating from 1931, is the next bridge south of Legií and is the least decorated of the Vltava bridges, but it does connect interesting areas that should be visited. At its eastern end is the famous modernistic Dancing House, an interesting curved building that has become a major Prague landmark. At its western end is Detsky Island, where you can investigate the workings of the locks on the Vltava.

Palacky Bridge dates from 1876 and is similar in appearance and structure to Legií Most. It also uses a riot of stone colors and textures to highlight the stone arches, piers, spandrels, and balustrades.

Another half-mile to the south is Vyšehrad Bridge. This is an industrial-looking black steel through-truss railroad bridge dating from 1901, and only becomes semi-interesting due to its location near the Vyšehrad fortress complex, an area that is of immense importance in Bohemian history and legend. The bridge has sidewalks on both sides but is generally off the beaten tourist path. It is a bit surprising then to walk out on it and find quite a few love padlocks, which are usually reserved for more romantic locations and popular tourist areas. The reason for this is not clear, although it may be related to the importance of Vyšehrad in Czech nationalism.

Having mentioned in Chapter 1 of *Bridgespotting: Part 1* that Charles Bridge is probably the best walkable bridge in the world, it seems almost ridiculous to suggest that there are other pleasant bridges over the Vltava to visit in Prague, but there are. After you get tired of the crowds on Charles Bridge, there is still plenty to see on the other bridges.

RIVER LIFFEY BRIDGE TOUR, DUBLIN

Dublin is not as large a city as many other European capitals, and its river is not nearly as familiar as those in other major European or US cities. When confronted with London, New York, Paris, Rome, Washington, Pittsburgh, Prague, or Budapest, millions of people can immediately name the prominent river that bisects the city, separating one major historic area from another, and being crossed all day long. Interact with the tourists on the street in any of these other cities, and nobody is going to ask you, "What is the name of the river?" Tourists in Dublin, on the other hand, seem a bit surprised to find a river there. A small river, to be sure, but cutting the city neatly in half, right in the middle of the action. So it is not unusual to be asked in Dublin "What is the name of the river?"

The river is the Liffey. Hardly a household name, as rivers go, but crossed by 15 interesting bridges in the four-mile stretch between the train station and the harbor in central Dublin. The bridges range from extremely old to brand new, from pedestrian to traffic-bearing, from plain to extremely ornate. All of them are just a short walk from the museums, churches, and pubs that you are going to visit. It is a great place to see a large number of bridges that have more pedestrians on them than cars.

The general setting of all of the bridges is similar. The River Liffey flows almost directly from west to east through central Dublin, which for purposes of this tour stretches from the Seán Heuston Train Station on the west to the Docklands district of the city near the harbor to the east. The river is about 150 feet wide near the train station, passes through the central Temple Bar district between Parliament Street and O'Connell Street, and then gradually widens to about 400 feet at the Docklands. The river is confined within stone quays along the entire stretch, and the surrounding city streets are elevated about 15 to 20 feet above river level. Along the western half of the tour, there are narrow sidewalks lining the top of the quay on both sides of the river, but no river-level sidewalks or promenades. In the Docklands area, the sidewalks along the quay are more of a riverfront promenade than a sidewalk. Also, the buildings in the Docklands are much newer, as this area has been redeveloped in recent years.

There is no concentrated area where you will find the "best" bridges, so you will need start at one end and walk to the other. Beginning at the western end, the Seán Heuston Bridge is located directly across the street from the train station of the same name. The bridge is a single cast-iron arch dating from 1821. It was built to commemorate a visit to Dublin by King George IV, so is elaborately decorated with ornate railings, lampposts, and cast-iron decorations on the spandrels, much of it incorporating a crown motif. The color scheme is a gleaming white base, with decorations applied in royal blue and gold. Intended for early nineteenth century horse traffic, the bridge carried cars and trucks up through 1980, at which time weight restrictions were placed on the bridge. Vehicle traffic was stopped, but the bridge still carries light-rail commuter trains and pedestrians.

A replacement traffic bridge, the adjacent Frank Sherwin Bridge, was constructed in 1982. Although a plain-looking cement bridge, it was designed with clean and simple lines, and is not unattractive. Also, its location is a good place to view the Heuston Bridge to the west and the equally lovely Rory O'More Bridge to the east.

The Rory O'More Bridge is almost a half-mile east of the train station, in a somewhat more working-class neighborhood halfway between the train station and the tourist center. The southern bank of the river between the Sherwin and O'More bridges is taken up by the enormous Guinness Brewery complex. Like Seán Heuston, the Rory O'More Bridge is an ornate, single-span cast-iron arch bridge. This bridge was built in celebration of the royal visit of Victoria and Albert in 1861. As opposed to the Seán Heuston Bridge, which is a closed-spandrel arch with applied decorations, the Rory O'More Bridge is an open-spandrel arch where the decoration of the sides is accomplished through the configuration of the supports, which are highlighted by the painted color scheme. The arch, spandrel supports, and railing are a sky-blue color that perfectly matches the color of the river on a sunny day, and the other structural elements are highlighted in white.

Right next to the Rory O'More Bridge is the James Joyce Bridge. The James Joyce Bridge is an interesting case because it is not large or historic, nor is it located in the center of the tourist area or carry major roadway, yet it somehow features more than one important attraction. Even though it is not in a prominent location where it would be seen by many people, it is an important public sculpture commissioned from Santiago Calatrava, a prominent modern bridge designer. As discussed in Chapter 6 of *Bridgespotting: Part 1*, it also attracts a literary crowd due to its location across the street from James Joyce's House of the Dead.

The next three bridges to the east are among the oldest in Dublin, all of them stone arch bridges. Moving east from the James Joyce Bridge, these are the Mellows Bridge from 1768, Father Mathew Bridge from 1818, and O'Donovan Rossa Bridge from 1816. The bridges are similar in structure, each being a three-span stone arch, carrying two lanes of traffic with sidewalks on both sides, and having almost identical balustrades composed of a granite frame enclosing white, urn-shaped balusters. This theme is also carried through the balustrades along the quay between the bridges in front of the historic Four Courts Building, which is home of the Irish Supreme Court.

O'Donovan Rossa Bridge marks the beginning of the tourist center of Dublin. Visible down the street a couple blocks to the south of the bridge is an ornate elevated walkway that is part of Christchurch Cathedral, and St. Patrick's Cathedral is just a few blocks further south. Dublin Castle is located just east of Christchurch Cathedral.

The next bridge to the east is the Grattan Bridge, which marks the beginning of the Liffey Boardwalk. The sidewalks on the top of the quay on both sides of the river are narrow, only a few feet wide, and are not amenable to riverfront strolling. To make the riverfront more of a resident and tourist destination, the Liffey Boardwalk was built in 2000. It is a promenade constructed as an extension out over the river from the sidewalk. Situated on the northern bank of the river, it extends from Grattan Bridge to O'Connell Street Bridge, and has riverside benches and vendors selling refreshments from kiosks. It is not a long or wide promenade, but given that the sidewalk itself is hardly more than a wide curb, it is definitely a major improvement for enjoyment of the river and its bridges.

Grattan Bridge dates from 1874. Although it is another stone arch bridge, it has some substantial differences from Mellows, Father Mathew, and O'Donovan Rossa. Grattan Bridge is firmly in the middle of the tourist action, and this is reflected in the pedestrian amenities on the bridge, in the surrounding buildings, and in its connection to the boardwalk. The major noticeable feature of Grattan Bridge is that, although it carries traffic, its sidewalks are so wide that it almost seems to be more of a pedestrian bridge. The sidewalks are much wider than the structure itself, and you can see from the side that they are supported from below by decorative, curved iron cantilevers that extend several feet out from the stone structure. The bridge's traffic lanes seem an afterthought—a narrow stretch of asphalt through the middle of a wide plaza of benches and delightfully decorative iron railings and lampposts. The railings are a sturdy lattice of diagonal iron strips, painted dark green. The bases of the lampposts are a cast-iron pair of seahorses, but not the actual sea creature you might think of. Instead, they are mythical-like creatures with a real horse head, upper body, and feet, and then a scaly lower body and tail, much like a mermaid, except a mer-horse. The bridge is only a few steps from the pub-packed neighborhood of Temple Bar. Make sure to stop on the southwest corner of the bridge to look at the amazing decorative glazed ceramic friezes on the Sunlight Chambers Building across the street.

Millennium Bridge, a few steps east of Grattan Bridge, is another of the four modernistic bridges in Dublin. Some modern bridges are deliberately designed with a complex engineering scheme in order to appear to be modern art works. Millennium Bridge, built in 1999, is just a simple, beautiful arch structure made of a few substructure steel supports, with no decorative embellishments at all. In a city with many decorative bridges, both old and new, the Millennium Bridge seems like a breath of fresh air, not trying to be anything more than an attractive, functional bridge.

The Ha'penny Bridge, a little further east, is the epicenter of Dublin's bridges and is an iconic landmark. In a city with so many interesting bridges, an internet search of Dublin bridges is likely to turn up more pictures of Ha'penny than any of the others. There are several reasons for its iconic status, including being the oldest and most decorative bridge in the tourist center, as well as being a steeply arched pedestrian-only bridge. The bridge, built in 1816, is a single iron arch. Because the bridge was built as a pedestrian-only bridge, it did not need to be wide, flat, or composed of heavy-gauge members to support heavy loads. As a result, the bridge is very light and airy. The arch and railings are made of light-gauge members, made even lighter looking by their bright white color. The bridge is only about ten feet wide and is so steeply arched that most of the length of the bridge is steps up one side and down the other. The most decorative part of the bridge is three lampposts held high above the middle of the bridge by curly wrought-iron structures that extend from the railing on one side, over the pedestrian area, and down to the railing on the other side. The iconic status of the bridge and its central location is documented by dozens of love padlocks attached to the lamppost structures.

Ha'penny was the only pedestrian bridge in Dublin for almost 200 years until Millennium Bridge opened. In fact, it is not immediately obvious why a second pedestrian bridge was needed just one city block over from Ha'penny. However, the bridgesofdublin.ie website discusses how the narrow Ha'penny Bridge was so tourist-centric and popular that it became overwhelmed, so another pedestrian bridge was constructed just one block away to take pressure off it.

The eastern end of the historic tourist area of Dublin is marked by the O'Connell Street Bridge. O'Connell Street is the grand thoroughfare in the "newer" section of the city north of the river, and includes a wide median in which there are a series of monuments extending about a mile from Parnell Square to the bridge. The median even extends onto the bridge, where it is landscaped with potted palm trees and beautifully ornate iron lampposts. Built in 1880, this is a stone arch bridge with attractive granite balustrades. The bridge is the most centrally located of all of the traffic bridges in the city, connecting the important monuments of O'Connell Street north of the river with Grafton Street, Trinity College, the government center, the art and archaeological museums, and St. Stephens Green to the south. It is also unusual in that it is an extremely wide bridge over a narrow river, and is one of the few bridges you will ever see that is effectively square, almost as wide as it is long.

O'Connell Street historically marked the eastern edge of the tourist center and the beginning of the more industrial Docklands area. The two or three blocks directly east of the bridge, between the bridge and the Custom House, are a little rougher than the main tourist area. A new traffic bridge, constructed in 2014, is located directly east of O'Connell Street. A short walk further is Butt Bridge, a 1930s concrete bridge that sits in the shadow of the Loopline Bridge, an elevated railroad bridge leading to Tara Station on the south bank. Butt Bridge is walkable and is a good place to view the painted decorations on the piers of the industrial-looking Loopline Bridge, which is not walkable.

Just on the east side of the Loopline Bridge, the area opens up again into the Docklands district. The north bank of the river immediately east of the Loopline Bridge is dominated by the enormous, ornate eighteenth century Custom House. On the eastern side of the Custom House is the 1978 Talbot Bridge. Like Sherwin Bridge near the train station, this is a plain cement girder bridge that is not specially decorated or interesting, but is attractive because of its simple and clean lines.

The river widens in this area, which was once the shipping center of the port of Dublin. No early bridges existed here due to the movement of ships, but the increased size of ships in the late twentieth century resulted in movement of the active docks further seaward, opening this area up

MULTIPLE BRIDGE TOURS

to redevelopment and to the construction of new sculptural bridges. The remainder of the Docklands, for about another mile between the Custom House and the Samuel Beckett Bridge and beyond, has been impressively redeveloped into a wide riverfront promenade lined by sparkling glass office towers and connected by modern bridges.

The two bridges in this area are the Seán O'Casey Pedestrian Bridge and the Samuel Beckett Bridge. The Seán O'Casey Bridge has incredible views of the newly developed Docklands, including the Custom House, a tall ship moored on the northern bank, the new glass-sided office buildings, and the towering Beckett Bridge. Being connected into the new, wide promenade on both sides of the river, this is the only bridge in Dublin that appears to be intended to support recreational jogging and biking activities for local residents.

The Calatrava-designed Samuel Beckett Bridge is about another half-mile further past the Seán O'Casey Bridge, and it is far enough out that it is beyond the limits of tourist center maps of Dublin. However, because it has a high superstructure more than 100 feet above the river, it is prominently visible once you are east of the Loopline Bridge, and it probably attracts a large number of tourists to this area just for its unusual appearance. In fact, buses between the airport and the city center drive right past the end of the bridge, probably resulting in more than a few tourists making a mental note to come back to check it out.

Few cities have such an amazing mix of old and modern, decorated and understated, bridges as Dublin. One important note, which applies to almost no other city, is that each of the bridges in Dublin has some attractive or other redeeming feature. In many cities, the interesting walkable bridges are mixed in with a few ugly railroad bridges, old abandoned bridges with weeds growing out of them, or boring highway bridges. There are no bad bridges in Dublin. Even the non-walkable Loopline Bridge at least has interesting painted decorations on its piers. The 1970s and 1980s-era bridges have nothing special about them, but they are at least clean and simple enough to be attractive. Not bad for a city where you might not have even expected to find a river.

RIVER AVON BRIDGE TOUR, BATH, ENGLAND

Much of the history of science, engineering, architecture, literature, and the Industrial Revolution in England all converge in the bridges of one city, Bath, between the late 1700s and mid-1800s. *Bridgespotting: Part 1* provided detailed profiles of both Pulteney Bridge near the center of town and the Palladian Bridge on the south side of town as two important tourist bridges not to be missed. Chapter 3 of *Bridgespotting: Part 1* also described Town Bridge, near the train station in the neighboring Cotswolds town of Bradford-on-Avon, as one of the few remaining examples of a chapel constructed on a bridge. In addition, Chapter 3 of *Bridgespotting: Part 2* discusses the development of the Kennet and Avon Canal during canal mania, as reflected in the Dundas Aqueduct, accessible by bus or long hike a few miles southeast of Bath.

In this area between Bradford-on-Avon and Bath, the River Avon, the Kennet and Avon Canal, and the Great Western Railway are all roughly parallel to one another, and there are historic bridges, designed and constructed by the most prominent engineers and architects in Britain, crossing all three. Of the bridges already discussed above, architect Robert Adam was responsible for the design of the 1774 Pulteney Bridge; Capability Brown, known as the leading figure in British landscape architecture, designed Prior Park and its Palladian Bridge; and John Rennie, best known as the designer of London Bridge and Waterloo Bridge, not only designed the 1810 Dundas Aqueduct but also surveyed the route for the Kennet and Avon Canal. A few years later, Isambard Kingdom Brunel, who designed Clifton Suspension Bridge in the 1830s, engineered one of the most important achievements of the early Industrial Age, the Great Western Railway. However, these structures are just the beginning of the historic and interesting bridges in and near Bath, and anyone visiting Bath to investigate these more famous bridges should make time to see several lesser-known bridges.

The railway, canal, and river all converge at the Bath Spa train station, which sits on the northern bank of the river, and this is the best place to begin a combined walking and boat tour. You will find the first interesting bridge entering the car park on the back side of the Bath Spa station. This is Widcombe Footbridge, dating from 1877. Also known as Halfpenny

MULTIPLE BRIDGE TOURS

Bridge for the cost of its toll back in the day, this is a narrow pedestrian-only bridge that crosses the river to provide access to the train station from Widcombe, the southern suburb of Bath. The original wooden bridge at this location collapsed in 1877, killing ten people. It was replaced by the current bridge, which is a simple, flat, wrought-iron truss, painted dark green and with distinctive trellis lattice sides. A small lodge on the southern end dates from 1867 and served as the tollhouse. A cast-metal plaque lists the constructor as Westwood Baillie and Company, with a date of 1877.

A short walk to the east along the River Avon is the location where the Kennet and Avon Canal joins the river through a lock. When the canal operated, the canal and river were separate only east of Bath. West of Bath to Bristol, the river itself was engineered with locks and served as the canal route. The canal and river joined here at Widcombe Lock, adjacent to a historic mill building known as Thimble Mill. At this location, the canal and railroad trend to the northeast and the river trends to the northwest, so they become separated by a distance of about a quarter-mile.

Continuing along the river directly north of Widcombe Lock, the North Parade Road Bridge is a pleasant stone arch bridge constructed in 1836. The bridge crosses the river on a single arch. It still carries traffic and has sidewalks on either side. The stonework on the spandrels is decorative, with textured stones set in relief around the arch ring. Textured stone is also used on the four corners to provide monument-sized supports for intricate, decorative iron lampposts. A plaque with the 1836 date lists David Aust as the constructor and W. Yierney Clark as the engineer responsible for the design.

Stairs within another small stone structure on the eastern end of the North Parade Street Bridge lead down to the riverwalk on the eastern side of the river. The riverwalk connects about one half-mile north to the 1774 Pulteney Bridge, which is the most prominent landmark bridge of Bath. Pulteney Bridge is discussed in detail in *Bridgespotting: Part 1*. The shops on Pulteney Bridge can be explored on foot, and the bridge is also a prominent attraction for the River Avon boat tours.

The next bridge north of Pulteney Bridge is the Cleveland Bridge. Connecting Cleveland Place to Bathwick Street, Cleveland Bridge is an ornately decorated cast-iron arch bridge constructed in 1827. The bridge is unique in that some decorations should be viewed by walking across, while others can only be viewed from a boat. The property on all four corners of the bridge is privately owned, so the only way to obtain a view of the sides is by taking one of the boat tours.

Walking across, the prominent features are four small stone lodges with Doric columns holding up pediments, one on each of the four corners. Once operating as tollhouses, these lodges now house small art studios and offices. The ornate cast-iron railing displays the 1827 construction date in large Roman numerals facing both inward toward traffic on the bridge and also outward facing boats on the river. The bases of the four lampposts display cast-bronze plaques commemorating the purchase of the bridge by the city from its private owner in 1925; the 1928-29 date for reconstruction of the bridge; the reopening in 1929; and the date the bridge was freed from toll in 1929. The bridge was also substantially renovated in 2021.

If you take the boat tour in order to see Cleveland Bridge, you will be taken further to the Bathampton Toll Bridge a few miles north of Bath. The navigable part of the river ends at a weir at the base of the stone arch bridge. The bridge, constructed in 1872, consists of a series of eight pointed arches made of Bath stone.

Returning to the walking tour, a short walk along Bathwick Street to the east of Cleveland Bridge leads to Sydney Gardens, a historic city park dating from 1795. Shortly after it was established, Sydney Gardens was bisected by the canal, thus requiring the construction of two footbridges over the canal to connect the main part of the park to its eastern corner. Then, in 1840, the Great Western Railway was constructed parallel to the canal, cutting more directly through the center of the park and again requiring footbridges to connect the two halves. As a result, Sydney Gardens is home to four lovely and historically important park bridges.

The two bridges over the canal are cast-iron bridges, each displaying a plaque stating "Erected Anno 1800." Both were designed by John Rennie as part of his plan for the canal, and both were cast at Coalbrookdale where, only 21 years prior, the first iron-arch bridge in the world, Iron Bridge, was cast. Although they are small footbridges only about five feet wide and

25 feet long, they both incorporate decorative cast-iron shapes into their arch designs and are both painted sparkling white. One of the bridges has a closed spandrel arch, while the other is completely open, consisting of a series of increasingly smaller circles. Both have railings composed of decorative cast-iron lattice.

The two bridges over the railway were designed by Brunel as part of his plan for the Great Western Railway. One of them is a decorative stone arch bridge dating from 1840, and the other is an open-spandrel, cast-iron arch. When visited in 2014, the cast-iron bridge was rusted and needed a fresh coat of paint, but it has a gorgeous, decorative cast-iron railing.

The literary connection to these bridges is, as with most things in Bath, associated with Jane Austen. From 1801 to 1804, Austen lived at No. 4 Sydney Place, which is across the street from the western entrance to the Sydney Gardens. It is known from Jane's letters that she enjoyed taking extended, wandering walks around Bath, and she frequently mentioned taking these walks and attending events in Sydney Gardens. Although the railway bridges were not constructed until later, the two white cast-iron canal bridges were new at the time. She would have walked over and underneath them multiple times in her three years' residence there.

RIVER DEE BRIDGE TOUR, CHESTER, ENGLAND

The River Dee in Chester, in northwestern England, is a good example of a place where the entirety of the bridges is greater than the sum of their parts. None of the Chester bridges would be a major attraction on its own. Bridgespotters passing through this area would likely skip Chester and head for the Menai and Conwy suspension bridges in Wales, which are a short train ride to the west. However, the city does have a few bridges of different styles and ages, situated a short walk from each other, making an enjoyable day trip for some light bridgespotting.

Tourists from outside of England may not be familiar with Chester as a potential tourist attraction. Casual tourists venturing this far from London are probably going to Liverpool, about 20 miles away, or Manchester, about 40 miles away. Chester, though, is an extremely old city and many of its historic attractions are still in place. The site of the city is a sandstone bluff, bounded on three sides by a bend in the river directly where the river widens into an estuary that once formed a harbor. In AD 70, the Romans built a fortress on top of the bluff to protect the harbor, and also constructed an early bridge across the river. Many of the Roman attractions can still be visited, including a large section of the fortress walls and a Roman amphitheater. William the Conqueror also recognized the strategic advantages of the setting. In 1067, he created the Earldom of Chester, and constructed a castle on top of the remains of the Roman fortress. The castle has been reconstructed many times, with the current castle buildings dating from between 1788 and 1822. The Normans also improved the harbor, including the construction of a weir across the river in 1092 to manage water levels.

The historic attractions of the city are mostly located on or near the river, starting at the Old Port on the west and ending at The Groves, a riverside park and promenade developed in the early 1700s, on the east. The Old Port and The Groves are connected by the Riverside Promenade Trail, which is a two-mile-long trail passing under or across four historic bridges. A detailed, large-scale exhibition plaque is displayed along the promenade at the northeastern end of the Grosvenor Bridge. This plaque shows a map of Chester, with a focus on the tourist and historical sites that can be seen along the Riverside Promenade, and includes photographs and narrative descriptions of all four bridges. A depiction of the same plaque can be found on the West Cheshire tourist website, and a quick review before starting will make your walk more enjoyable.

On the western end of the promenade, at the Old Port, is the railway bridge that was constructed in the 1840s to connect Chester to Holyhead, directly across the Irish Sea from Dublin. The original railway bridge, opened in 1846, was constructed of a cast-iron truss. Within six months, the cast-iron bridge collapsed under the weight of a passing train, killing five people, and initiating investigations into the structural stability of cast-iron when placed under tension as opposed to compression. This incident was one of the first major railway disasters to be investigated in Britain. The current bridge, which is not walkable, is a wrought-iron replacement. On the eastern side of the railway bridge is the Roodee, which is the oldest horse racing course in England, dating from 1540.

East of the Roodee is the Grosvenor Bridge, which was officially opened in 1832 by Princess Victoria, then 13 years old and who was not to become Queen Victoria for another five years. The stonework on the sides of the Grosvenor Bridge can be inspected from the promenade. The bridge crosses the Dee on a single stone arch that was, at 200 feet long, the widest single stone arch in the world when it was constructed. The bridge is constructed of sandstone blocks of colors ranging from beige to light red, giving the bridge a pink hue when viewed from a distance. The arch is anchored on each end by an enormous stone buttress, and the facing of both the buttresses and the spandrel are decorated by stones set in various depths of relief. The buttresses have large open niches that look as if they once housed statues, and which are topped by a series of columns and a pediment. The triangular shape of the closed spandrel is outlined with reddish, horizontal stones set in three depths of relief, and the arch ring is outlined in lighter-colored stone set parallel to the curve of the arch.

The bridge carries two lanes of traffic and has sidewalks on each side. The sidewalks are extremely narrow, barely wide enough for two people to pass each other, with high-speed traffic just a few feet away. The light red sandstone is used for the parapet, and the buttresses and the center of the arch are topped with magnificent, multi-armed iron lampposts. The sidewalk widens slightly at the buttresses, providing a place to view the scenery and read the engraved historical plaque.

Walking further to the east along the promenade, the first glimpse of the Old Dee Bridge comes as a bit of a shock because it is so incongruous with the surrounding architecture. The architectural style of the Grosvenor Bridge is Georgian, with ornate flourishes, and, although it is almost 200 years old, it is clean and in excellent condition. Similarly, all of the buildings along the river range from Victorian to modern, using beige to gray-colored stone.

In contrast to these clean, decorative, light-colored structures, the medieval Old Dee Bridge is deep red in color and looks ancient. It has a heavily weathered appearance, not in the sense of being neglected, but earned from centuries of honorable service. Bridges have crossed at this location since the Romans built the city walls, and the current bridge was constructed in 1387, making it more than 630 years old. The weathering of the red sandstone blocks has caused the individual blocks to stand out in relief, and also highlights the cross-bedding in the sandstone.

When approaching the Old Dee Bridge on the promenade from Grosvenor Bridge to the west, it is difficult to see, photograph, or investigate it, because parts of it are obstructed by overgrown vegetation between the promenade and the river, and by two small structures situated directly at the northern end of the bridge.

The structure closest to the bridge is a hydroelectric power station constructed in 1913. The structure blocks your ability to see the two northernmost arches of the old bridge, but it was constructed of the same deep red sandstone as the bridge itself. The name and date of the structure are carved in decorative letters into the sandstone wall along the promenade, reading "Chester Hydro-Electric Power Station A.D. MCMXIII." After the power station ceased being used in the 1940s the larger building, which is a water pumping station, was added to the complex and blocks views of the bridge from the promenade. The building has similar decorative letters carved into the sandstone, reading "W.G.W.B. MCMLII."

When viewed from the west side of the bridge, you can see how water is supplied to these structures. The river is crossed by a long weir, constructed by the Normans in 1092, which funneled water to mills for hundreds of years before the mills were removed and replaced by the hydroelectric station.

Before turning right to cross the bridge, the large, ornate Georgian structure on your left is the Bridgegate. Chester is situated on the boundary between England and Wales, and the roadway passing through the original medieval Bridgegate and across the bridge served as the route for medieval kings to conquer and control northern Wales. In the eighteenth century, the medieval gate became too narrow for the increasing traffic. It was torn down and replaced by the current Bridgegate in 1782. Turning left and passing through the Bridgegate leads into the walled section of the city, including the castle and the cathedral.

The Old Dee Bridge only carries one lane of traffic, using traffic lights to allow northbound and southbound traffic to alternate. The width of the bridge was expanded in 1826 to add the sidewalk, which is only on the eastern side of the bridge. The western side has the original stone parapet directly adjacent to the traffic lane, while the eastern side has the sidewalk bounded by an open, black steel railing. This allows crossers to have a good view of the river and riverside developments to the east. These include the weir, gardens, and pleasure boat docks of The Groves, and, about a half-mile distant, the northern end of the Queens Park Suspension Bridge.

On the southern end of the Old Dee Bridge, there is a much better view of the strikingly red structure from a park known as Edgar's Field, thought to have been the site of the palace for King Edgar in AD 973. From that vantage point, you can see the other five of the bridge's seven arches. The arches are constructed of the local red sandstone and are of varying sizes and shapes, with the two southernmost arches being wide and round and the three central arches being narrower and pointed. The bridge is not high, only about 20 feet above river level, and the river is not wide, so it would not seem that the bridge is visually prominent. However, the deep red color and highlights created by centuries of weathering, contrasted against the newer, lighter-colored buildings, make the bridge very distinctive.

The original Queens Park Suspension Bridge was constructed in 1852 to connect the new residential suburb of Queens Park, south of the river, to The Groves and, through that, into the city center on the north. The bridge was found to be unsafe and was replaced with a new pedestrian-only suspension bridge, in 1923.

As discussed with respect to other small-scale suspension bridges such as Waco, South Portland Street in Glasgow, and the bridges of Inverness, small-scale suspension bridges are appealing because they look like cute miniature versions of better known suspension bridges. The Queens Park Suspension Bridge is similar, except it has a twist that makes it even more appealing than those other bridges. The suspension towers of the bridge are a riot of decorative steel shapes and arrangements, applied decorations such as brightly colored coats of arms, and towers topped with golden orbs.

The entrances to the bridge pass through arch-shaped portals that provide bracing to the open-lattice suspension towers. The corners of portals such as this are commonly used for the placement of geometric decorative shapes, and those are present at the Queens Park Suspension Bridge. The center of each of these corner panels is filled with a brightly colored coat of arms, cast in lead, set within a wreath, and listing the names and dates of rule of seven of the Earls of Chester from 1070 to 1231. The wreaths are brightly painted in green and red, with the names and dates provided in raised lettering painted in gold. The coat of arms itself is in the form of a shield, topped with a crown. In each case, the crown is painted in bright gold. The shields vary, with some displaying a rampant lion, others displaying a wolf (for Hugh Lupus, of course), and still others displaying sheaves of wheat. All of the shields are brightly painted in deep gold, red, and/or blue. Several other panels on the portals and the sides of the suspension towers display similar brightly colored cast-lead decorations. Although the decorations were originally applied more than 100 years ago, they were restored in 2013. The bridge structure itself is painted gray, making the brightly-painted decorations stand out.

Escutcheon Commemorating One of the Earls of Chester, Queens Park Suspension Bridge, Chester, England

To visitors not educated in the extensive history of Chester, the coats of arms decorations are somewhat confusing. With the dates of the earldoms being so prominently displayed, it is not clear why a bridge constructed in 1923 is celebrating earls who ruled in the eleventh through thirteenth centuries. Some research shows that the earldom was created by William the Conqueror in 1070, as part of his doling out English lands to his Norman supporters. Being remote from London, the Earls of Chester ruled relatively independently from the monarch, making Chester a powerful city governing a large area. However, the title was transferred directly to the monarch in 1237 and then after 1377 was joined with the title of Prince of Wales, where it remains today. As the holders of the title no longer lived anywhere near Chester, the town lost its powerful status. The city has not forgotten, though, and still celebrates the independence of the Earls on a bridge constructed more than 700 years later.

Also worth mentioning, because of its proximity to Chester, is the stunning Aldford Iron Bridge situated about four miles south of the Old Dee Bridge. Constructed in 1824, the Aldford Iron Bridge consists of a single iron arch and carries a regional hiking path across the river. It is located on the grounds of Eaton Hall, the country home of the Duke of Westminster, and is therefore on private property. In addition, it is not easily reachable by walking because it is approximately four miles from the city center in Chester. The Eaton Hall website states that the bridge can be accessed on one of the four Open Days each year, when the public can visit the gardens. It can also be accessed on foot by taking the footpath along the western bank of the river from the village of Aldford. Before trying to visit, contact the Tourist Information Office in Chester to verify that the bridge is accessible and to identify bus, car, or walking routes to Aldford.

Why go to this extra trouble to see another bridge that is not technically within touring distance? Before going to Chester, perform web searches for the bridge and decide for yourself. The bridge is the perfect example of how cast-iron can be sculpted into intricate geometric shapes that are strong enough to support the arch of an iron bridge. The completely open spandrel is composed of quatrefoils, painted bright white, and set within a diamond pattern painted turquoise blue. This is one of the most beautiful bridges you will ever see, so is worth going to some extra effort to see it if you happen to be in Chester.

THREE RIVERS BRIDGE TOUR, PITTSBURGH

Philadelphia and San Francisco each have a large walkable suspension bridge dating from the early part of the twentieth century, but only one, and they are the most common type of single-span, steel-cable suspension bridge. Chicago, London, and Paris each have lots of bridges, but, except for Tower Bridge in London, these are all low-profile, small-scale bridges, and they are not visually prominent. Lots of cities have one or two historic bridges, or a couple bridges of interesting engineering design. However, only one city has a large number of old, large-scale walkable suspension bridges, most of them of unusual construction, and that city is Pittsburgh. Almost all of them are historic, dating from the 1880s to the 1930s.

Pittsburgh is defined by its rivers—the Allegheny on the north and the Monongahela on the south, converging to form the Ohio. From the downtown area there are at least seven historic bridges that can be walked over the Allegheny to the North Shore neighborhood, four that can be walked over the Monongahela from the south side of downtown, and two more over the Ohio west of downtown. Some of the bridges are not within walking distance of each other, so you would need to drive and park at several individual bridges to hit them all in one day. However, there are a group of bridges clustered near the western end of downtown that can be packaged into a great couple hours of bridge walking.

The central focus of this cluster is known as the Three Sisters—three identical suspension bridges dating from the late 1920s that cross from downtown to North Shore. These bridges each have two names, one for the street it carries, and one as a dedication to a famous former Pittsburgh resident. From west to east, these are the Roberto Clemente Bridge carrying Sixth Street, the Andy Warhol Bridge carrying Seventh Street, and the Rachel Carson Bridge carrying Ninth Street. As may be guessed from these street names, the three bridges are all within a few city blocks of each other. Since they are all large, visually prominent bridges, the sight of three perfectly identical bridges right next to each other is highly unusual.

The bridges were all built in the same timeframe. The Warhol Bridge was first, dating from 1925-26. The Carson Bridge opened in 1927, and the Clemente Bridge was built in 1928. Each bridge is about 1,000 feet long, and about 40 feet high over the river. Each has sidewalks on either side, outside of the support structure. The bridges connect directly into the street system in downtown Pittsburgh, so all have terrific views of the downtown skyline on their south ends.

None of the bridges is elaborately decorated, but none of them is plain, either. Instead, each has a few features that make them appear clean and understated. The bridges display a deliberate theme amongst almost all Pittsburgh bridges in that they are painted bright yellow. The railings are yellow steel-mesh plates between plain yellow posts. The lampposts are modern and spare, with nicely tended flower baskets on each. The bridges are covered with a variety of dedication and historical plaques, including large bronze reliefs dating from the 1920s, and plaques documenting aesthetic, historical preservation, and civil engineering awards.

The bridges are all suspension bridges with two prominent towers sitting on stone piers in the middle of the Allegheny River. However, instead of being suspended with cables, as we typically think of suspension bridges, the decks are suspended by steel eyebars. An eyebar is a flat, elongated steel plate with a hole in each end, not unlike the box wrenches hanging on the pegboard above your garage workbench. The main suspension structure strung between the towers is constructed of what are called eyebar chains. Each link is about 20 feet long and composed of eight side-by-side eyebars, which are each about two inches thick. The eyebars in each link are separated by gaps of two inches so that they mesh with the eyebars in the next link on each end. At the connections, the holes in the eight eyebars from one link are aligned with the holes in the eight eyebars from the adjacent link. A large bolt, connected with giant washers and nuts, runs through the holes and holds the eyebars together. From each of the connections, another eyebar on each side descends vertically to support the deck. The entire structure is reminiscent of how metal frame pieces are held together on a child's erector set, making the bridges look like gigantic, oversized toys.

The Three Sisters bridges are nicely integrated into the city's riverwalk system along both banks of the Allegheny. All three bridges connect to the street system at either end, and then have stairs or, in the case of Warhol, a ramp, connecting street level to river level. The riverwalk is on the north bank and extends for miles from the western tip of downtown out past several other bridges, passing under each of the Three Sisters, a railroad and interstate highway bridge, the Sixteenth Street Bridge, and then connecting into the city's bike trail system.

The Three Sisters bridges are just a short walk from Fort Duquesne Bridge, which leads into Point State Park at the confluence of the rivers that make up the Ohio River. It is not obvious that Fort Duquesne is a walkable bridge because the sidewalk is not visible from the Three Sisters area, and the northern approach to the bridge is a complex, multi-leveled mess of elevated on and off ramps that do not look pedestrian friendly. It is walkable, though. The riverwalk passes between the ballpark and the river, past the Pennsylvania Korean Veterans Memorial, and to a system of stairs and ramps from the parking lot directly beneath the bridge and up to its sidewalk, which is on its western side.

The Fort Duquesne Bridge is double-decked, with its roadways supported by steel cables from a steel arch superstructure. The bridge is not historic, having been opened in 1969, but it is structurally interesting and serves as an important pedestrian connection between the football and baseball stadiums on the North Shore and history-rich Point State Park at the western tip of downtown. The bridge provides a great elevated view of the state park, the confluence of rivers to form the Ohio River, the football stadium, and the Fort Pitt and West End bridges to the west. Like the Three Sisters, the Fort Duquesne, Fort Pitt, and West End bridges are all painted bright yellow, which is clearly a deliberate unifying theme meant to evoke the Golden Triangle, which is the local nickname for downtown Pittsburgh.

At the southern end of Fort Duquesne Bridge, the sidewalk follows a ramp down into Point State Park, which is located at what is known as the Forks of the Ohio, a designated Historic National Landmark. Point State Park was originally the site of Fort Duquesne, built in 1754, and of which only the outlines remain. After its destruction in the French and Indian Wars, it was replaced by Fort Pitt, some parts of which still stand and can be visited. Most of the park is occupied by lawns, a prominent promenade around the riverfront, and a large fountain at the western tip. Fort Duquesne Bridge continues as an elevated roadway across the park and connects directly into the Fort Pitt Bridge, which crosses the Monongahela. The Fort Pitt Bridge is of similar construction to Fort Duquesne, creating a unified appearance, but it is not walkable. The elevated roadway between the two bridges creates a substantial separation between

Point State Park and the downtown skyscrapers. A walkway underneath the highway connects the two, but the highway masks downtown such that the park seems quiet and isolated.

On the southern side of downtown is the Smithfield Street Bridge. This bridge is located about a half-mile walk up the Monongahela River from Point State Park and can be walked in a single large bridge tour with the Three Sisters and Fort Duquesne bridges. However, it is a much different bridge type with a different history, and makes an important bridge walk on its own.

Pittsburgh was an important location in the development of early technology for large-scale suspension bridges, and all of today's Pittsburgh bridges, as historic as they are, are replacements of even earlier bridges. The first bridges in Pittsburgh, one at the location of the current Smithfield Street Bridge over the Monongahela and another at the location of the current Clemente Bridge over the Allegheny, were wooden truss bridges constructed in 1818 and 1819. The Monongahela Bridge was destroyed in the Great Fire of Pittsburgh in 1845 and was reported to have burned in less than 15 minutes. Bridge engineer John Roebling then constructed a wire rope suspension bridge at the Smithfield Street location to replace the destroyed bridge in 1846 and another at the Sixth Street location in 1856. In 1883, Gustav Lindenthal designed the Smithfield Street Bridge as a replacement for the Roebling bridge at that location. At about the same time, Lindenthal also designed a suspension bridge at Seventh Street. In the 1920s, the Sixth Street (now Roberto Clemente) and Seventh Street (now Andy Warhol) bridges were constructed as replacements for the earlier Roebling and Lindenthal bridges. The Ninth Street (now Rachel Carson) Bridge was also constructed at the same time. However, the 1883 Lindenthal bridge at Smithfield Street was not replaced, and it is now the oldest of the existing Pittsburgh bridges.

The Smithfield Street Bridge is a lenticular truss bridge, which uses a steel arch above the deck as the main support. Instead of using cables to support the deck, an eyebar chain extends from one end of the arch to the other. The arches being convex upward, and the eyebar chains being convex downward, result in the bridge having a lenticular profile. The deck then connects to the eyebar chains by vertical steel girders. The superstructure of the Smithfield Street Bridge is constructed of three side-by-side lenticular trusses, one on each side of the bridge and one in the middle between the lanes of the roadway. Each truss is anchored on its end by a single, ornamental cast-iron tower, and each is connected to the adjacent one by a complex maze of girders.

The main structure of arches and eyebar chains are a dark marine blue color, but the two ornamental towers are dutifully painted in Pittsburgh bridge-yellow. In contrast to the simple, undecorated structure of the towers on the Three Sisters, the cast-iron towers on Smithfield Street are riotously decorated with castle-like crenulations, open-sided globe-like orbs, and, for no apparent reason, what appear to be medieval-looking coats of arms alternately sporting griffons and crosses. The juxtaposition of the yellow with dark blue is a nice change from the monotonous yellow of the other Pittsburgh bridges. However, the symbolism of the coats of arms is unclear, and there is a great deal of contrast between the medieval appearance of the towers, the industrial-age appearance of the arch-chain structure, and the glass-sided office towers a few steps away.

Despite, or possibly because of, this unusual appearance, Smithfield Street is the most prominent of the Pittsburgh bridges as far as being a tourist attraction. The southern end of the bridge leads into Station Square, a popular area of shops, restaurants, and bars with a great view of downtown across the Monongahela. While the Fort Duquesne Bridge has no tourists out walking, and the Three Sisters have only a few, the Smithfield Street Bridge is full of tourists strolling, taking pictures, and generally enjoying the bridge itself, as opposed to just using it to get from one side to the other.

If you have a car and are willing to drive and park several times, Pittsburgh has a handful of other bridges that are worth a visit. McKee's Rocks and West End bridges, dating from the early 1930s, cross the Ohio River northwest of downtown and are the largest of the bridges in the area. These are the more industrial areas of Pittsburgh, and the bridges are now rusted, dirty, and generally look run down. However, the structures are interesting, and worth walking. To access these bridges, you will have to drive, wander around the ends of the bridges, and hope to find a parking spot on the street.

Tenth Street Bridge, about a mile west of Smithfield Street on the Monongahela, is what we think of as a "normal" suspension bridge, dutifully painted yellow. Tenth Street will also require you to find on-street parking on either end, a short walk from the bridge. It is also in a more industrial area, so you will find it rusted and dirty, but it must have been beautiful in the 1930s.

A couple miles further east on the Monongahela is the Hot Metal Bridge, a lovely black steel truss bridge named for its former life transporting materials between two parts of a steel mill on either side of the river. The bridge is really two adjacent black steel truss bridges, one dating from the 1880s and the other dating from 1900. The portion of the bridge on the east is a traffic bridge, while that on the west has been modified in recent years to serve as part of the Great Allegheny Passage bike trail system. The southern end of the bridge ends in a newly developed commercial area of apartments, restaurants, and offices, and there is plenty of on-street parking. Alternatively, you can access the Hot Metal Bridge by bike from the trail system in Pittsburgh.

To finish your bridge walking day, there are additional bridges further east on the Allegheny River. Sixteenth Street Bridge, dating from 1922, is only a short walk up the riverwalk from Rachel Carson Bridge, and has lovely decorative stone towers topped with enormous bronze sculptures. The 31st Street and 40th Street bridges, which require a drive of a few miles up the Allegheny, are beautiful, old steel arch bridges. The 40th Street Bridge dates from the 1920s, and is also known as Washington's Crossing Bridge.

CENTRAL PARK BRIDGE TOUR, NEW YORK CITY

Probably the world's largest collection of decorative miniature park bridges is in Central Park, in New York City. However, Central Park is big—very big. The bridges in Central Park are small—very small. Small enough that, unless you go out deliberately to look for them, you might not even know they are there or know that there are dozens of them, how beautifully decorated they are, or in what beautiful settings they are placed.

Before discussing how to find them, here is how *not* to find them. If you drive around the edges of Central Park on Fifth Avenue, or Central Park West, South, or North, you will not see them. If you drive through the park on the four transverse roads (66th, 79th, 86th, or 97th Street), you will not see them. If you visit any of the major tourist sights on the edges of the park, such as the Metropolitan Museum of Art, American Museum of Natural History, or the Delacorte Theater, you will not see them. Finally, if you drive, bike, run, take a carriage ride, or go horseback riding on any of the interior surface roads (West, East, Terrace, or Center Drive), you may see a few. You will cross over them on these roads, but in most cases, you will not even know you are crossing a bridge and, if you do, you will not see any of the important decorative features from the road.

The only way to see these bridges is to set out on foot, onto the hiking paths of the park. This is because everywhere that a hiking path crosses under one of the interior surface roads or over a stream or part of a lake, there is a small, amazing, elaborately decorated bridge, almost all of them dating from the 1860s.

The bridges fall into distinct structural types based on their construction materials, methods, and manner of decoration. The most common type is the decorated stone arch bridges, which are found wherever the interior road system crosses a hiking path. There are 14 of these scattered throughout the park, with the bulk of them concentrated south of the Central Park Lake (referred to by New Yorkers as "The Lake") in the center of the park. These bridges are called Greyshot, Dalehead, Dipway, Green Gap, Greywacke, Winterdale, Driprock, Playmates, Inscope, Willowdell, Trefoil, Glade, Denesmouth, and Springbanks Arches. The decorated stone arches are all the same size and construction type. Most of them cross a hiking path that is only about ten feet wide, they all carry interior surface roads that are about 25 feet wide, and they were all designed to allow passage of a horse and small carriage. As a result, they are each about ten feet high, ten to 20 feet wide, and 30 to 40 feet long. These arches all have a flat deck and, except for a short length of railing that could be mistaken for a guardrail on the side of the road, you would not even know you are crossing a bridge. Because these bridges have low profiles and are located in wooded or lawn areas, the views available when walking over them are limited and not spectacular.

The most important feature of these tiny bridges is that their archways, interiors, and railings are elaborately decorated. The decorations are unique to each bridge and involve different stone types, colors, and textures, mixtures of stone and brick, and intricate stone carving. These are 14 completely unique works of art in stone and brick, each of them about 150 years old. It is not possible to discuss each in detail, but we will hit some of the highlights. There are websites and books dedicated to these Central Park bridges, so you are encouraged to access these if you would like more detail on each stone arch.

Probably the most elaborately decorated of the stone arch bridges is Playmates Arch, located between the Carousel and the Dairy, near the zoo in the southern part of the park. Constructed in 1863, the façade on both sides of the arch, as well as the interior, is constructed of a combination of gray stone, yellow brick, and red brick. The archway itself is outlined in gray stone, each block shaped smoothly around its edges but left rough-textured in the center. The facing between the arch and the abutments is made of brick in alternating horizontal red and yellow bands. The yellow bricks are of a larger size, creating wide yellow bands. The red bricks are smaller and set into the façade diagonally, so they present a textured surface. The façade is then topped by a horizontal band of the gray stone and a wrought-iron railing with a geometric design. If you wish to see this bridge on film, Zero Mostel and Gene Wilder emerge from it while walking around Central Park in *The Producers*.

Greywacke Arch, also dating from 1863, is situated in one of the more prominent and easily accessible locations in the park. It is located just a few steps away from the southwest corner of the Metropolitan Museum of Art, near the Great Lawn and almost directly under Cleopatra's Needle. The arch is decorated with alternating layers of red and yellow sandstone with carved flourishes, including claw feet at the base of the archway. The railing is composed of carved sandstone posts holding elaborate wrought-iron panels.

Trefoil Arch illustrates how the stone arch bridges were constructed. In photographs and from a distance, the trefoil shape of the archway, which is made of carved red sandstone, is unusual and appealing. However, up close you can see that the distinctive shape is only a surficial façade, and it is not the shape of the arch itself. In addition, it is only trefoil-shaped on the eastern end facing the Conservatory Garden, and it is not similarly shaped on the more heavily trafficked western end near the Bethesda Terrace and the Boathouse. The railing is made of trefoil-shaped arches in black-painted iron. The inside of the arch is the most disappointing of the stone arch bridges. Most of them have, at a minimum, red brick walls and ceiling with geometric patterns inset into the surface. Trefoil Arch has straight, flat red brick walls, and the ceiling is hidden by boring white wooden planks.

In addition to the decorated stone arches carrying the interior road system over the hiking paths, the park has six rustic, undecorated stone bridges. In contrast to the decorated stone arches, the rustic stone bridges are mostly made of a single type of stone, with the blocks having a uniform, rough texture. Although they are simple and undecorated, these are not unattractive bridges by any means. Even gray, unadorned stone blocks can be arranged in graceful arch shapes, and their locations over or near water are especially scenic. In general, the water bodies in the park have lovely views and not only because of the water, but because water means no trees, thus opening up the vista to the buildings facing the park on Central Park South or Central Park West.

Two of the rustic stone arch bridges are in particularly scenic settings. Gapstow Arch, dating from 1896, crosses the Pond in the southeastern corner of the park. The bridge is only about 30 feet long and five feet high over the water and does not lead anywhere. In contrast to the flat decks of the decorated stone arches, the deck of Gapstow is arched, resulting in a quaint appearance. The bridge has views that are among the best in the park. The Pond itself is lovely, and the clearing in the trees opens up a view that includes the Plaza Hotel and other Central Park South buildings only about a quarter-mile away.

The other amazing setting is that of the 1865 Glen Span Arch, which carries West Drive over the Loch, a small stream flowing in a ravine through the North Woods area of the park. The Pool, a small pond at the southern side of the North Woods, spills out into the Loch under a small

MULTIPLE BRIDGE TOURS   189

rustic wood bridge, designated as No. 30. On the opposite side of No. 30, the Loch plummets in a lovely waterfall, about 25 feet high, over a series of bedrock ledges. At the base of the waterfall, the Loch continues through Glen Span Arch, passing under more rustic wood bridges on its way northeast toward a body of water known as Harlem Meer.

The area presents ample opportunities to enjoy the views. From No. 30, the view to the west includes the apartment buildings of the Upper West Side across the Pool. To the northeast, No. 30 overlooks the bedrock ledges and Glen Span Arch. The bedrock ledges are a great place to sit directly next to the waterfall and take in Glen Span Arch. Another option is to take the hiking path over to West Drive to the top of Glen Span Arch. From there, you can enjoy the view of people sitting on the bedrock ledges next to the waterfall in the foreground, No. 30 and the Pool in the middle ground, and the apartment buildings of Central Park West in the background.

Further north on the Loch is Huddlestone Arch, dating from 1866. Huddlestone is unique among the stone bridges in that it is constructed entirely of local boulders from within Central Park. The rocks have not been quarried or shaped but give the impression of having been thrown into what looks like a large, haphazard pile. However, instead of being random, the design is actually ingenious, carrying East Drive over the stream at the base of another nice waterfall.

Aside from four or five rustic wood bridges made out of raw logs, Central Park has only one wooden bridge, constructed in 1860. This is Oak Bridge, also known as Bank Rock Bridge. This is a lovely bridge made out of carved wood pedestals supporting a wood beam deck, and lined with a railing of decorative iron panels held by carved wooden posts. There are beautiful views of the buildings on Central Park South and West across the Lake. Similarly, the bridge is visible from various paths, benches, and bedrock outcrops that surround this northern part of the Lake.

Near Oak Bridge, Balcony Bridge is a stone arch bridge carrying West Drive across a small stream entering the northern end of the Lake. Balcony Bridge was built in 1860, and is distinctive for the ornately geometric designs carved into its stone parapets, and for having small balconies with stone benches at either end of the arch, overlooking the Lake.

Also mixed in are five iron arch bridges dating from the early 1860s. These are probably the greatest collection of decorated cast-iron arch bridges in the United States, and possibly in the world. Each of the bridges is constructed of a single sweeping iron arch and railings, intricately decorated with curlicue designs and geometric patterns, and enhanced by the use of different paint colors to highlight various parts of the structure. Bridges Nos. 24, 27, and 28 all carry hiking paths over the Bridle Trail to access the running trails around the Reservoir in the northern part of Central Park. Bridge No. 24 has a filigree-style floral pattern in white, set against a gray arch and spandrel. A short walk away, Bridge No. 27 has the same color scheme, but with a curlicue vine-and-leaf pattern. Taken to its extreme, the open-spandrel arch of No. 28, also known as the Gothic Arch Bridge, is so convoluted that it is difficult to understand where the structural arch ends and the decoration of the spandrel begins. Pinebank Arch, built in 1861, crosses the end of the Bridle Trail near Columbus Circle in the southernmost part of Central Park. The loveliest location of all, Bow Bridge, spans a narrow neck separating two halves of the Lake. This is an iconic spot in Central Park, with amazing views of the Central Park West apartment buildings over the Lake, and the bridge has been used as a location for many films and television shows set in Central Park.

Gothic Arch Bridge (No. 28) in Central Park, New York City

Last, but certainly not least, the Bethesda Terrace Arcade does not fit easily into any of the other bridge types. It is certainly a bridge in that it is a decorated stone arch structure carrying Terrace Drive over part of the hiking path system, but any similarities to the decorated stone arch bridges end there. Built in 1869, Bethesda Terrace is more similar to the Pont Neuf in Paris, in that the bridge is only part of a larger park/plaza complex. The Arcade acts as a connection between the Mall in the southern part of the park and Bethesda Terrace overlooking the Lake to the north.

The Mall is not just a hiking path, but a wide promenade extending for more than a quarter-mile between the Zoo and the Terrace. Where The Mall meets Terrace Drive, it spreads out into a complex of gardens surrounded by carved sandstone and wrought-iron railings. At the northern end of the Mall, flanked by sandstone columns carved with deep reliefs, stairs lead down to an underpass beneath Terrace Drive. Instead of passing through a single stone arch, the stairs lead through three side-by-side carved sandstone arcades into an enormous subterranean room underneath the road and the Terrace.

The walls of this room are carved sandstone arcades painted with geometric designs, and the floor is red tile set in a pattern with granite. However, the highlight is the gorgeous tiled ceiling. The tiles are geometrically patterned in stunningly bright blue, white, red, and yellow, and each ceiling panel is framed in glazed dark blue and gold-colored trim. The design has a Moorish feel, like the Mezquita in Córdoba. The subterranean space is a popular place for musicians to play for the enormous crowds taking in the view from the Terrace. At the northern end of the large room, a series of seven more carved sandstone arches open out onto the Terrace itself. This area is overrun with more carved sandstone and polished granite decoration, statues, and views of the Lake.

If Central Park had only one bridge instead of more than 30 and that one bridge was Bethesda Terrace Arcade, then this would still be an important tourist bridge for your collection. The Arcade could easily have fit into one of the many different categories of attractions discussed in this book. The tile decorations are unique, as this is the only structure in the world that uses encaustic tiles to decorate the ceiling. The Arcade also satisfies anyone interested in exploring dimly-lit, unexpected interior spaces hidden inside an otherwise boring road bridge. Once you see the interior, you will realize that you have seen it on television and in movies for years, as a symbol of Central Park and the city of New York. The exterior of the Arcade is shown in the movie *27 Dresses*, and the tile-decorated interior has served as the setting for multiple sketches aired on *Saturday Night Live*.

There is no way that a simple bridge-to-bridge route can be suggested, as the park is so large and complex. Because the park is long and narrow, the easiest approach is to start at either the north or the south end and then move toward the other. Even this approach will require you to bounce back and forth repeatedly between Fifth Avenue and Central Park West. Some general observations may permit you to concentrate on the bridges most interesting to you:

- The northern part of the park, north of the 97th Street Transverse, is the location of the North Woods. This is where you will find Glen Span Arch and Huddlestone Arch, as well as the rustic wood bridges associated with the Pool and the Loch.
- Between the 86th Street and 97th Street Transverses is the Reservoir. This is the location of most of the cast-iron arch bridges, Nos. 24, 27, and 28.
- There are only a couple of bridges in the central area between the Metropolitan Museum of Art and the American Museum of Natural History. Greywacke Arch is located near the Metropolitan, and Eaglevale Arch is located across the street from the Museum of Natural History.
- There is a variety of interesting bridges in the area of the Lake, which is between the 79th Street Transverse and Terrace Drive. The area north of the Lake is called the Ramble, and this is where you will find Balcony, Bow, and Oak bridges. In addition, the Bethesda Terrace Arcade is at the southern end of the Lake.
- The area south of Terrace Drive is where most of the decorated stone arch bridges are located. This area also includes the lovely Pinebank Arch near Columbus Circle, and Gapstow Arch near the Plaza Hotel.

There are Central Park maps available that show the bridge locations, and they are highly recommended. A particularly useful one is available at the Metropolitan Museum of Art bookstore. These can be a little pricey, but they will ultimately save you a great deal of time from wandering around lost. This bridge walk is going to hurt your feet and legs—a lot. The good news is that no matter how lost or seemingly far off in the woods you are, you are never more than about a quarter-mile from either Central Park West or Fifth Avenue. At any point you can bail out, walk to one of these streets, hail a cab, and be back at your hotel in a matter of minutes.

Central Park is set in the middle of New York City, probably the most popular tourist city in the United States. As the major recreation spot for its residents, it is likely that a large number of people have stopped to admire one or more of the bridges, but millions more have passed by or crossed them without even noticing. This is because, as accessible as they are, you really need to plan ahead and seek them out. Even then, some will probably elude you, and you cannot plan ahead and seek them out if you do not even know they exist, or how wonderful they are. Now you know. Make sure to set aside a full day for them on your next trip to New York.

WIENFLUSS BRIDGE TOUR, VIENNA

Vienna is an ancient city that has been the major center of commerce, industry, and kingdoms and empires in central Europe for two thousand years. The city was founded on the banks of the Danube, the largest river in Central Europe, with the river forming the eastern wall of the medieval, fortified city. For hundreds of years, the river was critical to the life of the city. It provided a regional transportation route during the time before railroads, trucks, and airplanes, when shipping by river was the commercial lifeline. It was also part of the city's defenses, serving as the eastern barrier to which its medieval walls were linked.

This prominence suggests that, surely, the old city of Vienna, known as the Innere Stadt area within the Ring, must have constructed medieval stone bridges over the Danube. The city's leading role in industrialization of the empire must have led to early iron and steel bridges over the Danube in the nineteenth century. These early bridges may have been destroyed in times of war, but surely they were either reconstructed as originally designed or replaced with massive landmark suspension bridges shortly after. As a great commercial, industrial, and political center, the

Viennese must have done something monumental with their important river, right?

The answer is yes. They did do something monumental with their river. By the middle of the nineteenth century, improvement in railroad and road transportation had reduced the importance of the river in transportation. Improvement in armaments made quaint, old medieval walls ineffective, eliminating the importance of the river for defensive purposes. Meanwhile, the river occasionally flooded, which was inconvenient for residents and businesses in the center of the city. The river was also a public health problem, breeding pestilence in swampy mudflats in heavily populated areas. Finally, the river interfered with the growth of the city to the east, which was needed because expansion to the west was limited by the Vienna Woods and the foothills of the Alps. The river had slowly become more of a liability than an asset. To address this, the Viennese did something monumental with the river—they got rid of it. In the 1870s, the city simply moved the river. They straightened the channels on the eastern side of the floodplain, forcing the river to flow further east of the city. The relocated Danube is there today, about a mile and a half east of the historical city center, where few tourists will ever see it.

This reengineering of the river had a substantial effect on the bridges in Vienna today. As significant a tourist area as central Vienna is today, it does not straddle a major river with important sights on both sides linked by historical, decorated bridges, as in London, Paris, Budapest, and even Chicago. There is no large landmark bridge crossing a beautiful riverfront promenade, serving as a grand entrance into the central tourist area, as in Cologne or Lower Manhattan. In fact, you could easily spend an entire vacation in Vienna and never see a single bridge, but they are there, quite a few of them, and not that far from the central tourist area.

The bridges in Vienna are in three separate areas. The most obvious location, of course, is over the relocated Danube. The river was moved, in part, to allow the city to expand to the east. This expansion occurred, and the central business center of Vienna today, known as the Vienna International Centre (VIC), is located almost two miles east of the historic Innere Stadt.

MULTIPLE BRIDGE TOURS

The skyscrapers of the VIC are similar to the La Defense business center in Paris. Most tourists in the historical center may be completely unaware that a massive downtown area of glass-sided skyscrapers even exists until they climb to the top of a cathedral tower and see it hovering in the distance. An important bridge was built across the Danube to this area in 1872, and it was replaced with a decorative suspension bridge, the Reichsbrücke, in 1936. However, the Reichsbrücke famously collapsed in 1976, and it was replaced by the current modern bridge.

Several other modern bridges cross the Danube, including the Nordbahn Railroad Bridge and the steel-girder Brigittenauer Bridge. These bridges are all walkable and were designed to provide access for pedestrians and bicycles to the Donauinsel, a narrow 13-mile-long island that serves as a city park between the channels of the relocated Danube. Chances are, if you are visiting Vienna as a tourist, your destinations are the churches and imperial sites in the Innere Stadt, not the hiking and biking paths and restaurants in a city park a couple miles away. However, for the more than one million residents of Vienna who go about their lives outside of the touristy Innere Stadt, these modern bridges and the Donauinsel are major contributions to the urban environment. To access these bridges from the Innere Stadt, take the U6 U-Bahn line to Handelskai station at the end of the Nordbahn Bridge (also near Brigittenauer Bridge), or the U1 U-Bahn line to Donauinsel at the Reichsbrücke. Each of the bridges has ramps and stairs from the island up to the pedestrian sidewalks on the bridge.

The second set of bridges cross the Donau Canal, a narrow part of the original channel of the Danube forming the eastern border of the Innere Stadt. The Donau Canal area is interesting because, as a potentially attractive little piece of waterfront only a short walk from the main tourist area, you would expect that it has been developed and maintained to attract tourists. Perhaps it would have attractive landscaping and benches along street-level and canal-level promenades, small but attractively decorated bridges, riverfront restaurants and shops, tour boat docks, and great views of historic buildings. In fact, it has none of these and is actually a bit depressing. There is a canal-level promenade on the western side near the Innere Stadt, but the few attempts made at restaurants or clubs are closed. The buildings lining the canal are not particularly historic or attractive, and the walls, bridges, and stairways along the canal are covered with graffiti. There are bridges every few blocks, but they are mostly modern traffic bridges with sidewalks. The only one that is interesting is the Marien Brücke, which has a small plaza with a large bronze Virgin and Child statue in the middle of the bridge.

The interesting bridges of Vienna are located in an unexpected place, close to the tourist center, yet on the edge of it so that you may not know they are there. This is the Stadtpark, a small urban park forming the southeastern boundary of the Ring. Vienna was not built at a random place on the Danube. It was built at the confluence of the Danube with the Wienfluss, or Vienna River, which flows into the Danube from the Vienna Woods to the southwest of the city. The Wienfluss is little known because it is a small river and, like the Danube, the Viennese largely engineered it out of existence in the 1800s. Unlike the Danube, the Wienfluss was not moved. Because it was small enough, they simply built over it. Most of its length through the city is underground. It finally emerges through an ornate stone structure called the Wienflussportal, or Vienna Rivergate, about a half-mile from the Donau Canal, flows through the Stadtpark, and is crossed by six attractive walkable bridges on its way to the canal.

The Wienflussportal is worth a look while you are here. The final street to cross the Wienfluss in the area where it flows underground is Johannesgasse, at the Stadtpark U-Bahn station. The river flows out from under Johannesgasse through an elaborately decorated stone portal constructed in 1903. The river flows out of the tunnel into a concrete channel that is only about 20 feet wide, with stone walls about 30 feet high on either side of the river. The river itself is unattractive, but the portal is lined with carved and polished stone columns and monumental, open-sided stone pavilions topped with domes. Double-back grand staircases lead down from Johannesgasse and the Stadtpark onto wide promenades, about halfway up the stone walls, on either side of the river. The promenades are lined with stone benches, statuary, blue urns, and attractive light green, Victorian-style lampposts.

The first bridge over the Wienfluss is the Stadtparksteg, a modern, wood-decked pedestrian bridge dating from the 1980s. The supports for the bridge are two high, sweeping steel-girder arches, painted white. The deck is then a flat green steel-girder structure suspended in the middle of the white arches. The central part of the bridge is widened into a plaza to create a small gathering and viewing place in the middle of the river.

The other five bridges over the Wienfluss have structures and decorative elements that are similar to each other, so they appear to have been constructed at about the same time as the Wienflussportal. The structure on four of the bridges is a flat, steel-girder deck supported on each end by being built into the stone walls of the Wienfluss channel. All five bridges are painted the same shade of dark green, and each one has geometric designs applied on the outside of the steel girders of their decks. All five also have open, dark green steel railings with sun motifs in the center of each panel. Kleine Ungarn Brücke and Zollamts Brücke are both pedestrian bridges, while Stuben Brücke, Marxer Brücke, and Radeztky Brücke are small traffic bridges with sidewalks.

The most interesting of the bridges is Zollamts Brücke, which has a steel-girder deck thinner than the other bridges, and is held by a steel-girder arch soaring ten feet over the deck. Zollamts Brücke crosses at an angle over another bridge that carries U-Bahn trains, popping out of the wall on one side of the Wienfluss and then popping back into the other side.

Vienna's lack of bridges in the central tourist area has clearly frustrated potential love padlockers. Vienna is as iconic a tourist destination as Paris, Florence, Cologne, or New York, but it does not have a romantic bridge in its center to satisfy this need. Interestingly, love padlocks have broken out in fits and spurts in random places. In the South Tower of the Stephansdom, the windows in the stairwell have metal grate coverings, and padlocks have been attached on a few of those, near the top of the tower. The largest number of padlocks, maybe a couple dozen of them, is on the Marien Brücke over the Donau Canal. The bridge itself is uninteresting, and not in a romantically scenic setting, but the statue itself is attractive and, more importantly, it is surrounded by a bronze rosevine motif that is the perfect size for the attachment of padlocks. The final location for padlocks is on the Kleine Ungarn Brücke over the Wienfluss. This pretty little pedestrian bridge has an ornate geometric pattern on its railings that contains some components small enough for padlocks. Its location in the Stadtpark, close to the tourist center, is certainly a more romantic location than the canal.

Although neither the Donau Canal nor the Wienfluss are in the middle of the tourist action, they are both on the edge of it, a short walk away. The Wienfluss is lined with several major hotels, so you may easily be walking over these bridges between your hotel and the Innere Stadt.

DELAWARE RIVER BRIDGE TOUR, BUCKS COUNTY, PENNSYLVANIA

In our extensively settled and developed societies in Europe and North America, every stream, river, and harbor, no matter how large or small, has now been bridged multiple times and is therefore a potential subject for a river-focused driving tour of its bridges. Many rivers are dominated by uninteresting mid-twentieth century highway bridges or have few pedestrian-friendly bridges. Many have had all of their old bridges destroyed in floods or war, leaving nothing interesting to see. While other rivers are short and may have a limited number of interesting bridges to visit, there are not enough bridges to constitute much of a tour. This raises the question: Is there one river on which a bridge driving tour is far superior to that available on other rivers? The answer is yes, and that river is the upper Delaware, as it flows between Pennsylvania on its western bank and New York and New Jersey on the east.

To those unfamiliar with the region, the Delaware River may seem an unexpected choice. Most people's idea of the Delaware River is based on their knowledge of Philadelphia, Wilmington, Trenton, and the associated suburbs of these major cities. This region is home to millions of people, and the river is crossed every year by millions more on Interstate 95 and other mega-bridges at the ends of the New Jersey and Pennsylvania Turnpikes. The Delaware River in these areas is crossed by many relatively unattractive, large-scale highway bridges, and these are mostly not interesting targets for a bridge tour. Sure, the Benjamin Franklin Bridge directly in downtown Philadelphia is historically important. Similarly, the Delaware Memorial Bridge has many attractive qualities. However, these areas are on the lower Delaware River, the tidal portion of the river south of Trenton.

Similar to almost all other rivers along the Atlantic and Gulf Coasts of the United States, sea level rise following the most recent glacial period flooded river valleys with sea water, creating lengthy tidal estuaries such as the lower Delaware. At the time these areas were settled, the estuaries were deep enough to support the largest ocean-going ships, and they were also sheltered from storms, forming harbors. Because the harbors were the focus of trade, they became the large population centers of the eastern United States, including Boston, Hartford, New York, Baltimore, and Washington, DC. On the Delaware estuary, these population centers were Philadelphia, Trenton, and Wilmington. Once established based on the appeal of their harbors, these cities were then connected to each other by overland trade routes that became, over the centuries, the paths of major northeast-southwest highways such as US Route 1 and Interstate 95. These overland trade routes then contributed to further settlement of the coastal areas.

Inland of the estuaries, the story was different. The rivers consisted of fresh water flowing over bedrock, and an imaginary line connecting the downstream extent of the rapids and waterfalls on each of the rivers became known as the Fall Line. Settlement did occur inland of the Fall Line, but it was on a much smaller scale because these areas did not support the same high-volume shipping capabilities as the coastal cities. Even though the eastern states from Massachusetts south to Maryland are, mathematically, the most densely populated states in the United States, their populations are far from being evenly distributed. The populations are strongly concentrated along and southeast of the Fall Line. Even in the twenty-first century, once you cross from the coastal areas on the east to the areas northwest of the Fall Line, you almost immediately enter a different world.

The upper Delaware River is the perfect example of this contrast. The Fall Line passes just north of Trenton, which is one of the smaller cities on the Fall Line, but still with a population of about 85,000 people. The length of the upper Delaware River between the confluence of the two branches of the Delaware in Hancock, New York, and Trenton is about 200 miles. On that stretch of river, the largest cities are Easton in Pennsylvania, Philipsburg directly across the river in New Jersey, and Port Jervis,

New York. The combined population of these three largest cities on 200 miles of the upper part of the river is fewer than 50,000. Other than these small cities, every other settlement on the river is nothing more than a village. Many of them quaint and extremely attractive to tourists, but they are still far off the beaten track. A few major highways do pass through the area, hurtling traffic from central and western Pennsylvania toward New York City and New England. These include Interstates 78, 80, and 84. Although all three of these cross the upper Delaware River on modern, large-scale highway bridges, there are no major cities at these crossings. East-west travelers know they are entering a new state, and they might even notice that they are crossing a small river, but there is little reason or opportunity to stop.

The point of this lengthy account is to explain how there came to be such a large number of small, historic, decorated, and unusual bridges in what is generally thought to be the densely populated, over urbanized east coast. Southeast of the Fall Line, the descriptors of densely populated and over urbanized are accurate, and even partly responsible for a dearth of available tourist bridges in that area. However, northwest of the Fall Line less than ten miles north of Trenton, a tour of the bridges on the upper Delaware River is a complete lesson in historic and interesting bridge types. There are more than 20 walkable bridges along almost 200 miles of river, most of them dating from before 1940.

The valley where you will find most of the bridges is stunningly beautiful and rural. This portion of the Delaware River is the longest section of free-flowing river in the eastern United States, with almost no dams or reservoirs. Much of the area is owned and managed by the National Park Service, including the Upper Delaware Scenic and Recreational River between Hancock and Port Jervis, New York, and the Delaware Water Gap National Recreation Area between Port Jervis and Portland-Columbia. There are also multiple state parks encompassing historic canals on both sides of the river, offering former towpaths as lengthy, uninterrupted biking and hiking trails. The southern section of the area, between the Delaware Water Gap and Trenton, is the foothills of the Blue Ridge Mountains. The area near the Delaware Water Gap is the Poconos, and the area north of Port Jervis is the western slopes of the Catskills. Almost the entire length of the river is wooded hills, with the small river flowing through scenic valleys. The shores are often completely undeveloped for miles, and there are a few small, touristy towns, usually clustered around the end of an interesting, old, walkable bridge. Many of the bridges are special for their historical construction, aesthetics, and role in connecting hiking and bike trails on both sides of the river.

There are some common characteristics among the bridges that will provide context for your tour. Allowing the river to remain free-flowing, without dams or reservoirs, is certainly a way to ensure that the area remains rural and picturesque. It also ensures that floods on the river remain uncontrolled. Of the 27 bridges profiled in Frank Dale's *Bridges over the Delaware River, A History of the Crossings*, 18 of them began life as wooden bridges, most of them covered bridges, sometime between 1806 and 1869. All these bridges were systematically destroyed, some by fire, some by rot, but most by flooding, and then were rebuilt, some of them up to six or seven times. Many of the flood events were freshets, an annual spring flood due to a mixture of spring rains and thawing ice. The 1841 event known as the Bridges Freshet destroyed six bridges and damaged the rest. The 1903 Pumpkin Flood destroyed or caused enough damage to require reconstruction of 12 bridges. Back-to-back hurricanes in 1955 destroyed or caused enough damage to require reconstruction of seven bridges, including the last remaining wooden covered bridge at Portland-Columbia.

The rapidity with which these bridges kept getting destroyed and rebuilt makes it difficult to narrate the precise sequence of events at each bridge. When a bridge was destroyed, decisions were made that affected future generations of bridges at the location. In a few cases, the bridge was never replaced. At Portland-Columbia and Lumberville-Raven Rock, what had once been a roadway bridge was replaced with a pedestrian-only bridge. There are situations where the replacement bridge was constructed at the exact same location, and others where the replacement was constructed a short distance upstream or downstream.

Sometimes, only the deck was destroyed, so the next generation bridge consisted of a new superstructure and deck resting on the old piers. Because of differences in strength and weight, the size of stone piers needed to support a wooden bridge is much larger than that needed for an iron, steel, or suspension bridge. As a result, some of the bridges today look weirdly bottom-heavy, with relatively insubstantial steel superstructure and deck sitting on what appear to be massively oversized stone piers.

In other cases, only some of the spans on one side of the river were destroyed, so the bridge was only partially reconstructed. At Uhlerstown-Frenchtown and Lumberville-Raven Rock, a hybrid wooden-steel bridge existed for a number of years, with newer steel spans connected to the remaining wooden spans. In many cases, a bridge is reported to have sustained only minor damage and was repaired, but there is a major gray area between repair and reconstruction that makes it difficult to decide which bridges are "original" and which are not.

As a general rule, most of the wooden bridges on the upper Delaware were eventually replaced with a steel through-truss bridge, the bridge type that dominates the area today. Most of these bridges have a common appearance, consisting of a string of trapezoidal-shaped trusses, painted dark green. These bridges are primarily of two generations and of variable levels of interest. Four of the truss bridges, including the iron Calhoun Street Bridge in downtown Trenton, were constructed between 1884 and 1904 and are certainly attractive historical bridges. The Pond Eddy Bridge, also constructed in 1904, was demolished in 2018, but its replacement is a deliberate replica of the 1904 bridge. The New Hope-Lambertville and Washington Crossing bridges were similar through-truss bridges, both constructed in 1904, but both were damaged in the 1955 flood, requiring substantial reconstructions. Two additional bridges, the 1927 Centre Bridge in Stockton and the 1931 Uhlerstown-Frenchtown Bridge, are similar in appearance to the earlier bridges, with the same trapezoid-shaped trusses with a straight, horizontal top chord.

A later generation of through-truss bridges has a polygonal top chord instead of a horizontal top chord, making each truss appear to be arched. This includes the 1928 Lower Trenton, the 1933 Milford-Upper Black Eddy, the 1936 Hancock, the 1939 Mid-Delaware at Port Jervis, and the 1951 Cochecton-Damascus bridges. Most of these are larger in size than the earlier generation of trapezoid-shaped trusses.

In addition to wooden covered bridges, many of the locations were, at some point, crossed with early suspension bridges. Of the ten locations

MULTIPLE BRIDGE TOURS

that once had suspension bridges, four remain today, and these are some of the highlights of the driving tour. These include Lumberville-Raven Rock, Kellam's (also known as Little Equinunk), Riegelsville, and the Delaware Aqueduct (which was previously discussed in Chapter 2 of *Bridgespotting: Part 1*). Similarly, the Northampton Street Bridge connecting Easton and Philipsburg is an unusual cantilever truss and should be one of the main targets of your tour.

The story of the ownership of the bridges also acts as a summary of the history of the river valley. Almost all of the crossings were originally the locations of privately-owned ferries. The early bridges were then constructed to replace the ferries by a private individual or corporation, under charters from the states on either side of the river. These bridges were often funded by stock sale or by an industry, such as a lumber mill or a coal mine, that needed more economical transportation to markets on the other side of the river. The investors were then paid back from the collection of tolls.

Starting in 1918 and continuing through the early 1930s almost all of the bridges were sold, one after another, to one of the state-operated Joint Commissions for the Elimination of Toll Bridges, one Commission purchasing and operating the bridges between Pennsylvania and New York, and the other purchasing and operating the bridges between Pennsylvania and New Jersey. Today, the successor of the Pennsylvania-New Jersey Commission is the Delaware River Joint Toll Bridge Commission (DRJTBC), which owns 20 bridges. Eight of the bridges, mostly larger highway bridges, are operated as toll bridges, while 12, mostly the small, unique bridges making up this tour, are free to cross.

This ownership story results in a few interesting features that you will see on your tour. First, it is an important part of the history of each bridge, allowing a visitor to understand the reason that each was constructed and tying together the entire settlement history of the valley. The second feature is that the common ownership of the bridges since the 1920s has resulted in a commonality of appearance, which you will see on the tour. All of the walkable bridges owned and operated by the DRJTBC have been rehabilitated within the past 20 years. In addition to structural rehabilitation, each bridge has had a pedestrian sidewalk with decorative black railings installed and each is freshly painted the same appealing shade of dark green. All of them are clean and in impeccably maintained condition. Finally, most have one or both of their ends planted in a park, canal towpath trail, historic inn, or downtown area of a historic village.

Each DRJTBC bridge is staffed throughout the day by security guards housed in a little yellow administrative building at one or both ends of the bridge. Although these could be confused with a tollhouse, these bridges have not collected tolls since the 1920s or 1930s. The bridges are mostly narrow, with one lane each way. Many of them have sharp turns on the roadways leading to and from them, and it is not uncommon for traffic to become jammed and require assistance to keep moving. The security guard is in place to respond to these situations in real time rather than sending someone from a remote office. The security guard also monitors the video feed from security cameras, enforces size limitations on vehicles, and enforces bridge closures in cases of extreme weather.

These are all important functions, but the security guards also probably spend a good deal of their time trying to stop bridgespotters from being run over by cars while taking selfies in the middle of the roadway. It is unclear if taking photos of the bridges is allowed. During visits in support of this project, the author was stopped from taking photos of one bridge by a guard for security reasons. In contrast, most of the guards are eager to discuss their bridge with appreciative visitors, will point out unusual features you may not have otherwise seen, and will not stop you from taking photos. The best plan is to try to catch the attention of the guard and, if he or she is not busy, ask them what you are and are not allowed to do on that particular bridge. Chances are you will learn something new and will make a new friend who is as excited about bridges as you. Although the main objective of DRJTBC is certainly to keep traffic flowing between Pennsylvania and New Jersey, the fact that they do it while protecting their heritage and maximizing tourist interest in their bridges and surrounding communities is a bonus.

Although the description above applies to the entire 200-mile stretch of river between Trenton and Hancock, the driving tour described below will focus on the segment mostly bordering Bucks County, Pennsylvania, between Easton and Trenton. This Bucks County tour comprises nine

MULTIPLE BRIDGE TOURS

important bridges within about 60 miles of river and will probably take a full day on its own, without the northern segment. This does not mean that there are no important bridges to be seen on the 140-mile segment north of Easton to Hancock. There are a few, but they are much more widely separated and are probably better being visited as one-offs.

In general, the best route from bridge to bridge is to stay on the Pennsylvania side of the river. From the Pennsylvania side of the river opposite Trenton, State Route 32 will take you about 40 miles north to Kintnersville, where it connects to PA State Route 11, which continues another 20 miles to Easton. Both routes pass a short distance from each of the bridges and provide scenic views of the river. On the New Jersey side, NJ State Route 29 parallels the river for about 32 miles from Trenton to Frenchtown. However, the route in New Jersey becomes more complicated north of Frenchtown, and you should cross the Uhlerstown-Frenchtown Bridge and complete the tour on the Pennsylvania side.

Starting in Trenton, the first interesting bridge is the Lower Trenton Bridge on the south side of downtown. This is already discussed in some detail in Chapter 4, due to its prominent display of the slogan "Trenton Makes, the World Takes."

On the northern side of downtown approximately one mile north of Lower Trenton Bridge is the Calhoun Street Bridge. This bridge is unusual in that most early bridges in heavily populated downtown areas eventually become too small for the increasing amount of traffic, and they get replaced with newer and less interesting highway bridges. The Calhoun Street Bridge is certainly early, having been constructed in 1884, making it the second oldest bridge remaining on the Delaware River. The only older bridge on the river is the Delaware Aqueduct, which is in a much less populated area.

The Calhoun Street Bridge is about as large as you would expect for an 1884 bridge. It carries one lane of traffic in each direction, is limited to car traffic only, and has a speed limit of 15 miles per hour, which means it is certainly too small to function as a major part of the urban transportation network. The bridge is made of wrought-iron, which is a material more prone to corrosion and brittleness than steel. The era of iron bridges was short-lived because steel, a vastly superior building material, was invented shortly after iron bridges became common. Although preservation of historic bridges is a major movement protecting this bridge today, this has not always been the case during its long life, so it seems like a stroke of luck that the Calhoun Street Bridge escaped demolition and replacement in the name of progress.

However, it did escape and, on top of its historical importance, it is quite charming. The bridge consists of seven wrought-iron through-trusses sitting on stone piers. The bridge is the oldest and longest bridge owned and operated by the DRJTBC, as well as the only one made of iron. The bridge shares the features common to other DRJTBC bridges—the trapezoid-shaped trusses, dark green paint color, yellow administrative building at one end, and a sidewalk for pedestrians that is separated and protected from the traffic lanes. The bridge also has some decorative features not found on most of the other bridges. It has an ornate construction plaque courtesy of the Phoenix Bridge Company and finials capping the corners of each truss. The bridge also offers a good view of downtown Trenton and the golden dome of the New Jersey State Capitol Building from across the river.

Without the history of its location, the Taylorsville-Delaware Bridge, also known as the Washington Crossing Bridge, would be an attractive, interesting bridge to visit as part of the tour, but it is not particularly unique. The bridge is the furthest downstream bridge on the free-flowing upper Delaware, situated about eight miles upstream of the Falls of the Delaware. The bridge can be reached from Trenton by staying on the Pennsylvania side of the river and following PA State Route 32/River Road about ten miles north of the Calhoun Street Bridge.

The history of the bridge location is similar to that of most of the upper Delaware bridges. The location was the site of a private ferry crossing as early as the late 1600s. By 1774, the ferry was being operated by one Samuel McKonkey. He, in turn, sold the ferry to Benjamin Taylor in 1777, and the settlement on the Pennsylvania side of the river became known as Taylorsville. In 1831, the Taylorsville-Delaware Bridge Company was formed and a wooden covered bridge was in place by 1834. The wooden covered bridge was then destroyed in the Bridges Freshet in 1841, reconstructed as a wooden covered bridge, destroyed again in the Pumpkin Flood in 1903, reconstructed as a steel through-truss bridge, and destroyed yet again in the hurricane flood in 1955. That bridge was immediately reconstructed and remains in place today. Similar to Calhoun Street, the bridge is a single lane in each direction, restricted to car traffic, and has a 15 mile-per-hour speed limit, thus limiting its use to a small volume of local traffic and tourists. The bridge has a sidewalk on its south side, offering a view over the wide river. Because this is the farthest downstream location, the bridge is the longest of those on the free-flowing part of the river, consisting of six trapezoid-shaped trusses.

Of course, the primary reason for visiting this location today is to explore the events that occurred here almost 60 years before the first bridge was constructed, during the brief time the ferry was operated by McKonkey. On December 25, 1776, George Washington's Continental Army, having been driven out of New York and New Jersey by the British, desperately needed some sort of a victory to stop the Army from disintegrating due to desertions and expiring enlistments. It was at this location the Army, consisting of about 2,400 soldiers, crossed the river on Christmas night, using the docks of McKonkey's Ferry on both sides of the river. In addition to Washington, the crossers included a young Alexander Hamilton and 18-year-old James Monroe. The Army then defeated Hessian mercenaries in Trenton the next day, December 26. After withdrawing to Pennsylvania, the Continental Army recrossed into New Jersey again a few days later and won a victory over the British at the Battle of Princeton. Neither victory achieved much militarily, but they boosted morale, stopped the disintegration of the Army, and are considered to be the turning points of the Revolutionary War.

Although the bridge was not in place at the time of these events, it today serves to connect state parks on both sides of the river. In Pennsylvania, the Washington Crossing Historic Park, created in 1919, is operated by the Pennsylvania Department of Conservation and Natural Resources and the Friends of Washington Crossing Park, a non-profit partner. Washington Crossing Historic Park includes the original McKonkey's Ferry Inn, built in stages from 1752 to 1790, and several other houses and village buildings dating from the early nineteenth century. In New Jersey, Washington Crossing State Park is operated by the state Department of

Parks and Forestry. Both sides operate visitor centers with museum displays, and have stone monuments marking the spots where the crossing is thought to have taken place. In addition, the parks host a famous reenactment of the crossing of the river every year on Christmas. Although the bridge itself does not take much time to see, it would be unfortunate to miss the other historic sites, so you may end up spending some extra time here.

Of the many tourist attractions in and around Bucks County, the towns of New Hope and, a short walk across the bridge, Lambertville in New Jersey, are among the most popular. Situated about 30 miles north of Philadelphia, both towns are packed with day tripping tourists on summer weekends and during fall leaf-viewing season. Both towns were founded around 1700, and their early history includes supporting a ferry across the river and, eventually, canals and railroads parallel to the river. After these transport systems and any associated industry declined in the mid-twentieth century, the two towns were reinvented in the 1980s as arts-focused tourist destinations. Lambertville is the larger with about 4,000 people compared to New Hope's 2,500. Attractions include quaint downtown areas off each end of the bridge, well-preserved Victorian houses, restaurants, dozens of art galleries and antique shops, nostalgic train excursions, and the world-famous Bucks County Playhouse in New Hope.

Like Washington Crossing about seven miles to the south, the New Hope-Lambertville Bridge, on its own, would be interesting enough to stop at even if it were not in the middle of a major tourist area. The location started life as a ferry crossing, which was replaced with a wooden covered bridge in 1814.

The bridge's experience during the 1841 Bridges Freshet illustrates one of the lesser-known threats to bridges during floods. Flowing water that is high enough to reach the bridge deck can detach the trusses from the piers and carry the deck and trusses downstream. However, even if a bridge is high enough to avoid this calamity, it still may be a target for the detached pieces of its upstream neighbors. In 1841, the water and ice were so high that the locals expected the New Hope-Lambertville Bridge might not survive. In the end, it was not the water that destroyed the bridge. Instead, water and ice upstream detached the Centre Bridge at Stockton from its piers. The truss was floated about four miles downstream, where it scored a direct hit on the New Hope-Lambertville Bridge.

The bridge was reconstructed as a wooden covered bridge and destroyed again in the 1903 Pumpkin Flood. It was then replaced by a steel through-truss bridge. One of the six spans of the 1904 bridge was taken out in the 1955 flood but was quickly replaced, leaving a (mostly) 1904 bridge in place today.

Like many of the other 1904-era bridges in the region, the bridge consists of a series of dark green, trapezoid-shaped trusses, a single sidewalk, a yellow administrative building, and traffic that is limited to cars at 15 miles per hour, one lane each way. The bridge also has a marked difference from the other DRJTBC bridges, which is that the sidewalk is much wider—and for good reason. More than any other bridge on the upper Delaware, this bridge gets a large amount of foot traffic from tourists, which was apparently considered during a 2004 rehabilitation of the bridge. Much like some European tourist centers where there are important attractions on both ends of a bridge, it is unlikely that anyone would visit just to spend time in one town without visiting the other. Both towns are equally appealing, should be considered a single attraction, and a visit without the need to drive from one to the other is made possible by this well-kept bridge with its oversized sidewalk.

Less than four miles north of Lambertville, the Centre Bridge is located in Stockton, New Jersey. The situation of the bridge is similar to that of New Hope-Lambertville, with the historic inn and some touristy shops located just off the end of the bridge. However, Stockton is a village with only a few hundred people, and there is no town on the Pennsylvania end of the bridge, so its tourist industry is on a much smaller scale than New Hope and Lambertville.

The Centre Bridge structure and history are similar to those of New Hope-Lambertville. The bridge is six spans long, with the obligatory yellow administrative building, and a wood plank sidewalk on the south side of the bridge. The location began life as a ferry in about 1700, and the wooden covered bridge was constructed in 1814. The bridge was destroyed in 1841, and reconstructed. Somehow, the bridge managed to survive the 1903 Pumpkin Flood, while most of its neighbors both upstream and downstream were destroyed. The bridge was then struck by lightning and burned in 1923. The remnants were sold to the Joint Commission for the Elimination of Toll Bridges, which constructed the current steel through-truss bridge in 1927. This bridge then survived the 1955 flood unscathed.

One feature present here that is not seen at the other bridges is a large stone monument on either end, with two bronze plaques installed by the Joint Commission in 1927. These plaques describe the entire history of the bridge up to its construction by the Joint Commission. While some of the DRJTBC bridges have an original date plaque that pre-dates the purchase by the Joint Commission, and most of the bridges also have a recent bronze plaque commemorating the rehabilitation of the bridge by the DRJTBC in the early 2000s, this appears to be the only bridge constructed entirely by the Joint Commission.

From Centre Bridge to Lumberville-Raven Rock Bridge, the next bridge located only two miles to the west, it is recommended that you remain on the New Jersey side of the river, on NJ State Route 29. This is because this area presents what is one of the greatest challenges facing a bridge tourist who is trying to see everything before sundown, which is the "bonus bridge." The focus of the tour is supposed to be historic bridges crossing the Delaware River, but about halfway between Centre Bridge and Lumberville-Raven Rock, requiring a detour of less than a half-mile up Federal Trail Road to Raven Rock-Rosemont Road, there is a tiny gem of a bonus bridge that should not be missed. This is the Rosemont-Raven Rock Bridge, crossing narrow Lockatong Creek on one iron through-truss.

One of the unexpected features of the Delaware River bridges is their lack of decoration. They are historic, of unusual construction, have sidewalks, connect to trails, and are often linked to other tourist attractions. However, except for a few date plaques and some finials scattered on the corners of some trusses, the through-truss bridges are spare and utilitarian in appearance. Once you consider how important these bridges were to their local communities at the time they were constructed, the lack of decoration on these bridges seems remarkable.

This is even more reason to make a short side trip to Rosemont-Raven Rock. Although the decoration on this bridge is not overwhelming, by any means, it is more ornate than most other bridges in the region.

Instead of finials on the truss corners, the bridge sports finials on top of every vertical column, all along the top chord of the truss. The bridge also has geometric designs, comprised of interlaced circles, in the corners of the truss over the roadway. Geometric decorations on the top chord over the roadway are common on historic through-truss bridges, but they are found only twice—on Calhoun Street and on the Skinner's Falls-Milanville Bridge—on the upper Delaware River. Finally, the top chord over the roadway displays a lovely ornate plaque presenting the construction date of 1878 and the name of the Lambertville Iron Works, Builders.

Hunterdon County, which owns the Rosemont-Raven Rock Bridge, is clearly aware of, and proud of, its special features. There is a parking lot at one end to accommodate visitors and a large exhibition plaque, placed by the Hunterdon County Cultural Heritage Commission, describing the bridge as one of the earliest uses of Phoenix columns in an iron Pratt through-truss bridge in the United States. Phoenix columns, in which a compound vertical column is created by riveting several curved iron bars together to form a hollow column, were a development that revolutionized iron bridge construction in the United States. Invented in the 1860s, the hollow columns drastically reduced the weight of the iron (and later steel) truss. Only two bridges on the Delaware River, Calhoun Street and Dingman's Ferry, were constructed with Phoenix columns.

Returning to the main tour, the early life of the Lumberville-Raven Rock Bridge is a bit different from that of many other bridges across the Delaware River. There is no record of a ferry at this location, and there has never been any substantial town on either end. Settled in the early 1700s, the village on the Pennsylvania end consisted only of a pair of sawmills, a quarry, a general store, and a few small homes. Like the other locations on the river, the first bridge was a privately-owned, wooden, covered toll bridge. However, this bridge was not constructed until 1856, making it one of the latest locations in the region to be bridged. The bridge was damaged by floods and rebuilt a couple times but remained mostly in its original condition until 1944. At that time, inspection revealed that the wooden spans had been deteriorating and the bridge was no longer safe. At most Delaware River locations where this had occurred, the bridges were immediately replaced with new steel through-truss bridges. The situation at Lumberville was a little different. First, the incident occurred during World War II, a time when steel for reconstruction of bridges was not available. Second, Lumberville had never grown into a substantial town and by 1944 the quarry and sawmills were long gone. With the large Centre Bridge at Stockton having been built just two miles away in 1927, a new traffic bridge at Lumberville was simply not needed.

The reason for the construction of the current bridge, a pretty little Roebling and Sons Company suspension footbridge, is not obvious. Today, in the twenty-first century, we see communities building pedestrian bridges and turning historic areas into parks all of the time, which is a good thing. However, we tend to think of this as a recent development and assume earlier generations did not care as much about historic preservation, environmentalism, and recreation as we do. It does not seem to make sense that they were building bridges to support recreational parks and trails in the 1940s. The current Lumberville-Raven Rock Bridge was built for just this purpose. The piers of the original 1856 bridge were still in the river, in fine condition. Therefore, the DRJTBC decided to use the piers to construct a pedestrian bridge linking the parks on either side of the river. It is a good thing they did, because the little bridge is lovely and is now the central focus of the state parks, nationally important trails, and resort areas.

There were historic canals on both sides of the Delaware River in this area. The Delaware Canal on the Pennsylvania side of the river was connected to the Lehigh Navigation System at Easton and operated from 1832 to 1931. After it closed, the land was transferred to the state and the Delaware Canal State Park was established in 1940. Today, the towpath trail on the Pennsylvania side is 60 miles long, beginning near Easton and continuing to Bristol. Congress designated the area as the Delaware and Lehigh National Heritage Corridor in 1988, and the towpath is designated as a National Recreation Trail.

The Delaware and Raritan Canal on the New Jersey side of the river operated from 1834 to 1932. When it ceased being used for shipping it was converted to a water supply canal. The 70-mile-long towpath was designated as the Delaware and Raritan Canal State Park in 1974 and as a National Recreation Trail in 1992.

The Lumberville-Raven Rock Bridge is in the middle of all this. On the New Jersey end the bridge leads to a large parking lot at the visitor center for the Bulls Island Recreation Area of the Delaware and Raritan Canal State Park. On the Pennsylvania end the bridge ends at the front door of an original stone house dating from 1825. Right next door is the Black Bass Inn, which is a beautiful historic inn dating from 1745, and the stone Lumberville General Store.

The bridge serves not only to connect these areas but is also a beautiful aesthetic enhancement to these other features. Because it uses the five stone piers of the original covered bridge, each suspension span is short and the towers are small, about 25 feet high. Each tower holds a decorative light fixture above the deck, and is painted dark green. The suspension cables, vertical supports, and railings are painted a bright white. This contrasts nicely with the green towers and gray stone piers, and makes the bridge stand out in appearance against the earth tones of the surrounding hillsides. Unfortunately, the railing is lined with an unattractive chain-link fence, which detracts from the appeal. On the other hand, the chain-link fence is the perfect size for attaching love padlocks, and the appeal of this bridge to tourists visiting the area is documented by the presence of a few padlocks scattered here and there.

North of Lumberville, there are two more steel through-truss bridges that you may or may not want to see. These are at Uhlerstown-Frenchtown, about ten miles north of Lumberville, and at Milford-Upper Black Eddy, another four miles past Frenchtown. Both follow the same model as Centre Bridge and New Hope-Lambertville. Both were constructed as wooden covered bridges in the 1840s, were damaged and rebuilt in 1903, and were reconstructed as steel through-truss bridges in the early 1930s. The construction type is different, with Uhlerstown-Frenchtown having the flat top chord of the trapezoid-shaped truss, while Milford-Upper Black Eddy has the polygonal top chord. Both have the common features of the DRJTBC bridges: they are well-kept, painted dark green, carry one lane of car traffic in each direction, have a sidewalk with a decorative black railing, and have a small yellow administrative building on the end. In both cases, the bridge leads directly into the downtown area of a small village on the New Jersey end in Frenchtown and Milford, respectively.

While each town has some tourist appeal, neither is as popular as New Hope and Lambertville. Also, neither has a substantial town on the Pennsylvania end. Both are historic, scenic bridges that might attract a few bridge tourists if they were not situated directly in line with the more unusual Lumberville, Riegelsville, and Northampton Street bridges.

Twenty miles north of Lumberville, Riegelsville is a small town with a population of fewer than 1,000. The town is so small that you do not expect, when turning the corner, to be confronted with an unusual, lovingly decorated, well-maintained century-old bridge. Like other bridges on the Delaware, this was the site of an early wooden covered bridge, constructed in 1837. That original bridge was damaged in the 1841 and 1862 floods, but most of the original structure persevered until the 1903 Pumpkin Flood, when it was entirely destroyed. The current bridge was constructed in 1904 to replace the covered bridge. The new bridge is a suspension bridge constructed by the Roebling Company, designer of many of the early suspension bridges in the United States.

At about 1,000 feet wide, the river at Riegelsville is narrow, and the bridge crosses the river on three spans. Therefore, each individual span is not long, and the towers, correspondingly, do not need to be high. As a result, the bridge structure looks bottom-heavy. On large suspension bridges, we are accustomed to seeing giant towers sitting on smaller piers. At Riegelsville, the opposite is true, with cute little oil derrick-shaped towers about 15 feet high sitting on massive white stone piers 30 feet high. The tiny towers straddle the sidewalks on either side of the bridge, seeming to make the sidewalks part of the structure and not an appendage added on to its side. Plaques above the roadway on the suspension towers signify the construction by John A. Roebling's Sons Company of New York, in fancy decorative script. At the eastern end, the carved stone date plaque from the original bridge, showing its date of 1837, has been incorporated into the 1904 anchor block.

An interesting mystery here is why, following the 1903 flood, this bridge alone was reconstructed as a decorative suspension bridge, while most of the other damaged bridges were reconstructed as utilitarian through-truss bridges. Of ten wooden bridges damaged or destroyed in the Pumpkin Flood, one—Milford-Upper Black Eddy—suffered only minor damage and was reconstructed as a wooden covered bridge, and eight more were completely or partially rebuilt as through-truss bridges. Only Riegelsville was replaced with a suspension bridge—and with one uniquely decorative. The town of Riegelsville clearly takes pride in being the location of a lovely Roebling bridge. The western approach to the bridge crosses the remains of the Delaware Canal, the towpath of which has been converted into part of the regional Pennsylvania Highlands Trail Network of hiking and biking trails. Historical plaques along the towpath discuss the history of the canal, the 1837 covered bridge, and the 1904 Roebling bridge. The village is a National Historic District, and the best access to the bridge is to park at the historic Riegelsville Inn, which features the image of the little oil derrick-shaped suspension towers on its sign.

Although Riegelsville is the northernmost bridge in Bucks County, the tour must be extended another nine miles to the north in order to capture what is the most unique and decorative bridge on the Delaware River, and one of the most amazing bridges in the United States. The Northampton Street Bridge connects Easton, Pennsylvania to Philipsburg, New Jersey. Easton is a historic city located at the confluence of the Lehigh River and the Delaware. The Lehigh River is the largest tributary of the upper Delaware and was the transportation route for access to the anthracite coal fields in the nineteenth century, making Easton an important transportation hub for shipping coal between central Pennsylvania and the population and industrial centers in Trenton, Philadelphia, and Wilmington. Northampton Street is the main street in Easton, passing east-west through downtown and then crossing the Delaware River into downtown Philipsburg just upstream of the Lehigh River.

The location of the Northampton Street Bridge was one of the earliest and most durable bridge locations on the entire Delaware River. The Delaware Bridge Company was chartered by the state governments in Pennsylvania and New Jersey to build a bridge at Easton in 1795, making it the earliest charter for a bridge on the river. Actual construction was delayed by flooding and financial problems, so the original Lower Trenton Bridge was completed a few months before the bridge at Easton. However, the Easton bridge, completed in 1806, was just the second covered wooden bridge constructed in the United States. It was apparently well-constructed because this bridge was never destroyed, while neighboring bridges up and down the river were washed away, rebuilt, and washed away again. The original 1806 wooden bridge was replaced in 1896 due to a general increase in traffic and plans to run electric trolleys between Easton and Philipsburg. The Northampton Street Bridge you see today is now more than 120 years old. It is not the oldest remaining bridge on the river, as Kellam's Bridge at Hankins and Calhoun Street Bridge in Trenton date from the 1880s, and the Delaware Aqueduct dates from 1848. Northampton Street is, though, the most interesting and ornate bridge on the Delaware River.

The structure type of the Northampton Street Bridge is not obvious. From the side, it looks like a normal eyebar chain suspension bridge, like the Three Sisters in Pittsburgh. It has two main towers sitting on piers in the middle of the river, the central portion of the superstructure drops through an arc between the towers, and vertical supports between the arc and the flat deck are evenly spaced across the bridge. The bridge type, however, is not suspension but a combination of a cantilever and steel through-truss. The arc is composed of eyebar chains, but the vertical composite girders and diagonal eyebar supports hold the arc up, rather than the other way around.

The surprising and appealing feature of the bridge is the decoration of the towers and lampposts. Eyebar chains and composite girders are decorative wherever you find them because the individual components can be shaped into complex geometric patterns. Added to these are elongated, lattice-like finials on the tops of the towers. On the top chord over the middle of the roadway, a frieze displays gilded allegorical figures of Liberty and Prosperity on either side of a heraldic shield, which sits over a gilded plaque reading "1795-1895." Another gilded plaque on the lower horizontal support shows the significance of these dates, with 1795 being the date of incorporation of the Delaware Bridge Company, and the bridge construction in 1895 marking the centenary of the company. The lampposts are nicely-shaped, frosted-glass globes sitting on decorative black iron bases. The bridge carries two lanes of traffic on a steel mesh deck and has wide sidewalks on both sides, outside of the truss.

There are two major characteristics of older bridges that affect their desirability for supporting recreation and culture within their community.

MULTIPLE BRIDGE TOURS

These are the condition of the bridge and the proximity of the bridge to other prominent community developments. You can have the most interesting and decorative bridge imaginable, but if it is covered with graffiti and the sidewalks are littered with garbage, nobody is going to want to visit, except to drive across the river as quickly as they can. Similarly, it is important that the bridge is integrated into other desirable community neighborhoods and parks. If the ends of your bridge lead into industrial or commercial neighborhoods without direct access to parks, trails, or pedestrian friendly shopping and restaurant areas, then your bridge is unlikely to attract visitors. It is not enough to design and maintain an interesting bridge. You must also integrate that bridge into the community.

Northampton Street Bridge between Easton, Pennsylvania and Philipsburg, New Jersey

At the Northampton Street Bridge, it would have been easy, over more than 120 years, to allow the bridge and its surrounding area to fall into decline. The industries that built Easton and Philipsburg are long gone, and other similar-sized industrial cities with interesting bridges can be depressing to visit. Easton has not allowed this to happen or, if it happened in the past, it has been successfully reversed. Downtown Easton, just a block or two from the bridge, is an attractive and well-maintained shopping and restaurant area. Philipsburg, being much smaller, is a little rougher around the edges, but still has some attractive historic downtown buildings just off the end of the bridge. Most importantly, the entire riverfront in Easton has been converted into a park and integrated into a large hike and bike trail system. The park includes historical plaques, statues, benches, trails, and outdoor performance spaces. The riverwalk and park begin at the Easton-Philipsburg Bridge about a half-mile north of the Northampton Street Bridge, continue underneath its western end, and then proceed another half-mile south to the confluence of the Lehigh River. The park at the confluence has connections to other trails along the Lehigh River. Northampton Street Bridge, rehabilitated in 2002 and freshly painted a pleasant dark green color, is the centerpiece of this redevelopment.

You have now traveled about 60 miles and seen nine historic, unusual, and decorative bridges, some just from a drive-by, but most on foot. This has probably taken most or all of your day. There are fewer bridges, and more widely spaced, north of Easton, and there are still about 140 miles left to the confluence of the east and west branches of the Delaware at Hancock, New York, making it tempting to cut off the tour here. The problem is that, even though there are only a few more bridges to be seen, they are awesome bridges. Therefore, we will abandon the bridge-by-bridge tour here, and instead highlight a few of the treasures that await to the north, which you may want to set aside for another day.

If you are doing the research for a driving tour of Delaware River bridges on your own, the next bridge to the north of Easton may not even appear on your radar. This is the Interstate 80 bridge. It is neither historic, nor of unusual construction or attractive, but it does have one important feature: it crosses the river at the Delaware Water Gap, one of the scenic wonders of the eastern United States. The Water Gap was one of the earliest outdoor recreational destinations in the United States, made popular through a series of paintings by George Inness in the mid to late nineteenth century. The area is well-known to generations of geologists who have knocked off a piece of its strata to take home, and the Water Gap focused the locations of trade routes because it was the only passable gap in the first ridge of the Blue Ridge Mountains.

For obvious reasons, walkable sidewalks are usually not incorporated into the design of major interstate highway bridges. The Delaware Water Gap is an exception for an important reason. This is because a bridge is needed, at some location, to carry the Appalachian Trail across the Delaware River, and the Delaware Water Gap was the only option for many miles in each direction. The sidewalk, adjacent to the southbound lanes, can be accessed from either end of the bridge. On the western end in Pennsylvania, the Appalachian Trail passes through the small touristy town of Delaware Water Gap. You can park in town and walk on city streets, such as Delaware Avenue, toward Interstate 80 on the east side of town. Just before reaching the interstate, near the toll plaza, the Appalachian Trail enters the sidewalk. On the eastern end in New Jersey, you can take the first exit to River Road and then double back about a mile to where River Road passes underneath Interstate 80. You will find a pull off along the road and a ramp that leads up to the sidewalk. Even with the understanding that you are doing a driving tour instead of a hiking tour, and also understanding that there is no quaint, scenic bridge to see here, it is still worth driving over this bridge for the scenery.

Dingman's Ferry Bridge, 25 miles north of the Water Gap, was never purchased by the commission, and is distinguished by its status as one of the last privately-owned toll bridges in the United States. However, there are many more reasons to visit, as attested by the popularity of the bridge and its surroundings as a tourist attraction. Dutch settlements associated with the Old Mine Road, considered one of the oldest continually used roadways in the United States, and the forerunner of US Route 209, began in the seventeenth century. Members of the Dingman family are documented to have settled the site, and began operating a ferry and several mills by 1735. As with many of the other current bridge crossings, the ferry was replaced by a wooden bridge by 1836, beginning a cycle of wooden bridges being constructed, destroyed, and constructed again, with ferries being reestablished in the intervals. The charter for the bridge was purchased from the Dingmans, along with the surrounding land, in 1899, by members of the Perkins family. The current iron through-truss bridge was constructed in 1900 using salvaged iron trusses from an older bridge on the Susquehanna River.

The bridge, along with the adjacent 1803 stone Dingman house, is now owned by the Dingmans Choice and Delaware Bridge Company (DCDBC), which is still in the hands of the descendants of the Perkins family. As a result, the ferry and bridge at this location have been operated by only two small family businesses in the past 300 years. The DCDBC takes great pride in maintaining the structure of the bridge, as well as its appearance, which is prominent among the other historic tourist attractions in the area. The bridge is narrow, barely wide enough for a car to pass in each direction. It has no sidewalks and pedestrians are prohibited, but it still attracts tourists due to its history and picturesque location. There is a large parking lot provided on the Pennsylvania end and attractive signs display the names and dates of the house and the bridge. A quaint feature of the bridge is a small wooden tollhouse on the Pennsylvania end of the bridge that includes an extension of its roof covering both lanes of traffic.

The Delaware Aqueduct, already discussed in detail in Chapter 3 of *Bridgespotting: Part 1*, is approximately 40 miles north of Dingman's Ferry. If your primary interest in the tour is the early history of bridge construction in the United States, then this must be at the top of your list.

The Skinner's Falls-Milanville Bridge is located approximately ten miles north of the Delaware Aqueduct and is most easily reached by continuing on State Route 97, on the New York side of the river. The first bridge at this location, a steel through-truss, opened in 1902, and was almost immediately damaged in a flood in 1904. The current bridge was rebuilt in 1904. There is a large parking lot on the New York end, with a boat ramp. The National Park Service has provided exhibition plaques with a map of the Upper Delaware Scenic and Recreational River, along with information on wildlife, recreational opportunities, and other attractions in the region. Nearby businesses rent inner tubes for leisurely floating down the river.

The bridge itself is a prominent attraction. It consists of two trapezoid-shaped trusses, painted white and nicely maintained, with a wooden deck and decorative ironwork on the top of the truss and along the railings. One attractive feature on the stiffening bar across the roadway is a decorative date plaque, displaying the 1901 date that the Milanville Bridge Company was chartered, rather than the 1902 date when the bridge opened to the public.

Kellam's Bridge, also known as Little Equinunk, is located approximately 13 miles north of Skinners Falls. Kellam's Bridge is one of the four surviving suspension bridges on the upper Delaware. Although old, Kellam's Bridge is not among the most historic bridge locations in the region when compared with its neighbors. As early as the 1850s, there were already 20 or more bridges crossing the upper Delaware, yet there was no bridge at the Kellam's location until 1889. The 20 existing bridges were not just wooden covered bridges but, by 1872, 17 years before Kellam's was built, there were already seven suspension bridges in place. Through a choice of the safest location or proper construction or luck, Kellam's survived the decades of floods, fires, rotting wood, and rusting iron better than any other bridge on the river. Alone among the upper Delaware bridges, Kellam's Bridge did not go through the cycles of destruction and rebuilding that occurred at every other location. Although the original wooden deck has been replaced with a steel grid, the rest of the bridge is relatively original, dating from 1889. This makes it the oldest bridge on the river that is in its mostly original condition, and the only location where no bridges have had to be rebuilt after being destroyed.

While the history of the four surviving suspension bridges on the Delaware is an attraction, it is probably their quaint appearance that is most charming. Because they cross a small river in a sparsely populated region, all four of the suspension bridges are of a relatively small scale. Kellam's is no exception, as it is a single lane wide. This would be a major delay for traffic if the bridge were located in a place where there was actual traffic. In addition, the narrow width of the river, and the fact that the free-flowing river never supported sailing ships, meant that the bridge deck did not need to be high above the river. This, in turn, meant that the towers holding up the suspension cables did not need to be high, resulting in a miniature suspension bridge. Miniature versions of larger bridges are always attractions, just due to the visual novelty.

What is most amazing about this tour of more than 20 interesting bridges in a mostly rural and natural setting is that it is so close to home for millions of people. Even though it is mostly off the beaten track, it is remarkably close for day trippers or weekenders from Philadelphia, most of New Jersey, and even the Baltimore and New York suburbs. While the entire trip cannot be done in a day, it can be done in two, especially if you use the information in this book, and from other sources, to select specific bridges that would be of particular interest.

CHAPTER 10
BRIDGES NOT FOR TOURISTS

BILLBOARD BRIDGES, VARIOUS LOCATIONS

One of the most obvious attractions of bridges is their visual appeal to amateur, professional, and aspiring professional photographers. Bridges, especially those with a high superstructure, are prominent features of our city skylines and viewscapes, even to the point where individual bridges or groups of bridges serve to symbolize the city itself. Many bridges are decorated with sculptures, geometrically-shaped components and railings, and ornamental color schemes. In addition, the structural forms of many bridges serve as beautiful public works of architecture. Bridges are also often found in particularly scenic locations with water views. Because they are recognizable symbols of their locations, many bridges serve as the backgrounds for selfies, allowing the photographer to document their visit and tell the world about it.

Every visitor will have a different reason for photographing a bridge. Most of the tourists will be casual, amateur photographers, taking pictures of anything that seems remotely interesting, to be posted on their social media sites. Others are more serious, with photography being the primary purpose of their visit. These more serious photographers will be trying to capture the bridge at sunrise, sunset, in fog, in shadow, or with a bright blue sky. They may be trying to capture photographs of the bridge silhouetted against the city skyline lit at night, or with the full moon in the background, or in specific rain or snow conditions. Some may seek photographs of the bridge swarmed by tourists, while others may wait for hours to see if they can manage to get a shot of the bridge, for a brief moment, completely unoccupied by people. A few of the more serious bridgespotters will be found scurrying in the shadows underneath the deck of the bridge, attempting to document specific construction details, to be posted on one of the available bridgespotting websites.

With all of these various reasons to photograph a bridge and the different objectives that each photographer may have, there is one common situation that is probably dreaded by almost all of them—the prominent display of advertising on, or in the background of, an important photogenic bridge. Although bridges that are prominent and a highly visible part of the city viewscape attract bridge photographers, this prominence also makes them an irresistible target for advertisers. There is no better way to ruin a good photograph than to have the subject lie hidden beneath a commercial. Even if the advertisement is tasteful and aesthetically done, it has nothing to do with the bridge itself. Following are a few of the more egregious examples.

Brooklyn Bridge is probably one of the most photographed and recognizable bridges in the world. The decorative stonework, double-pointed gothic arch towers, and complex web of supporting cables are instantly recognizable to millions of people. A photograph of almost any part of the bridge, from almost any angle, is both documentation of the photographer's visit to New York City and an appealing work of art. Detailed photographs of the structural components are unusual and interesting. Longer-range photographs of the towers and cables looking east from Manhattan toward Brooklyn are also popular.

There is one view, from one particular angle, that is more important than the others. Almost no bridge photograph, anywhere in the world, is more satisfying than Brooklyn Bridge from the east, silhouetted against the Manhattan skyline. This photograph captures New York City's past, present, and future all in one gorgeous view. It can be taken from the bridge deck itself, from boat tours crossing under the bridge, or from the riverside parks on the Brooklyn side of the East River. However, one item seriously damages this view: the enormous logo of a well-known telecommunications company displayed atop a 32-story office building directly on the Manhattan end of the bridge.

It is almost impossible to take a picture of the Brooklyn Bridge against the Manhattan skyline without this hideous logo dominating the view of the bridge itself. You can spend hours trying to clip the building outside of the view, or somehow have it hidden behind something else, but the resulting pictures are just awkward and contrived. The logo is so perfectly placed to be visible in all photographs of the iconic bridge that no conclusion can be reached other than that its placement was deliberate, for the purpose of ruining the photos of millions of bridge photographers.

There are hundreds of other buildings within this viewscape, and it is likely that every other company on every floor of all these buildings would love to have a similarly prominent advertisement. Somehow, though, none of these other buildings has such a display. It is theoretically possible that these hundreds of other building owners all agreed to restrain themselves for the good of the community. It seems more likely, though, that once the city government saw the damage they had done by approving the first display in 1976, they clamped down and prohibited similar advertisements on later buildings.

Worse than the placement of advertisements in the background is their attachment directly to the bridge structure itself. A bridge superstructure is a steel framework that is not dissimilar to those used for billboards, so its use for advertisements is convenient. Also, the features that allow you to see the cityscape from a bridge, such as elevation above its surroundings and separation from buildings and trees, work in reverse. Not only do they allow people on the bridge to see the city, but they also allow people in the city to see the bridge. The higher and more prominent a bridge, the more it must make advertising executives lose sleep at night, trying to figure out how to get their message up there.

In some cities, a bridge is visually prominent and attractive from almost any angle and distance. Using the Brooklyn Bridge example above, except for the unfortunate placement of an advertisement in its background from one direction, it is quite difficult to take a bad photograph of this bridge from any other angle. Therefore, even though the advertisement ruins the most important camera angle, many other excellent camera angles are unaffected.

In other cities, though, there is one and only one direction and angle that will create the perfect picture. Chapter 3 of *Bridgespotting: Part 1*, discussed how the view of the sides of five bridges in Newcastle-upon-Tyne was so iconic that it had become a symbol, used in tourist advertisements for the city and as the inspiration for musical compositions. The highest bridge in this view, an enormous green arch sitting atop the other four bridges, is the Tyne Bridge. A picture of these bridges from almost any distance and angle is just a picture of some old bridges, but a photograph from the quay on the northern end of the Gateshead Millennium Bridge, directly along the straight line axis through the five older bridges, is magical. So magical, it appears, that the city cannot resist the revenue that is generated by allowing advertisers to despoil the view with gigantic messages, lit at night. During the field visit for this book in 2018, an advertisement for a running event occupied much of the enormous space between the deck and the arch of the Tyne Bridge, ruining the iconic photograph.

Using attractive, prominent bridges as advertising space is so objectionable that the bridgesofdublin.ie website discusses how the beauty of the Ha'penny Bridge, in Dublin, was disrespected by "unsightly advertising" until the 1950s. Therefore, it is a shame that, during a visit in 2014, both sides of this gorgeous bridge, the most important tourist bridge in Dublin, were again covered with a gigantic, unsightly advertising banner. More interesting is the culprit responsible for this advertisement. At the same time the bridgesofdublin.ie website was criticizing the placement of banners on the bridge, it was also advertising itself on a banner displaying the name of the website.

Bridges tarnished by the placement of advertising can technically be resolved by the removal of current advertisements, as well as decisions by city managers to stop leasing the space for this purpose. In general, most of these advertisements are temporary anyway, so removal does not impose additional costs. Municipal governments have the authority to review and approve signage and advertisement, usually within well-defined parameters established to protect the aesthetics of the community. In most cases, though, the city is also the owner of the bridge in question and stands to bring in revenue by allowing private entities to lease these prominent advertising spaces. This means that the entity that is supposed to protect the aesthetics of a community benefits financially from authorizing these activities, creating a potential conflict of interest. It is likely that advertisements are so ubiquitous that the negative impacts on a community's visual aesthetics do not register with most residents. However, advertisements are a major headache for bridge photographers.

MANHATTAN AND WILLIAMSBURG BRIDGES, NEW YORK CITY

Two of the more historically important bridges in the world are Williamsburg and Manhattan bridges, both located within walking distance of the Brooklyn Bridge. Opened in 1903, the Williamsburg Bridge carries Delancey Street across the East River to the Williamsburg neighborhood of Brooklyn. Williamsburg Bridge took over the title of world's longest suspension bridge from the Brooklyn Bridge and held it until 1924. This was also the first bridge in the world to use steel towers. Suspension bridges prior to this, including Wheeling, Roebling, and Brooklyn, have towers built of stone, while Waco's towers are made of brick.

Dating from 1909, only a few years after the Williamsburg Bridge, Manhattan Bridge is located between the other two bridges, much closer to the Brooklyn Bridge. Manhattan Bridge is also a classic suspension bridge with steel towers. Although it did not set any length records, it was the world's third longest suspension span at the time it was built. A historical plaque on the bridge indicates that this is considered the first "modern" suspension bridge in which the towers that hold up the main suspension cables are slim, two-dimensional structures. Earlier suspension bridge towers, whether stone or steel, were almost as thick as they were wide, having a cross-sectional area roughly shaped like a square. You can see this on the Brooklyn and Williamsburg bridges. However, for the Manhattan Bridge, designers understood that the stresses on towers of suspension bridges are almost completely vertical, with no forces pulling to one side more than the other. This means that the towers can be almost flat, as is seen in later suspension bridges such as the Golden Gate and Mackinac.

From a distance, Manhattan Bridge is one of the most attractive bridges in the world. It is a gorgeous, ornate, and historic bridge that dominates the view of the upper Manhattan skyline for tourists walking across the Brooklyn Bridge. In addition, the sidewalk on Manhattan Bridge connects to the same riverfront park on the Brooklyn shoreline as the sidewalk of Brooklyn Bridge, making a four-mile round trip across one bridge and back on the other an enticing walking tour for bridge enthusiasts. Manhattan Bridge was designed with lovely decorative flourishes in metal and stone at the ends of the bridge on top of the anchor towers and suspension towers. The western entrance to the bridge is in what is now Chinatown, at the historically important corner of Canal Street and The Bowery. The bridge entrance at The Bowery was graced with an enormous monumental arch flanked by stone colonnades, all made out of sparkling white granite and elaborately carved with allegorical motifs. Traffic passes through the arch between the wings of the colonnades, as well as around the outside of the colonnades. The plaza formed by the colonnades is accessible but because it is hemmed in by busy traffic lanes, it is not pedestrian friendly, and the only people there are teenaged skateboarders and the occasional bridgespotter.

The mammoth-sized anchor towers on Manhattan Bridge are made of granite blocks. The towers, and the rest of the approach to the bridge on the Brooklyn end, are so large that the area beneath them is its own neighborhood, called DUMBO, an acronym for "Down Under Manhattan Bridge Overpass." The anchor tower is bisected with an arch so large that it shelters an outdoor food court with numerous vendors and picnic tables. On top of the anchor towers the sidewalk spreads out into a small plaza with stone columns and railings forming viewing platforms, all elaborately carved. There is also amazing decoration on the suspension towers, both at the top and at sidewalk level. The steel towers are formed with a pointed arch that mimics the pointed arches on the Brooklyn Bridge, but with only one arch instead of two. The pointed arch is flanked by "X-crossed" panels of steel girders, and the tops of the towers are lined with four gigantic, open steel orbs. The main part of the structure is painted a lovely marine blue and the suspension cables and supports between the two decks are highlighted in white. Where the sidewalk passes the suspension towers there are large bronze plaques with bridge dedications, topped by elaborate iron metalwork caps.

As historically important and, at least in the case of Manhattan Bridge, decorative as these bridges are, they are both disappointing for bridge tourists. On Manhattan Bridge, apparently for safety reasons, the entire length of the sidewalk has been enclosed with a chain-link fence, and steel grates preclude visitors from walking between the columns to the viewing platforms. These measures make it impossible to get a good view of Lower Manhattan and the Brooklyn Bridge, although these views would have been spectacular before the sidewalk was fenced. Similarly, the pedestrian sidewalk on Williamsburg Bridge seems like a later appendage added to the bridge as an afterthought. It consists of a metal cage variously next to, between, above, or below the train and traffic decks. On both bridges, the enclosure of the sidewalk presents major challenges for getting optimal photographs in an area where good views and photographs are a major part of the attraction.

Even more disappointing on both bridges is the overwhelming amount of graffiti. The graffiti is not only on the bridge components and the rooftops crossed by the bridges, but it covers the ornate, 100-year-old bronze plaques honoring Manhattan Bridge's engineers and designers in a manner that repels bridge tourists instead of attracting them.

The issues at Manhattan and Williamsburg bridges are likely beyond redemption. Both will continue to perform their traffic-moving function, retain their historical significance, and continue to attract bridgespotters. In addition, both will, from a distance, continue to be attractive enhancements to the city skyline. However, for pedestrians walking on these bridges, the visual results of neglect will continue to be evident.

The problem is that the bridges are both simply too big for the city to be able to keep up with the proliferation of the graffiti. Any attempt to deal with graffiti in any location is complex. It is not feasible to have security patrols on the sidewalk of a bridge one or two miles long, just to discourage would-be vandals. In an era of tight budgets, with the enormous costs required just for structural maintenance, few municipalities will devote resources to non-structural graffiti removal. Finally, it is not only the graffiti directly on the bridges that repels tourists. Both bridges have lengthy approaches crossing a large swath of residential neighborhoods, and there is even more graffiti on the roofs of the apartment houses than on the bridges. This graffiti falls outside the control of bridge authorities. As a result, a short-term solution to the despoilment of these two beautiful, historic structures does not seem likely.

Both Manhattan and Williamsburg bridges are amazing structures to marvel at from the shore, but both are disappointing and, in fact, a little creepy to walk over. They should be walked anyway for their history and decoration, but be sure to go in with your expectations lowered.

HANOVER STREET BRIDGE, BALTIMORE, MARYLAND

The complex of marshes and harbors that comprise the Middle Branch of the Patapsco River south of Baltimore, Maryland, was crossed in the late 1800s by a series of wooden bridges, and finally by construction of the cement-arch Hanover Street Bridge in 1916. The importance of the bridge was recognized by incorporating substantial architectural decoration, effectively providing a grand entrance into the city of Baltimore for visitors from Annapolis, Washington, and areas further south. A drawing and photographs of the bridge from a 1934 thesis written by John F. Maynard shows the bridge constructed of intricate arches, the drawbridge towers topped with capitals, and the entire structure sparkling white in color, making a prominent statement on the importance and prosperity of Baltimore. However, the bridge has been largely bypassed and forgotten except by a small number of local residents.

The central section of the bridge, marked on its corners by four small concrete structures extending about 15 feet above the bridge deck, is a Rall-type bascule drawbridge, as mentioned on two historical plaques in the middle of the bridge. The drawbridge was operated by motors at each of the four corners under the span and controlled by an operator in the structure on the northeast corner, known as the operating house. The other three structures have a similar outward appearance for symmetry but were not used for operating the drawbridge. Constructed of concrete, the structures each have a door at deck level and windows on an upper floor, and each is topped by a copper light.

That the bridge was so attractively designed is the good news. However, due to the construction of interstate highway approaches to downtown in the 1960s and 1970s, the importance of the bridge in serving as a major traffic artery from the south has long ago withered away. The bridge is still in use, carrying traffic of Hanover Street, also known as Maryland Route 2, from the southern suburb of Brooklyn into Locust Point, and from there into downtown. Although the bridge carries local traffic, it would never be used for traffic from the Annapolis or Washington areas today. Downtown Baltimore is now accessed by three major highways, one from the north (Interstate 83) and two (Interstate 95 and the Baltimore-Washington Parkway) from the southwest. While the Hanover Street Bridge serves to provide access over Middle Branch to Locust Point, a further drive of about two miles through the industrial Locust Point area and then the narrow, congested residential streets of Federal Hill is still needed to reach downtown. The two highways from the south, on the other hand, empty directly into downtown with no need to pass through neighborhoods on surface streets. Even residents of Brooklyn, at the southern end of the bridge, could find it quicker to drive a few miles west to the parkway and be funneled directly into downtown, thus bypassing surface streets in Locust Point and Federal Hill.

The unfortunate end result is that the beauty of the bridge is almost completely unknown to Baltimore residents. The bridge is located about two miles south of downtown and is separated from it by the Inner Harbor and the port facilities of Locust Point. The bridge can be seen vaguely, in the distance to the right, by drivers approaching downtown from the south along the much higher Interstate 395 bridge. Even then, if those drivers are looking around for scenery, their attention is likely to be directed to the downtown skyline on their left rather than the flat, featureless area on their right. Also, the bridge cannot be seen at all from cars leaving downtown to go south or from cars on Interstate 95 or the Baltimore-Washington Parkway.

Worse than being forgotten, this bypassing of the bridge has led, unfortunately, to neglect. The concrete of the intricate arches is flaking, exposing the steel underneath. The sidewalks are littered with debris and garbage. The lovely operating houses at the four corners of the drawbridge, which no longer operates, are locked shut, and the upper windows of some have been broken and replaced by plywood. It is a sad sight for such a beautifully designed bridge that has seen better days. Unless you happen to stop by while riding bike trails in the Baltimore area, you are going to have to make a deliberate trip out of your way to visit this forgotten treasure. Having Mr. Maynard's drawings and pictures from 1934 is a great pleasure because it allows us to see the bridge as it was in its glory days.

THEODORE ROOSEVELT BRIDGE, WASHINGTON, DC

Perhaps the best or, more accurately, worst example of a non-tourist bridge is the Theodore Roosevelt Bridge in Washington DC. Completed in 1964, the Roosevelt Bridge is located close to the Arlington Memorial Bridge, so close that it is a conspicuous part of the scenery as viewed from Arlington. The bridge carries Interstate 66 and is one of only two primary routes carrying commuters from northern Virginia into downtown Washington. In its defense, it does have a pedestrian sidewalk connecting the area known as Foggy Bottom with an urban park on Roosevelt Island, but the sidewalk is on the northern side of the bridge facing away from the monuments of the National Mall. Residents in Foggy Bottom may use the bridge to cross to the island, but they need to walk all the way around to the northwestern tip of the island to access it, and there is nothing on the sidewalk to entice them to stop and enjoy the view. Otherwise, the bridge is not historic, was not constructed with innovative engineering, and has no decorations or plaques.

These issues would not be a problem if the bridge were located in a non-descript industrial or urban setting, but the bridge is, in fact, located in the middle of one of the most scenic locations in a major tourist city. The bridge is highly visible from the monumental areas to the south, which include Arlington Memorial Bridge, the Washington Monument, and Arlington Cemetery. From the north, the bridge is visible from attractions such as the skyscrapers of Rosslyn, the National Cathedral, Georgetown University, the wooded hillsides of the park on Roosevelt Island, the glistening white Kennedy Center for the Performing Arts, and the Watergate Complex. Right in the middle of these prominent landmarks is . . . the Roosevelt Bridge. It is a steel-plate girder bridge—the most unattractive bridge type imaginable. To add insult to injury, the bridge is unkempt, with its white paint peeling from its side, leaving large irregular, rusting patches. The bridge is a visual blot on what would otherwise be an impressive viewscape of the monuments in the nation's capital.

Roosevelt Island is an urban oasis crossed with hiking and running paths. These paths pass over small wooden-plank bridges over creeks, and are lined with benches and plaques discussing the history and ecology of the island. The one thing the island does not have is a spur leading a couple of hundred feet out to the shoreline, which would offer visitors a view over the Potomac River toward the Kennedy Center on the opposite shore. There may have been many reasons for this, including funding limitations and environmental concerns, but another reason may be that the unattractive Roosevelt Bridge crosses the southern tip of the island and effectively hovers over any viewing spots that may have been considered.

Roosevelt Bridge at the Kennedy Center for the
Performing Arts, Washington, DC

The view to the south from the Kennedy Center is similarly dominated by the bridge. Without Roosevelt Bridge, the terrace of the Kennedy Center would overlook Arlington Memorial Bridge, Arlington Cemetery, the Lincoln Memorial, and the Washington Monument. The Roosevelt Bridge does not just detract from this view, it completely blocks it. Again, in defense of the bridge, it was constructed before the Kennedy Center existed. There is no doubt that, if a similar bridge was proposed today, the community outcry would be enormous and the effect on the view from the

Kennedy Center terrace would be the first and foremost objection. Once you have seen what other cities have done to enhance their urban environment with sculptural bridges that have recreational attractions, it is hard to look at the Roosevelt Bridge as anything other than a disappointment.

Correcting the issues presented by the Roosevelt Bridge is technically possible, although not likely in the near future. Eliminating this blot on the landscape would probably require removal of the current bridge and replacing it with a new one. This would open up the location to unlimited possibilities for a tourist bridge. However, any structure proposed for this location would be subject to the restrictions in the Building Height Act of 1910, which limits the height of all architecture in the city to a maximum of 130 feet. In addition, all proposals for new construction in the city are subject to review and approval by the US Commission of Fine Arts.

Imagining the ways in which the location of the bridge could be enhanced by a different bridge requires comparing and contrasting the city's differing approaches to its bridges over the Potomac and the Anacostia Rivers. For well over 100 years, the shoreline and viewscape of the larger Potomac River have been mostly protected, albeit with some unfortunate exceptions, to maintain the vistas of the Capitol dome, monuments of the Mall, and tree-lined parks and trails along the shoreline. Protection of the monumental vistas along the Potomac River has long precluded all but low-profile bridges there. This implies that any replacement bridge would need to be a low-profile, neoclassical-style bridge, similar to Arlington Memorial, which would blend in with the white granite and marble of everything else in sight.

While this new copy of Arlington Memorial Bridge would fit in with the monumental character of the area and would likely be acceptable to regulators, could it really become an important tourist bridge? It would just be a copy of Arlington Memorial Bridge but situated in a less prominent location, so the answer is "probably not." It would no longer be an eyesore, but it would not have any other attractions.

Instead of building a replica that would be concordant yet not special, it is worthwhile to look at recent developments on the District's other river, the Anacostia. A small tributary of the Potomac, the Anacostia River has long been a red headed stepchild where Washington's riverfront is concerned. The Anacostia shoreline is out of view of the monumental areas along the Potomac and was historically lined with industrial and military facilities. The river was famously polluted and passed through what were considered less than desirable neighborhoods. The area existed within the shadows of the dome of the US Capitol building, but in a direction that nobody looked or cared about.

As discussed in Chapter 3, this condition persisted until about 2010, when Nationals Park had been opened and redevelopment of the Anacostia shoreline began. That redevelopment included the first new bridges constructed in the District in almost 50 years, including the 11th Street Bridge and the Frederick Douglass Bridge. Perhaps because this area is out of the sight of the monumental areas along the Potomac, the new development along the Anacostia, including the new bridges, has not been constrained by the overwhelming hand-wringing that would likely be associated with new developments along the Potomac. The designers have been free to consider community-enhancing features such as a modernistic bridge with a prominent superstructure and glass-sided office towers and condos, all of which would probably be considered discordant with the neo-classical monumentality of the Potomac waterfront. The new developments along the Anacostia have not only been approved by the regulators, but they have proved to be enormously successful in terms of the economic redevelopment of a large area of the city.

A bridge similar in design to the modernistic new Frederick Douglass Bridge would look terrific at the Roosevelt Bridge location. Like Frederick Douglass and other new high-profile, cable-stayed bridges, the bridge would be white so that it could be lit in deep colors at night. During the daytime, the white color would blend perfectly with the adjacent Kennedy Center and the granite and marble of all the other structures visible along the waterfront. The arches would partially obscure the view of the Kennedy Center but, on the other hand, the structure would be very open so that the Kennedy Center, Roosevelt Island, and the monuments of the Mall would be visible through the web of cables.

The bridge would also enhance the area's network of bike and hiking trails. The current bridge already crosses the urban park on Roosevelt Island, and the western end of its sidewalk connects to the parking lot there. The Roosevelt Island parking lot serves to connect all kinds of local and regional trails, including the C&O Canal trail and its connections into Montgomery County in Maryland, the hiking trails on the island, and the Mt. Vernon bike trail along 17 scenic miles of the Potomac River. On its eastern end at the Kennedy Center, the sidewalk of the current bridge merges with city sidewalks. With a few approaches and extensions, a wide sidewalk on the new bridge could be connected to other trails near Ohio Drive and could ultimately provide bike and pedestrian access to the Mall not far away.

Where the bridge crosses the southern tip of Roosevelt Island, spiral ramps would descend from bridge level to island level so that hikers and runners would not need to walk all the way around to the northwestern end of the island to access the island trails from the bridge. The hiking paths on the east side of Roosevelt Island would have spurs leading out to a riverfront promenade at the base of the glittering new bridge, overlooking the Kennedy Center. Like the Frederick Douglass, Woodrow Wilson, and so many other recent bridges, there would be expanded sections of the sidewalk with benches, to entice walkers, runners, and bikers to stop and take in the scenery. In addition to historical plaques, there would be a panoramic photo pointing out all of the landmarks that are visible from the spot, including the Capitol dome, Washington Monument, Lincoln Memorial, the Old Post Office, the Air Force Memorial, Arlington Memorial Bridge, and Arlington Cemetery. The only attraction our new replacement bridge would lack would be history, but even that would come with time.

CHESAPEAKE BAY BRIDGE, ANNAPOLIS, MARYLAND (UPDATE)

The Chesapeake Bay Bridge in Maryland was presented as the premier example of a non-tourist bridge in Chapter 10 of *Bridgespotting: Part 1*. When that critique was written in 2021, the Maryland Transportation Authority and Federal Highway Administration were actively seeking public comment on the Tier 1 Bay Crossing Study, which evaluated alternatives for the location of a new crossing of the Chesapeake Bay in order to alleviate traffic congestion on the current bridges. Tier 1 was completed in April 2022, with the unsurprising decision to construct a new crossing within the same corridor as the two existing bridges. Although the nature of this new crossing has not yet been defined, it will almost certainly result in a third bridge being constructed adjacent to the two existing bridges.

The next phase of the process, Tier 2, began in summer 2022, and will select a specific design for that new bridge. Tier 2 is likely to take several years to complete, and will offer additional opportunities for the public to become involved and demand that the new bridge incorporate aesthetics, recreation, and other community-centric features into its design. Hopefully, the decision-makers, with local community input, will recognize the enormous damage that was done to the viewscape 50 years ago by constructing the existing mismatched bridges and will work to correct the situation, or at least strive to not make it worse.

Moving forward, the state of Maryland has three general approaches available. Approach A would be to replicate the process used in the early 1970s, ignore the fact that two bridges already exist, and construct a third bridge that has nothing visually in common with them. There is no question that great effort would be expended to make the third bridge as aesthetically pleasing as possible, as a stand-alone bridge. The problem, though, is that no matter how wonderful the new bridge is, it would still be viewed within the context of the two existing bridges and would never overcome their mismatched styles. This would certainly be the least costly approach and, given that the aesthetics of the area have already been damaged and probably would not be made much worse, may be selected

Approach B would involve consideration of ways to not only have the third bridge fit in to the location, but also possibly correct some of the errors made with the second bridge. One way to do this would be to restore symmetry without making any modifications to the existing bridges. This would involve construction of a third span stylistically matching the northern bridge, but equidistant on the opposite (southern) side of the first bridge. This would result in two identical three-lane bridges with horizontal braces on the towers, and the older two-lane bridge with crossed-X braces in between them. This solution would also eliminate the current practice of reversing the flow of traffic on one of the three lanes on the northern bridge on Fridays—a practice called contraflow, which seems particularly dangerous. Instead, eastbound traffic would flow permanently on the three lanes of the newest bridge, westbound traffic would flow permanently on the three lanes of the northern bridge, and the two lanes of the first bridge would be reversible, but they would be reversible together. This would allow the bridge to reverse two lanes instead of the current one lane and eliminate the need to have contraflow traffic on adjacent lanes of a single bridge.

A variation on Approach B could be modeled after the three mismatched bridges crossing the Firth of Forth at Queensferry, near Edinburgh, Scotland. At both Delaware Memorial and the current Bay Bridge, the second span was constructed perfectly parallel to the first and so close, within a few hundred feet of each other, that viewers are forced to consider them to be "twins." It is this parallelism and close proximity that drives the apparent need for symmetry. At Queensferry, there are three enormous bridges close to each other, and of radically different design types. Although the bridges are neighbors, they cross the Firth at different angles and are not parallel. They are also separated by a distance of about a half-mile apart. Implemented at the Bay Bridge, the parallelism of the two existing bridges cannot be corrected. However, a third bridge could potentially be constructed some distance away and at a different angle, so that it would not be considered, visually, to be a twin (or a triplet?) of the existing bridges. This would allow freedom to construct a completely different style of bridge without needing to consider symmetry. The farther the new bridge is from the existing bridges, the more it will visually stand on its own, and the more its aesthetics can be considered separately without regard to the other two bridges.

Approach C is admittedly and completely disconnected from the reality of budgets and other constraints. However, it is an approach that could be used to develop a world-class, iconic bridge that would not only enhance the aesthetics of this portion of the Chesapeake Bay, but would create a prominent, bridge-centric tourist and recreational attraction. This would require the state of Maryland to rip off the Band-Aid, wipe the slate clean, and start over.

This approach would involve construction of a new bridge, or a matching pair of bridges, that are large enough to accommodate the current and projected future traffic, followed by demolition of the two existing bridges once the new bridge is opened. In fact, this approach has been adopted in resolutions by both Anne Arundel and Queen Anne's counties, which are connected by the bridge. The model would be similar to that used for the Ravenel Bridge in Charleston, which included construction of a large-scale cable-stayed bridge over a nationally significant viewscape, followed by demolition of the obsolete and unattractive Grace and Pearman bridges.

To increase capacity from the currently available five lanes, the new bridge would either be a single eight-lane bridge, or twin matching four-lane bridges. Obviously, by demolishing the two existing bridges, the incorporation of aesthetics into the design of the new bridge would not be constrained by a need to match or be symmetrical to any other man-made structure. The designers would be free to consider only the vistas available in the bay and along its shores. Replacement of the existing bridges by a single, sparkling white, new cable-stayed bridge, or twin cable-stayed bridges, would be lovely. The same approach could be used at the eastern channel crossing, where the mismatched cantilever spans could also be replaced by cable-stayed spans that are designed to match the new cable-stayed spans over the main channel.

EPILOGUE

THE MESSAGE TO BE CONVEYED here in *Bridgespotting: Part 2* is the same as that provided in *Bridgespotting: Part 1*. This is to stress that one of the primary objectives of both books is to provide ideas, supported by specific examples of design types, decorative elements, recreational features, events, and other enhancements from existing bridges that can be used by you, the reader, to make both the old and new bridges in your neighborhood more community-friendly. It is hoped that you will use this information to directly participate in the public engagement activities that your local, state, or federal government is legally required to implement before they spend money or issue permits for bridge projects.

One common mistake made by public commenters on proposed government construction projects, such as bridges, is to simply object to the government's plan without citing specific reasons or offering alternative solutions. However, the detailed information and specific examples discussed in the *Bridgespotting* books and other sources can be used to persuade your fellow community members, resulting in amplification of your comments. Because many of these ideas are relatively low-cost compared to the overall cost of the bridge, it is likely that the decision-makers can be persuaded as well, resulting in a more attractive, recreation-friendly, and community-centric bridge.

Both *Bridgespotting* books have cited the myriad ways in which people visit and use bridges today as tourists or for hobbies or recreation.

EPILOGUE

However, once you have watched people using these bridges, you will begin to see far more than just what is occurring on a bridge today. You will also see into the past, at what your local bridge looked like, and how people used it, tens or hundreds or thousands of years ago. Instead of the flaking concrete and plywood covering the windows of the tender houses on the almost forgotten Hanover Street Bridge, you instead see Model A Fords crossing the glittering white, grand entrance into downtown Baltimore. Almost 200 years of reinforcing concrete and steel supports fall away from Dunlap's Creek Bridge in Brownsville, Pennsylvania, leaving the ornate iron arch being crossed by ladies wearing hoop skirts and carrying parasols. Further west on the National Road, Conestoga wagons slow down to navigate the curves of the S-bridges. Suddenly, the Roman citizens walking across Ponte Fabricio are wearing togas instead of blue jeans.

Even better, using your imagination, you will start to see not how the bridge was used in the past, or how it is used today, but how it can be used, and how it can transform the community, in the future. As documented throughout the *Bridgespotting* books, bridge designers and community leaders are not planning their new bridges solely based on current residential, commercial, and recreational needs. Instead, they are planning the locations, designs, and features of these bridges based on their vision of what the local community can be in the future with a little help from the new bridge.

In Glasgow, Dublin, Newcastle, and dozens of other port cities, you no longer see crumbling, abandoned former docks. Instead, you see clean, glass-sided office towers and brick warehouses reimagined into lofts and connected on both sides of the river by modernistic, sculptural bridges. The land area on the ends of the Kerrey Bridge in Omaha is no longer empty fields but is covered with condos and restaurants, drawn by the modernistic bridge and easy access to miles of recreation trails on both sides of the Missouri River. In southwest Washington, DC, the formerly unattractive and neglected Anacostia Riverfront is alive with music from performances on the reimagined 11th Street Bridge Park.

Further into the future, the nationally important viewscape of the Chesapeake Bay is no longer diminished by a pair of mismatched, unattractive bridges that provide almost no economic or recreational benefit to the local community. Despite there being many different purposes and uses of the Chesapeake Bay Bridge, the vast majority of its traffic is suburban Washingtonians and Baltimoreans driving to the beach. Thus, not only does the unattractive bridge not attract tourists and recreational users to its local area, but any economic development and tourism benefits that are created are distributed in the Washington and Baltimore metro areas, on Maryland's Eastern Shore, and, increasingly, in Delaware. These benefits completely bypass Annapolis and Anne Arundel County, where the bridge is located. It is unfortunate that costs and impacts associated with this bridge rest completely on the residents of Maryland and Anne Arundel County, but largely benefit development in Delaware.

Once the choice was made to demolish the existing bridges, the crossing became a completely blank slate for the consideration of every other tourist bridge enhancement discussed in the *Bridgespotting* books. The new bridge is a large, bright-white cable-stayed bridge, or possibly a matched pair. The state of Maryland followed the lead provided by so many other localities and now brands and markets the new bridge as a stand-alone tourist attraction. The logo for the Maryland Transportation Authority was changed overnight, and the state of Maryland's new commemorative license plates proudly display the new design. Stylized versions of the new design are now logos for local businesses, emblazoned on the sides of their delivery vehicles.

Business at the shorefront restaurants and marinas on Kent Island is brisk, with diners making reservations to get a table near the large plate-glass windows or on the outdoor terraces overlooking the bridge. They arrive early in order to get settled in just before dusk, when the new sculptural bridge is silhouetted against the sunset. New condo developments on the island offer residents views of the bridge, clean and bright in the daytime and lit in deep color at night.

The water beneath the bridge is full of boats of all kinds. Instead of ignoring the industrial-looking bridge as they pass underneath, they slow down to take in the vista. The outer decks of cruise ships calling on the Port of Baltimore only a few miles away are now packed with passengers who do not leave the deck until the bridge is out of sight behind them. Instead

EPILOGUE

of the utilitarian Francis Scott Key Bridge, the front page of the cruise line website now features a photo of the new Chesapeake Bay Bridge.

The bridge carries a bicycle-friendly sidewalk, with benches in the middle of the bay. On the east, the sidewalk connects directly to the existing bike trail network on Kent Island. On the west, the sidewalk connects directly to trails in Sandy Point State Park and, through the new Broadneck Peninsula Trail that is currently under construction, to the existing Baltimore and Annapolis Trail. The Baltimore and Annapolis Trail, in turn, already connects to the enormous network of bike trails in and around Washington and Baltimore.

The name of what was once called Sandy Point State Park is now Sandy Point-Bay Bridge State Park, advertising the association between the park and the stunning bridge that it overlooks. The park visitor center includes displays on the history of the location, including the period when ferries operated, the construction of the original bridge, the addition of a second bridge, and then the rebirth of the area as a bridge-centric tourist area. The park and its website provide a shop where tourists can purchase bridge books (including the *Bridgespotting* books), as well as coffee cups, T-shirts, and refrigerator magnets displaying the image of the new bridge. The Bay Bridge Walk is now an annual event, attended by tens of thousands of Marylanders celebrating this connection between the two parts of the state.

After studying more than 600 tourist bridges over nine years, this is now the future I envision for the Chesapeake Bay whenever I cross the Chesapeake Bay Bridge. The information is out there, on full display at hundreds of other bridges. It has been synthesized and summarized in the *Bridgespotting* books. Now, the challenge is to catch the attention of the decision-makers and bring them to understand how a little extra effort now can pay enormous dividends to the local community in the future.

BRIDGE INDEX

11th Street Bridge (Washington, DC) 235, 241
20 Mile Road Bridge 157
31st Street Bridge (Pittsburgh) 185
40th Street Bridge (Pittsburgh) 185
59th Street Bridge. *See* also Queensboro Bridge
133rd Avenue Bridge 157
Alcántara Bridge 116–118
Aldford Iron Bridge 179
Andy Warhol Bridge 180, 183
Arlington Memorial Bridge 52, 124, 232, 233, 234, 236
Ashtabula County Covered Bridge Festival 5, 67–73
Balcony Bridge 189, 192
Bank Rock Bridge. *See* Oak Bridge
Barrage Vauban 81–85
Bathampton Toll Bridge 172
Bauer Road Bridge 43, 157
Bear Mountain Bridge 142–147
Benetka Road Covered Bridge 73
Benjamin Franklin Bridge 54–58, 146, 198
Bethesda Terrace 188, 190, 191, 192
Boston University Bridge 66
Bow Bridge 190, 192

Bridge at Remagen (Ludendorff Bridge) 60–63
Bridge Between Continents 77–78
Bridge No. 24 190, 192
Bridge No. 27 190, 192
Bridge No. 28. *See* Gothic Arch
Bridge No. 30 189
Bridge of Sighs (Venice) 118–119
Brigittenauer Bridge 195
Brooklyn Bridge 33, 34, 146, 224, 225, 227, 228
Burnside Bridge 58–60
Butt Bridge 168
Caine Road Covered Bridge 71
Calhoun County Historic Bridge Park 43, 155–158
Calhoun Street Bridge 89, 202, 205, 206, 207, 211, 216
Calvin Coolidge Memorial Bridge 90–91
Čechuv Bridge 161, 162
Center Street Bridge. *See* Iowa Women of Achievement Bridge
Central Park Bridge Tour (New York City) 185–193
Centre Bridge 202, 208, 209, 212
Charles Bridge 161, 163
Charles River Bridges 65–67

Charlotte Highway Bridge 156
Cherry Hill Road Bridge 41
Chesapeake Bay Bridge 5, 159, **236–239**, **241–243**
Choate Bridge 26
Cleveland Bridge (Bath) 171, 172
Clifton Suspension Bridge 170
Clyde Arc 36, 102, 104
Cochecton-Damascus Bridge 202
Columbia-Wrightsville Bridge 48–54
Conwy Suspension Bridge 173
Cornish-Windsor Covered Bridge 70
Creek Road Covered Bridge 73
Dalehead Arch 186
Delaware Aqueduct 33, 203, 205, 216, 220
Delaware Memorial Bridge 159, 198, 238
Delaware River Bridge Tour 198–222
Denesmouth Arch 186
Dingman's Ferry Bridge 211, 219
Dipway Arch 186
Doyle Road Covered Bridge 72
Driprock Arch 186
Dumbarton Bridge 96–98
Dundas Aqueduct 78–81, 170
Dunlap's Creek Bridge 241
Eads Bridge 29–33
Eaglevale Arch 192
Easton-Philipsburg Bridge 218
Father Mathew Bridge 165, 166
Fifth Avenue Bridge (Des Moines). *See* Green Bridge (Des Moines)
Fort Duquesne Bridge 182, 183, 184
Forth Railroad Bridge 8–9
Forth Road Bridge 9
Fort Pitt Bridge 182
Four Points Bridge 41, 42
Francis Scott Key Bridge (Baltimore) 243
Francis Scott Key Bridge (Washington, DC) 52, 124
Frankford Avenue Bridge (Philadelphia) 26
Frederick Douglass Bridge 85–87, 235, 236
Frederick Douglass Bridge (demolished 2021) 86
Gale Road Bridge 157
Gapstow Arch 188, 192
Gateshead Millennium Bridge 102–103, 104, 226
George Washington Bridge 145
Giddings Road Covered Bridge 71
Glade Arch 186
Glen Mill Bridge 26
Glen Span Arch 188, 189, 192
Golden Gate Bridge 227
Gothic Arch 190, 192. *See* Central Park Bridge Number 28
Graham Road Covered Bridge 68, 69
Grasbrug 17
Grattan Bridge 166
Gray's Lake Park Bridge 104–105
Green Bridge (Des Moines) 154–155
Green Gap Arch 186
Greig Street Bridge 113, 114, 115
Greyshot Arch 186
Greywacke Arch 186, 187, 192
Grosvenor Bridge 174, 175, 176
Halfpenny Bridge (Bath). *See* Widcombe Footbridge
Hammersmith Bridge 88–89
Hancock Bridge 202
Hanover Street Bridge 52, **230–232**, 241
Ha'penny Bridge 167, 226
Harpersfield Covered Bridge 69, 72
Harvard Bridge 66
Hassenplug Covered Bridge 4, **21–28**
Hells Gate Bridge 128
Higginsville Road South Bridge 44

BRIDGE INDEX

High Trestle Trail Bridge 105–109
Hoofdbrug 17
Hot Metal Bridge 185
Huddlestone Arch 189, 192
Hyde Hall Covered Bridge 4, 21–28
Infirmary Bridge 114
Inscope Arch 186
Interstate 80 Bridge (Delaware Water Gap) 218
Iowa Women of Achievement Bridge 103–104, 154
Iron Bridge 172
Jackson Street Bridge. *See* Green Bridge (Des Moines)
Jacques-Cartier Bridge 128, 132
James Joyce Bridge 165
Jiraskuv Bridge 162
Keeseville Suspension Bridge 45–48
Kellam's Bridge 203, 216, 221
Kenneth F. Burns Bridge 65–67
Kerrey Bridge 241
King's Bridge (Dublin). *See* Sean Heuston Bridge
Kleine Ungarn Brücke 197
Krämerbrücke 73–75
Lanterman's Falls Bridge 112
Lanterman's Falls Covered Bridge 112
Lars Anderson Bridge 66
Legion Bridge 162
Liberty Bridge (Greenville, SC) 99–102
Liffey Bridge Tour (Dublin) 163–169
Little Equinunk Bridge. *See* Kellam's Bridge
London Bridge (Lake Havasu City) 80, 170
Longfellow Bridge 66, **118**
Loopline Bridge 168, 169
Lower Toddsville Road Bridge 43
Lower Trenton Bridge 89–90, 202, 205, 215
Lowry Avenue Bridge 104

Lumberville-Raven Rock Bridge 201, 202, 203, 210, 211, 212, 213, 214
Mackinac Bridge 227
Main Street Bridge (Cooperstown) 5
Main Street Bridge (Greenville, SC) 99
Manesuv Bridge 161
Manhattan Bridge 76, **227–230**
Marienbrücke (Neuschwanstein) 140–42
Marien Brücke (Vienna) 196, 197
Market Street Bridge (Chattanooga) 148, 149, 150, 151
Market Street Bridge (Harrisburg) 52
Market Street Bridge (Wilkes-Barre) 52, 91–93
Martin Luther King Bridge (St. Louis) 32
Marxer Brücke 197
Masemore Road Bridge 38
McKee's Rocks Bridge 184
Mechanicsville Covered Bridge 69, 72, 73
Mellows Bridge 165, 166
Menai Suspension Bridge 173
Mid-Delaware Bridge 202
Middle Road Covered Bridge 68, 72, 73
Milford Swing Bridge 45–48
Milford-Upper Black Eddy Bridge 202, 213, 214
Millennium Bridge (Dublin) 167
Mittlerebrücke 64–65
Monongahela Bridge (destroyed 1845) 183
Navajo Bridge, Arizona 158–160
Ness Bridge 113
Netcher Road Covered Bridge 71, 73
Newburgh-Beacon Bridge 145
New Hope-Lambertville Bridge 202, 208, 209
Newport-Southbank Bridge. *See* Purple People Bridge
Noble's Mill Road Bridge 5, 39, 40, 41

Nordbahn Railroad Bridge 195
Northampton Street Bridge 203, 214, 215, 216, 218
North Parade Road Bridge 171
Nurse Fairchild Memorial Bridge 4
Oak Bridge 189, 192
O'Callaghan-Tillman Bridge 125–128
O'Connell Street Bridge 166, 168
O'Donovan Rossa Bridge 165, 166
Old Dee Bridge 175, 176, 177, 179
Olins Covered Bridge 72, 73
Padlocked Bridges (Paris) 132–35
Palacky Bridge 163
Palladian Bridge 170
Panther Hollow Bridge 93–96
Parapet Bridge 112
Passerelle Debilly 134, 135
Passerelle (Luxembourg) 20
Passerelle Senghor 132, 133, 134
Passerelle Simone de Beauvoir 134, 135
Penobscot Narrows Observatory 159
Pinebank Arch 190, 192
Playmates Arch 186, 187
Poffenberger Road Bridge 42, 157
Pond Eddy Bridge 202
Pont Adolphe 18–21
Pont Alexandre III 135
Pont d'Arcole 135
Pont de l'Alma 135
Pont de l'Archevêché 132, 133, 134
Pont des Arts 132, 133, 134, 135
Pont d'Iena 135
Pont du Stierchen 21
Ponte degli Scalzi 6
Ponte dell'Accademia 6
Ponte della Costituzione 6
Ponte di Rialto 6–8
Ponte Fabricio 241
Ponte Vecchio 73, 82
Pont Fragnée 5
Pont Marie 135

Pont Neuf 134, 191
Pont Notre Dame 135
Ponts Couverts 81–85
Poplar Street Bridge (St. Louis) 31
Portland-Columbia Bridge 201
Public Garden Footbridge 109–110, 111
Pulteney Bridge 73, 82, 170, 171
Pumpkin Run Road Bridge 44
Purple People Bridge (Cincinnati) 152–153
Queensboro Bridge 76–77
Queensferry Crossing Bridge 9, 238
Queens Park Suspension Bridge 177
Rachel Carson Bridge 180, 183, 185
Radeztky Brücke 197
Ravenel Bridge 239
Red Bridge (Des Moines) 103, **154–155**
Reichsbrücke 195
Reichsbrücke (destroyed 1976) 195
Rhine Falls Bridge 136–140
Riegelsville Bridge 203, 214, 215
Rip Van Winkle Bridge 120–122
River Avon Bridge Tour (Bath) 170–173
Riverdale Road Covered Bridge 72, 73
River Dee Bridge Tour (Chester) 173–179
River Ness Bridges 113–115
Riverside Park Drive Bridge 103, **154–155**
River Street Bridge (Boston) 66
Riverview Bridge 69, 71
Roberto Clemente Bridge 180, 183
Roebling Suspension Bridge 33–36, 152, 153, 227
Roman Bridge (Córdoba) 10–13
Romerbrücke 13–14
Root Road Covered Bridge 72, 73
Rory O'More Bridge 164, 165
Rosemont-Raven Rock Bridge 210, 211
Rue Münster Bridge 21
Samuel Beckett Bridge 169
Schenley Bridge 95
Seán Heuston Bridge 164, 165

BRIDGE INDEX

Seán O'Casey Bridge 169
Sherwin Bridge 164, 168
Sint-Michielsbrug 16–18
Sixteenth Street Bridge (Pittsburgh) 181, 185
Skinner's Falls-Milanville Bridge 211, 220
Smithfield Street Bridge 183, 184
Smolen-Gulf Covered Bridge 69, 70
South Denmark Covered Bridge 69
South Portland Street Footbridge 36–37, 177
Southwest First Street Trail Bridge. *See* Riverside Park Drive Bridge
Springbanks Arch 186
Springfield Memorial Bridge 52
Stadtparksteg 196
State Road Covered Bridge 71
St. Martin's Bridge (Toledo, Spain) 117
Stone Arch Bridge (New Hampshire) 5
Stone Bridge (Regensburg) 14–16
Stuben Brücke 197
Swing Bridge (Newcastle-Upon-Tyne) 103
Sydney Gardens Bridges 172, 173
Sydney Harbour Bridge 128–132
Talbot Bridge 168
Tappan Zee Bridge 145
Taylor-Southgate Bridge 35, 153
Taylorsville-Delaware Bridge. *See* Washington Crossing Bridge (near Trenton)
Tenth Street Bridge (Pittsburgh) 185
Theodore Roosevelt Bridge 232–236
Three Rivers Bridge Tour (Pittsburgh) 179–185
Tower Bridge 8, 88, 180

Town Bridge (Bradford-on-Avon) 170
Trefoil Arch 186, 187
Tyne Bridge 128, 226
Uhlerstown-Frenchtown Bridge 202, 205, 213
Valley Drive Suspension Bridge 110–113
Vltava Bridge Tour (Prague) 161–163
Vyšehrad Bridge 161, 163
Waco Suspension Bridge 177, 227
Walnut Street Bridge (Chattanooga) 148–152
Walt Whitman Bridge 54, 56
Washington Crossing Bridge (near Trenton) 202, 206, 207
Washington's Crossing Bridge (Pittsburgh). *See* 40th Street Bridge (Pittsburgh)
Waterloo Bridge 170
Weeks Footbridge 66
Wenceslas Wall 21
West Cornwall Covered Bridge 28–29
West End Bridge 182, 184
Western Avenue Bridge 66
West Liberty Street Bridge 69, 71
Wheeling Suspension Bridge 227
Widcombe Footbridge 170
Wienfluss Bridge Tour (Vienna) 193–198
Wienflussportal 196
Williamsburg Bridge 146, 227–230
Willowdell Arch 186
Windsor Mill Covered Bridge 72, 73
Winterdale Arch 186
Woodrow Wilson Bridge 123–124, 236
Wright's Ferry Bridge 51
Wrought Iron Bridge Company 38–45
York Haven Bridge 39
Zollamts Brücke 197

ABOUT THE AUTHOR

BOB DOVER IS A PROFESSIONAL GEOLOGIST with degrees from Beloit College and the University of North Carolina—Chapel Hill, and additional graduate study at Cornell University. He has more than 35 years of professional experience as a petroleum geologist and environmental geochemist, and has spent most of the past 20 years leading environmental planning efforts for transportation, solar power, nuclear power, and pipeline projects. Aside from his professional experience, his personal interest in geology is the role of topography, hydrology, and geologic materials in influencing human geography, architecture, and history.

He is a contributor of bridge photos and documentation to the historicbridges.org website, having contributed many of their Maryland bridges, as well as photo-documentation of a key bridge in the United Kingdom. Recently retired from his day job, he lives in Columbia, Maryland.

Made in the USA
Middletown, DE
03 December 2022